The Sailor's War
1914~18

Saturday Aug. 1. 14.

H.M.S. Laerties,
Third Destroyer Flotilla.

Harwich.

I am writing to you today, my dearest Father, because I think I may not be able to tomorrow.— We may be at sea. I do not think we shall avoid this war — if Germany mobilises we certainly cannot leave our ally to her fate — I will not I trust. There is to my mind one hope & one only. If the food in Germany reaches famine prices she _may_ give her word to remain neutral — otherwise I see now clearly enough that it _must_ come. Meanwhile we stand before the God of Battles —, not a sparrow falls

PETER H. LIDDLE

THE SAILOR'S WAR
1914~18

BLANDFORD PRESS
POOLE · DORSET

First published in the UK 1985 by Blandford Press Ltd,
Link House, West Street, Poole, Dorset, BH15 1LL

Copyright © 1985 Peter H. Liddle.
Distributed in the United States by Sterling Publishing
Co., Inc.; 2 Park Avenue, New York, NY 10016

Reprinted 1985

ISBN 0 7137 1397 6

British Library Cataloguing in Publication Data

Liddle, Peter, *1934–*
   The sailor's war 1914–1918.
   1. World War, 1914–1918—Naval operations,
   British
   I. Title
   940.4'5941   D581

Filmset in 10/12 pt Plantin by August Filmsetting,
Haydock, St Helens.
Printed in Great Britain by BAS Printers Ltd, Wallop,
Hampshire.

Contents

Foreword

This history of the Navy's part in World War I differs from other histories in that the author has set out to record the 'feel' of the period by extensive extracts from the memoirs, papers and letters of individuals who took part in the various happenings, actions and operations. The individuals in question are so varied between officers and ratings at all levels that it can be claimed to give some indications of how events appeared to a wide spread of those involved.

Since the author is a dedicated historian and has built up the 1914–18 archives stored at Sunderland Polytechnic, which are probably the biggest collection in the country of personal records of all three services in private hands, he has a vast storehouse of information of this nature at his disposal.

Further he has expanded the narrative by including much detail of life on board HM Ships at this time which will give readers a considerable insight into the conditions the officers and ratings of those days lived and fought under – very different from the present day!

The picture painted is accurate and is a record of the times which will help to preserve the memory of a past age which should not be forgotten as it undoubtedly tends to be these days. It brought back memories of my younger days and in particular reminded me of an episode in my first ship – the old battleship *Vengeance*.

The midshipmen's bathroom was a dark compartment below decks with only cold water laid on. We midshipmen bathed in shallow metal tubs, hot water being brought down in cans from the ship's galley two decks higher up. The galley stove was a huge square erection and had several tanks in which liquids could be heated, each fitted with a tap to enable the contents to be drawn off. On the day in question the lights failed suddenly, leaving us in darkness in the bathroom waiting for the hot water cans to arrive. At that moment our servants were in the process of drawing off the hot water from the galley which was also in semi-darkness, but they managed to grope their way down to the bathroom and pour the water into our bath-tubs in the glimmer of light that was coming from somewhere. We got on with washing ourselves conscious that the water smelt slightly peculiar. The lights came on again with equal suddenness and we discovered we were bathing in weak coffee!

I am grateful to have been asked to write this foreword, my only qualification being that I served as a very junior officer throughout the war and there are not many of us still alive.

I hope readers will enjoy and appreciate this book and can but end by wishing Peter Liddle every success with it.

Sir Charles Hughes Hallett

Preface and Acknowledgements

This book has grown from seeds planted almost twenty years ago. It was in 1964 that I began to feel that the heritage of personal experience in the Great War was under the threat of time, with all those constantly threatening hazards which time brings. There were the memories of participants to record; there were diaries, collections of letters and memorabilia to be preserved. Men, women and their families had to be traced and then persuaded that the objective was a worthy one. This was by no means all; the material being gathered had not merely to be conserved, but also to be carefully examined and listed, and cross-references taken to make its significance more immediately accessible.

Gradually, I built up an archive of personal documentation of the 1914–18 war. Since 1967, it has been housed within Sunderland Polytechnic, where I hold a lectureship in Modern History and War Studies. The archive has become a centre for scholarly research on the Great War and its resources assist authors, researchers and students keen to examine primary source material on all aspects of the war.

It is with regard to Royal and to some extent Merchant Navy experience that I have chosen to illustrate first in any depth what it was like to serve in one of Britain's actively-engaged forces during the war. *The Sailor's War* attempts to do this in an historical and broadly chronological setting. On this basis, service afloat will be looked at through the eyes of young officers and ratings. Naval action will of course be a main theme, but life in the gunroom, or on the messdeck will be described. A wide range of work and responsibility will be represented, and some idea of the breadth of this range will be gathered as different classes of ship, different types of operation and different locations are considered. There was, for example, an obvious kinship between the submarine service in the Baltic and in the Dardanelles – but striking differences between them. The North Sea was not quite the same sea for the sub lieutenant of a destroyer of the Harwich Force, as it was for a sub lieutenant in a Scapa Flow-based battleship. Atlantic convoy duties provided a different form of life and stress from that which had been accepted by those involved in naval support to the Gallipoli landings.

My concern has been to outline a particular war circumstance, and then to select extracts from original diaries, letters or official journals, to choose photographs and artwork and, occasionally, to use the well-founded recollections of men who were closely involved to illustrate that circumstance at a personal level.

The expression 'at the sharp end' of war service has unfortunate ambiguity if used for naval as opposed to army service, but if it were taken as an indication of closeness to the point of personal involvement in the drama being described, then it precisely expresses the focus of the book.

The selection of the material is a personal one, but reflects my judgement as to what might properly be viewed as a document interesting in its own right, while frequently containing the essence of the experience of others. It has always seemed to me exceptionally hard to make valid general observations from evidence of individual personal experience; especially is this the case if it were to be based upon perceptions or attitudes. Nevertheless, an attempt has been made to reproduce evidence which is, at least to some extent, an indication of what it was like for others suffering or sharing the experience.

Few, if any, historical records have an authenticity which in every point is beyond question. The third and fourth volumes of the excellent *Official History of the Naval Operations of the Great War* certainly earned their share of controversy over Jutland. The task of the Official Historian is as vulnerable as it is burdensome. How much, then, are we to scrutinise the letters or diaries of the sub-lieutenant or rating before they may be responsibly selected for publication? There is a well-known story of New Zealand soldiers on the banks of the Suez Canal, early in 1915. Some wrote home of a fierce defensive action against a Turkish onslaught on the Canal. To their embarrassment before their fellows they found their letters returning to them published in home-town newspapers describing 'bloody events' which no-one who took part in them could have considered as more than a slight skirmish!

Critical examination, then, is required but we may well note that this is a two-sided coin. The average man certainly did not want his family to be too alarmed at his danger and so might avoid mention of any circumstances of peril or understate them. There were, however, various impulses towards making a written record of all that was happening, as and when time permitted. Sheer habit, inculcated at home, must explain why so many soldiers and sailors broke the strict regulations against keeping a diary. As for letters, affection, habit, duty, and a natural desire to bridge the separating miles, all reinforced each other in stimulating an effort to keep an anxious soul or family informed. But I believe there was something else. Was there not an inner drive to record vivid, new, perhaps searing experience, while its detail was still clear in the mind? There would indeed be many a time-server in all the forces to whom each day was a day at work and, as such, scarcely meriting note – still less anything which might smack of a lurid 'writing-up'; but there would be others, who were surely conscious of being participants, however lowly, in dramatic and even in great events. Their papers might contain graphically detailed word-pictures of telling accuracy; they might reflect, too, a sense of history being made.

With such varied motives encouraging or deterring the diarist or letter writer, it will not be judged surprising that sometimes it has seemed to me necessary to use several sources to catch the full flavour of an event. On other occasions, a single document has, in my judgement, achieved a justifiable self-sufficiency.

In all cases, the style as in the original is retained, and therefore frequently is at variance with that of the main text, except that vessels' names have been italicised. Editorial interpolation is indicated by square brackets [], and omissions by three points . . .

I would like to add here that it is fortunate that I have a number of outstanding collections of the papers of ratings. Historical and archival circumstance have combined to lead to a dominance of midshipman, sub-lieutenant, and surgeon-probationers' papers in my archives: educational and social background, habit, opportunity, living-space, all play their part in explaining this phenomenon. Family circumstances and attitude towards the vestigial evidence of their history, have ensured the preservation of a goodly proportion of the material recorded at the time by the young officer. That there is an unbroken continuity of British seafaring tradition, itself an element in the victory at sea in the Great War, was demonstrated yet again to me recently in a personal way. A letter from one of two brothers, both naval officers in the two World Wars, outlined what the writer called, with attractive understatement, their 'strong naval connection'. 'My father was Admiral Sir Arthur Farquhar KCB, my Grandfather was Admiral Sir Arthur Farquhar KCB, and my Great Grandfather was Admiral Sir Arthur Farquhar KCB and I never had an idea of doing anything else except joining the Royal Navy if it would have me.'[1]

To the surprise, I presume, of no-one, *The Sailor's War* must be dedicated to the sailors themselves and in particular to those men and their families whose trust has ensured the preservation here of 1914–18 papers. It may be that this book will bring in more such documentation; my debt will then be the greater. I thank especially the donors of material selected for inclusion in this book; their names are listed separately, and the source of each illustration is appropriately noted.

In connection with the development of the Royal Navy and Merchant Navy section of the archive, many men may be mentioned. I hope it will not be thought invidious to thank by name the late Captain L.A.K. Boswell, Professor W.H. Bruford, Mr W.G. Cave, Tim Dumas, with his rare distinction of a father and a father-in-law of flag rank, the late Dr H.V. Edwards, the late Dr A.B. Emden, John Falconer, William Crick, Fred Foxon, Cdr T.S. Fox-Pitt, the late Admiral Sir Henry McCall, Vice Admiral Sir Charles Hughes-Hallett, the late C.E. Keeler and his family, Dr W.W. King Brown, Rear Admiral K.M. Lawder, Cdr C. Longden Griffiths, Percy May, Mr F.W. Harry Miller, the late Cdr J.B. Mitford, Cdr J.G.D. Ouvry, the late Professor G.R. Potter, Vice Admiral J.S.C. Salter, the late Rear Admiral B.L. Sebastian, Dr James Shaw, Captain H.N. Taylor (MN), Cdr D.S.E. Thompson, the late Cdr H. Vetch, Cdr C.G. Vyner, Mr T.W. Walker, Vice Admiral Sir Peveril William Powlett and Mr A.E. Wood.

While the book was being prepared, there were my lecturing commitments to fulfil, in addition to the constant archive-work of cataloguing, cross-referencing, correspondence, making new contacts, maintaining old links and travelling to collect papers and to tape-record. I have been invaluably supported by voluntary help, and in acknowledgement of this, I must not neglect to express my appreciation of the fact that I have an institutional base from which to conduct my research. At Sunderland, congenial colleagues have in recent years made it more relaxing to approach two jobs at one and the same time, the one a contractual engagement, the other a self-imposed burden of pleasure and fulfilment.

The help I have had from Charlie Ward, Squadron Leader Nobby Clark, Kevin Kelly and more recently Vera Stevens and Joyce Henshaw, all based in the North East, has provided a life-boat in practical terms for the archive and a lifebelt for me. I have on occasion, through the pressure of tasks facing me, felt threatened by a nightmare fusion of the tolling of the Lutine Bell and the bell of Hemingway's ominously titled Spanish Civil War novel. The generous assistance of friends of the archives has reduced the occurrence of the nightmare.

Quite specifically with this book, Nobby, Kevin, Vera and Joyce have helped in a variety of ways. Margaret Close and Andrew Davison did research work in the early stages, Margaret also began the decyphering of my appalling manuscript. This challenging task was continued by Birgitta Scott, Gillian Mushens and Kathleen Barnes. Vice Admiral Sir Charles Hughes Hallett and Vice Admiral J.S.C. Salter made enlightening critical comments on the resultant typescript of each section of the book as it was written. Time and again, I profited significantly from their observations and Kathleen then re-typed the newly altered text. Vera toiled at the photocopying of faded documents. For the photographic reproduction of items from the archives I would like to thank Raymond Heppell, a technician in the Geography, History Department at Sunderland Polytechnic and for the maps, Howard Williams, Head of the Geography Department, Thorneyclose School. The reader will be able to judge the enhancement of the book resulting from their skills. Of the institutional sources of help I would like to mention in particular the Royal Marines Museum at Eastney but I must refer again to the patience and good will of Sir Charles Hughes Hallett, Admiral Salter, William Crick and Harry Miller who responded so generously to rapid fire questions projected by letter and telephone.

I would like appreciatively to acknowledge that I have been fortunate in my editor at Blandford Press, Michael Burns. The final shape of the book owes a good deal to Michael who has invariably offered constructive advice.

The 'ship', I feel sure, has been made the more secure by the way the pilot has brought her into port.

Last, but really first as well, and throughout every area of my work, my thanks are due to my wife, Louise, who has provided the sort of contentment and stimulus from which could be tackled the daunting prospect of doing justice to the theme of this book.

Peter H. Liddle, FR Hist. Soc.,
DIPITY COTTAGE, LIME STREET, WALDRIDGE FELL,
CHESTER-LE-STREET, DURHAM.

Introduction

It may seem curious that there is both a general assumption that the Royal Navy provided the decisive factor in the allied victory in the Great War and also that the Navy's 1914–18 record is defaced with an embarrassing number of disappointments or even disasters. An explanation of this phenomenon makes it seem a good deal less extraordinary. It lies in the vast scale of the Navy's role in the war. There can be no disagreement whatever that the task facing it was one of awe-inspiring dimensions. The material and statistical factors in relation to the numbers and classes of ship, the naval personnel establishment and all its specialisms, the source, sufficiency and supply of oil, coal, ammunition, victuals, stores, the question of communications, the progressive expansion of the Navy through new building, improvement in design, scientific development, repair, refitting, recruitment and training and re-training are all separate but related matters which together should encourage a pause for thought by anyone rash enough to express a sweeping assessment of what was involved in the naval effort. All the above would have to be considered in relation, first, to what the Navy had to do and, then, to how and with what success it was carried out.

The British Expeditionary Force had to be safely transported to France. The essential cross-channel support of this force as it expanded from its original 100,000 to just less than two million at the end of the war, was a constant major naval responsibility. The obvious but too infrequently stated fact was that not a single British or Commonwealth soldier came to active service in the Great War except by courtesy of the transportation and convoy escorts vessels of the Royal or Commonwealth Navies. It was by no means for the drama of Gallipoli alone that the soldier relied upon the sailor. No advance to, never mind retirement from Mons was possible without the Navy. Much more is concealed behind such a generalisation. Canadian, New Zealand, Australian, South African and Indian army units needed transportation over enormous distances. Expeditionary forces were bound for Britain, Egypt and Gallipoli but also for West Africa, East Africa and the Persian Gulf. Troops had to be routed for China to assist the Japanese in the capture of the German station at Tsing Tao and New Zealand and Australian ships took their Commonwealth troops to Samoa and New Guinea respectively. A whole new front was created in Macedonia late in 1915 and all these diverse operations or incipient campaigns had to be maintained and supplied. Yet these tasks, with all their high priority and their formidable range, must still be judged as support work. We have yet to come to the fulfilment of any primary role, like the defence of Great Britain from invasion, clearing the seas of German commerce and commerce raiders or maintaining the nation's supply routes for food, munitions and trade. Then, having thus dealt with German naval vessels outside the North Sea, it was generally perceived that the German High Seas Fleet must be brought to decisive battle. Even these awe-inspiring burdens do not clearly specify what were to become tasks of overwhelming importance: the battle against the German underwater threat by submarine to our commerce – a threat so serious that it brought a prospect of British defeat – and the distant blockade strangulation of the German economy and war effort.

In the light of this outline, one can scarcely be surprised that there were occasions when policy, men or materials failed, or the enemy exerted a local superiority. The result on such occasions was variably significant but, with the exception of the 1917 U-boat crisis there was always spare rope which could replace or repair damaged cable. A loss or a defeat were to be regretted and slowness to learn lessons was reprehensible, but the 'fleet in being', ready for action, was maintained and pressure upon German supplies was more and more strongly applied. No authority more reasonably sums up the extent of the flawed but superb record of naval achievement than Professor A.J. Marder.

'It was the function of British sea power to ensure the use of the sea for Allied purposes and to deprive the enemy of its use. This sea power had four major components – the Fleet, bases, the merchant navy, and the ship building industry. All played their part – to say nothing of the tremendous natural advantage of Britain lying like a breakwater across the exits from the North Sea – but it was above all the Grand Fleet taking full advantage of the favourable geographical position and constantly holding the High Seas Fleet in check, that underpinned the entire Allied war effort.'[1]

The way in which the Naval High Command perceived the opportunities and constraints offered by the war and then the policy upon which it embarked, have not been free from criticism. Briefly, but I trust fairly, summarising the charge which was vigorously put forward within the service and during the war, the criticism lay in the adoption of a passive strategy. Additionally, the critics, led by Admiral Sir Herbert Richmond and Vice Admiral K.G.B. Dewar, asserted that the Navy had been unprepared for the war. It had furthermore made a series of blunders in its conduct of the war.

Most fundamental, however, was the question of strategy. The Navy had failed to assert the advantage of the mobility it might have given to British military power and it had done insufficient to bring about decisive battle with the High Seas Fleet. The threat of mine and submarine, Richmond felt, had quite unrealisti-cally wrested all initiative from the controlling brains of British naval strategy: risk had submerged opportunity. For Britain to maintain a distant watchfulness, awaiting a German move, was as counter to the glorious tradition of victory in battle as it was strategically and technologically an unjustifiable response to the potentiality of twentieth century warfare at sea. It might wryly be observed that much the same line of philosophical thought had led to the French military plan XVII and the grim harvest of its hopes in the 1914 Battles of the Frontiers, but the argument does have, even today, a seductive attraction. A decisive naval victory in 1914 or 1915 would have enabled far greater resources to be devoted to countering the German submarine menace which would, in consequence, never have reached the calamitous proportions of 1917 following the opening of unrestricted U-boat warfare.

The argument seems to me, even in its superficial allure, to concentrate too little on the intentions of the High Seas Fleet command and to exaggerate British capacity to influence these intentions. Just as the Germans had seized in 1914 a strategic initiative on land in Belgium and France, they possessed a frustrating initiative of a different sort as their fleet lay secure in its North German river estuary bases. Would the High Seas Fleet come out or not? The British High Command had to prepare and wished to prepare for a German emergence leaving sufficient safe sea room for confrontation and battle. The Grand Fleet was, however, quite unable to bring about such a circumstance. This devastatingly simple reality invited the making of virtue from incapacity. What need was there to risk capital ships against mine or submarine when the object of such a hazardous exercise chose to remain inert positionally but, presumably, alert to its capacity to use modern technology against incautious approach? The penalties of failure in such a suspiciously inviting enterprise were well couched in Churchill's famous phrase of Jellicoe's heavy responsibility at Jutland. Whether the war could have been lost in an afternoon or not, it has been pointed out that

Nelson's last and greatest victory had by no means won the war against Napoleonic France. It was, in any case, a British response to French initiative which led to Trafalgar, and the victory was merely an added bonus to the time-taking overall strategy to respond to one system of economic starvation by another – the blockade.

With the easily assembled wisdom of hindsight, I think that it can be fairly judged that the British naval response to the unknown elements of modern warfare was realistic. Perhaps the Commander in Chief, Grand Fleet, Admiral Sir John Jellicoe, as has been argued so convincingly for Sir Douglas Haig by John Terraine, was in closer touch with the reality of war under the prevailing technology time-scale than both his contemporary and his later critics. After all, it was the High Seas Fleet which was escorted into the Firth of Forth for internment in November 1918.

There is much more that might be discussed here on the naval direction of the war. The question of tactical rigidity, the use of the air arm, the subjects of ship design and weapon, shell and communications development are all matters worthy of consideration and appropriate reference will be made to some of them in different sections of this book. In any case, *Sailor's War* is no attempt at even the palest imitation of Professor Marder's *chef d'oeuvre*. In my view, with the qualified exception of the year 1917, the higher direction of the maritime war effort does stand up well against critical assessment but the concern of this book is to show what it was like for the ratings and their junior officers at the forefront of the great naval endeavour.

1

Men, Morale and Preparedness

MEN AND MORALE: PREPAREDNESS, JULY–AUGUST 1914

Reflective thinking on the performance of British forces in August 1914 concentrates with justifiable pride on the high degree of professionalism displayed by the small British Expeditionary Force. It was not just discipline and marksmanship, but the efficiency of mobilisation procedure, the type and level of training and pre-August 1914 service experience which had produced so fine a force. The only area of inadequacy was, of course, in size in relation to the sort of war in which the force was to be involved.

For the sailors, the grand material scale, not shared by their khaki counterparts, was there and so was the same superb professionalism which, for the army, so swiftly won renown. Naval mobilisation plans, training, service and spirit were to respond successfully to the demands of the occasion. Confidence prevailed among the young officers and men, just as it did in the Nation, that the Navy would decisively deal with the German threat to its command of the sea. As far as the Senior Service was concerned, the roots of that confidence lay in a thorough knowledge of their shipboard duties and a healthy degree of tacitly acknowledged interdependence of officers and men.

It is tempting to consider policy and technology as exclusive determinants in twentieth century naval conflict, yet no less an authority than the late Professor A.J. Marder, in succinctly summarising the reasons for the victory at sea in the Great War, emphasised the significance of personnel in no uncertain terms: 'officers and men were equally superb.'[1]

THE EDUCATION OF OFFICERS: THE ROYAL NAVAL COLLEGE

Sub-lieutenants and midshipmen had, in the main, received their education at preparatory school and then, after application, medical and written examination and Admiralty interview, they went to the Royal Naval College. Lest anyone were to believe that the examination for a twelve-year-old was a formality, question number 15 of a 1911 Arithmetic paper read: 'What is the weight in tons of a wall 80 feet long, 6 feet high and 9 inches thick, built of materials weighing 112 lbs per cubic foot?' There were three days of Geography, History, English, English Dictation, Latin, Arithmetic and Algebra, German and French dictation, French or German written and Geometry examination papers.

From 1903 the first stage of the College education was no longer in the old wooden-walled *Britannia* and *Hindustan* but in newly built, though designedly temporary accommodation in the grounds of Osborne, Queen Victoria's home on the Isle of Wight. Two years at Osborne were followed by transfer to the magnificently sited and impressive buildings of Dartmouth College, proudly overlooking the river Dart itself. For those whose education was not interfered with by the outbreak of war, the final stage was a six-month training cruise in *Cumberland* or *Cornwall*. Alternation was necessary as cruiser time was six months and a term of students at Dartmouth came due for its cruiser time every four months. With a reduced ship's company, the cruise provided practical experience in all departments from upper deck to engine and boiler room for the cadets who

Top left
HMS *Hindustan*, left, and HMS *Britannia*, right, on the River Dart, seen from Dartmouth College Landing Stage. (Rear Admiral B. Sebastian)

Bottom left
Royal Naval College, Dartmouth. (Rear Admiral B. Sebastian)

Above
HMS *Cumberland*. (Rear Admiral B. Sebastian)

were at the same time continuing their academic studies. Halifax, Nova Scotia, American ports or West Indian stations, the Baltic and the Mediterranean might be the locations for such cruises. There would be especial excitement and ceremony at Kiel but then delightfully relaxed picnics when Scandinavian ports were visited.

In many ways life at the naval college conformed to the English public school tradition but with an individual variation of both principle and detail. The principle was, of course, that the

cadets were embarking upon the necessary formal educational introduction to their chosen service profession. The difference in detail would vary as one might expect from one school to another. Life was communal, rather monastic and prefectorial but under the different nomenclature of cadet captaincy. The 'house' structure, incorporating boys of different ages, was replaced by one of 'term of entry'. Games and other physical activities were compulsory and there were distinctive conventions of dress and conduct characteristic of English public school life.

At Osborne, there were about four hundred and fifty cadets in six terms, each term named after a distinguished admiral. A term was under the command of naval officers and petty officers and there were schoolmasters for the formal education offered by the college. Captain Bush in *Bless our Ship* wrote evocatively of the daily routine which began with the 'Two gongs turn-out' shouted out by the cadet captains at 7 a.m.

A Dormitory at Royal Naval College, Osborne. Note the huge chest at the end of each cadet's bed. (Rear Admiral B. Sebastian)

Bottom left
Osborne Cadet R.M. Dick between rounds of his winning Bantam Weight Boxing Semi-Final, summer 1911. (Rear Admiral R.M. Dick)

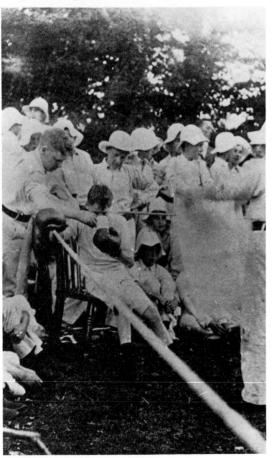

ordering a hasty emergence from bed to bedside prayers, a cold plunge bath, ship's biscuit and cocoa, an hour's work before breakfast, inspection parade at 9 a.m. followed by prayers and then a march off to lessons. After lunch there were further lessons then games, tea, prep (or homework) and bed at 9 p.m.

The programme for the July–August 1914 Dartmouth passing out examinations included three-hour papers in History, Mathematics (two papers), French or German (with vivas accordingly), English Composition, Engineering (two papers), Navigation, Pilotage, Seamanship (and viva) and Electricity, finishing on Monday, 3 August with Mechanics and the second navigation paper. In separate instructions, candidates who were soon to face enemy guns were enjoined: 'Take care to spill no ink on the floor, by knocking out your pen.' The last question in the European section of the History paper concerned the fall of the second French Empire in 1870, there being no question whatsoever on international relations beyond that date. R.M. Dick, who passed out twenty-fifth in order of merit from the results in these examinations, earned a French and English prize and a share of the History prize. From his term, one boy was killed at Coronel three months later,

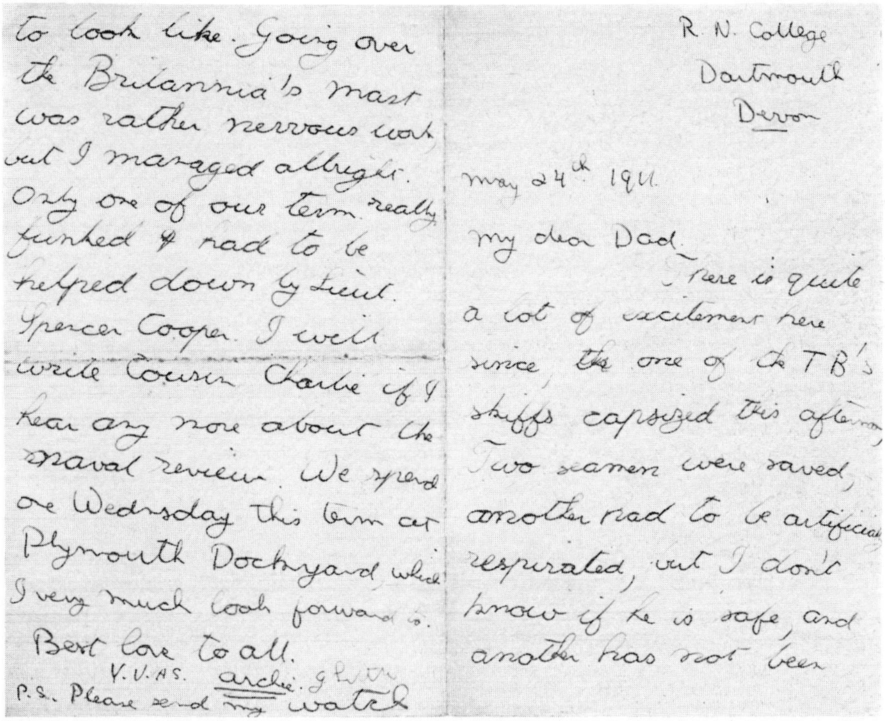

R.N. College
Dartmouth
Devon

May 24th 1911

My dear Dad,
There is quite a lot of excitement here since the one of the TB's skiffs capsized this afternoon. Two seamen were saved, another had to be artificially respirated, but I don't know if he is safe, and another has not been found yet. There was a very strong tide running at the time. I did not actually see it but heard a noise and saw a steam boat charging off. Prince Albert was there and was in the gig that took the two rescued men back to the Bathing stage. The 'Pomone' is here and is not nearly such an old ship as the 'Racer'. She has had some of her boilers taken out, and is fitted with oil-fuel, for instructional purposes. Prince Albert is kept down in the papers. Prince as watching a cricket match at the oval the other day, whereas he was playing cricket here. Such are the trials of Royalty. Some French officers have been here last week & were just like I should expect a typical Frenchman to look like. Going over the Britannia's mast was rather nervous work, but I managed alright. Only one of our term really funked & had to be helped down by Lieut. Spencer Cooper. I will write Cousin Charlie if I hear any more about the naval review. We spend one Wednesday this term at Plymouth Dockyard which I very much look forward to. Best love to all.
V.V.A.S.
archie glwyn
P.S. Please send my watch

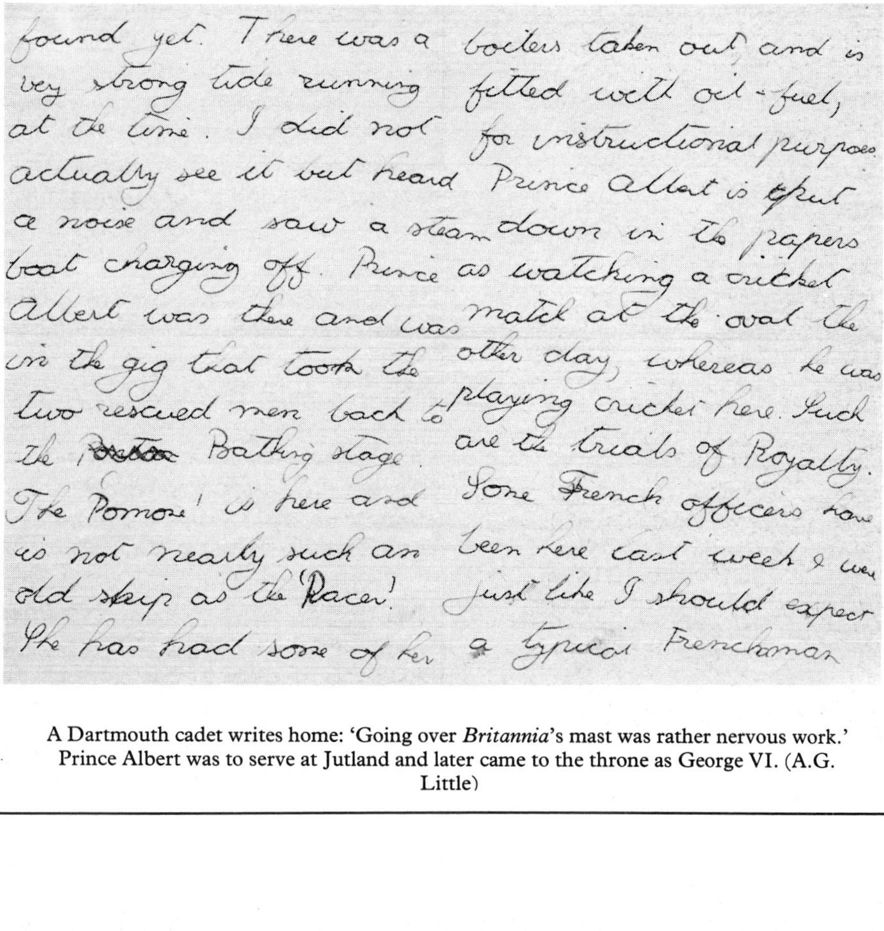

A Dartmouth cadet writes home: 'Going over *Britannia*'s mast was rather nervous work.' Prince Albert was to serve at Jutland and later came to the throne as George VI. (A.G. Little)

one at the Dardanelles and four at Jutland. These grim details, together with a record of Falklands and Dardanelles service, are annotated in Dick's hand on his pass list.[2]

There was much in the life at the Royal Naval College common to all boarding schools, but perhaps not the more specifically naval relaxation of Saturday evening dances of which Captain Bush records: 'No girls being available, we partnered each other. Officers and masters joined in.' He added philosophically 'As I was small, it was always my lot to be "lady".'

At Osborne, cadets progressed by seniority through a more angled wearing of their caps; at Dartmouth they ran 'at the double' to all activities. Each establishment had its transient dramas, from endemic pink eye to the scandal of poor cadet Shee, a sad little story of the mistaken identity of the culprit in a theft of a postal order. For various reasons, the incident became a national *cause célèbre*, with judicial proceedings, and it left a famous literary legacy in Terence Rattigan's play, *The Winslow Boy*. Memorable with a host of anecdotes for many a cadet was a cheek by jowl schooling beside two future Kings, Prince Edward, to be Edward VIII, and Prince Albert, the rather undistinguished cadet who became so well-loved a monarch.

Bullying at Osborne and Dartmouth seems not to have been in the least excessive. Juniors encountered on Sunday afternoons might well have to perform some song or such like activity for the amusement of their seniors but it might be wryly observed that this was a vital even if informal part of their education in view of what they would have to face as junior midshipmen in the gunroom. Incidentally, there are former cadets who recall with something of a shiver official investigations to secure the name of an anonymous transgressor of college rules. On discovery, the malefactor might, on rare occasions, earn himself 'official cuts' and his fellows, the chilling spectacle of being assembled to see the blows administered upon a clothed but humiliatingly prostrate body bent over a gymnasium horse.

There were workshops at both establishments for practical training in engineering, a distinctive element of the change introduced in 1903 to give cadets an all-round education from which specialism could develop later. In fact, this well-intentioned reform was not to work. Specialist engineering training at Keyham College was needed to provide the answer for those whose future lay as engineers, or 'plumbers', as they were known colloquially.

At Dartmouth, there was a greater concentration upon seamanship and boat work. It was at Dartmouth also that an interesting feature of self discipline was successfully practised. This was the keeping of a six-day log in which an activity recognised as a 'log', like an organised games match, or a 'half log', like a swim or a run or a game of squash, had to be completed and recorded for each working day of the week.

Beagling was perhaps an unusual opportunity for Dartmouth cadets, though the comfortable middle class background for many, particularly those from rural areas, would make it by no means an unfamiliar pursuit. Long treasured photograph albums attractively illustrate splendid facilities for cricket, the complex arrangements of assaults at arms, elegantly costumed amateur dramatics, superbly appointed workshops and the disciplined competitiveness in a gracious setting of the river Dart regattas.

Not easily defined, but clearly an implicit part of cadet experience at the senior establishment, was the preparation for the assumption of command even as the knowledge from which to exercise it was being gained. Dartmouth was a part of a long, continuous process in this matter and it might be maintained quite reasonably that if the process were to fossilise at any stage, even including that of flag rank, then danger for all concerned would set in while that officer held his rank. Almost every former midshipman with whom I have spoken has dwelt on what to the outsider must seem a very special mystery of the young officer's first step on the ladder of naval advancement. It was then that he was

Above
Dartmouth College Assault at Arms, summer 1913.
(Commander P. Haig-Ferguson)

Right
A midshipman in command – but with a little help! (F.A. Foxon)

Below
Dartmouth Assault at Arms Prizegiving, July 1914, Exmouth Term winning the three big cakes on display. (Captain L.A.K. Boswell)

'HIS FIRST COMMAND'

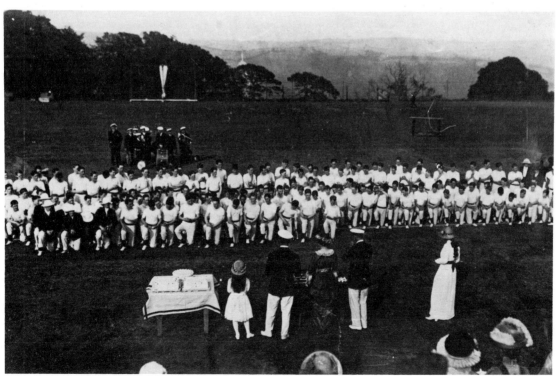

guided by his working relationship with an experienced senior rating looking after the young innocent, saving him from the errors of his ignorance of men, boats, wind and tide, yet remaining unquestionably his junior in all formal standing. The first stages of such a special relationship were laid down at Dartmouth where in boat handling on the Dart more than that skill was being learned than was apparent at the time to the young cadet.

A former cadet, Charles Hughes Hallett, writing of the values inculcated at the Royal Naval College and then in service life, unaffectedly listed: 'leadership, loyalty, an extreme sense of duty and obedience as the main virtues one acquired'. Of leadership he wrote: 'Nobody ever mentioned the subject but we were constantly finding ourselves having to take charge of a body of cadets and I think it became a habit forming practice which stood us in good stead when we went to sea and had to take charge of seamen.' Concerning loyalty, Hughes Hallett made the point that 'Naval officers are not "sworn" men but nevertheless in my day we all accepted without question that we were called upon to be loyal to our King and Country and to the Navy. I suppose inculcation of a sense of duty might be said to hark back to Nelson's days with his constant affirmation of the need to do one's duty and his dying words "Thank God I have done my duty." It bred a spirit of devotion to the Navy and in most people the unspoken principle that you put the service first and your own affairs second. The habit of putting the service first did result in a closely knit band of officers but most of them had few interests outside the service and their outlook was in consequence undesirably narrow! Of obedience as a virtue Hughes Hallett also had some reservations as it could lead, he suggested, to an 'unquestioning obedience particularly in officers with low calibre brains and little imagination'.[3]

Returning more exclusively to Dartmouth in the period immediately prior to the outbreak of the Great War, I have questioned many former cadets on another matter of some interest. To what extent were the young cadets consciously prepared for the day when the 'insolence' of the German challenge to British naval supremacy would have to be dealt with? In formal lessons and in informal discussion, were the cadets taught to think in terms of the German enemy and a day of facing them in battle? Inconclusive but stimulating has been the uniform response to this question. 'There was no specific teaching but it was generally understood and accepted by all'.

For the midshipmen already at sea in June 1914, some reference must be made to one aspect of their life as they gained experience of watch keeping, gunnery and the full range of their responsibilities, particularly at action stations. C.L. Morgan in his novel *The Gunroom* scandalised naval authorities and the freemasonry of naval officers in drawing attention to the bullying which could occur as the most

A naval engineering drawing of a torpedo from Midshipman Mitford's journal. (Commander J.B. Mitford)

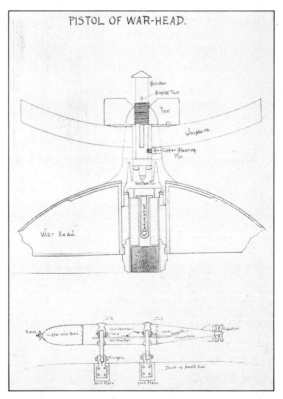

junior midshipmen were subjected to a routine of initiation drills, or evolutions, as they were called. In the confinement of the crowded gunroom, the junior officers' mess, the most senior, usually a sub-lieutenant, in some cases would order the juniors to perform tasks of differing degrees of humiliation. Solo singing or recitations under taunts were the least of their ordeals. On hands and knees 'Creeping for Jesus', was one refinement, the blindfolded following of a trail of angostura-bitters while occasionally being beaten with a variety of implements. Another, signalised symbolically by a gesture, 'Fork in the beam' immediately urged the juniors on an obstacle course to reach and return from some point or to secure some trophy from an awkward location. 'Fork in the beam' dated from sailing ship days when it was literally stuck in the overhead beams. Originally, it was only a signal for midshipmen to get out of the mess because the sub-lieutenant of the Mess wished to talk to the few other slightly older members alone. Severe penalties could be vested on the laggardly in such a race. For a few men even today such memories remain uncomfortable as they remember a young manhood associated too frequently with fearful recall or dreaded anticipation as the long days at sea were endured. Naturally, such memories are associated with gunrooms ruled by someone of a particularly sadistic mien and it should be made clear that, for many, evolutions were merely good fun for the inflictors and something briefly to be endured by the sufferers. That there were gunrooms where things went too far was as true then as it is true today in civil life, at school or among apprentices where the conventions of initiation rites lead to abuse.

THE TRAINING SHIPS AND SCHOOLS FOR SEAMEN BOYS

Despite the reforms which set up numerous shore establishments for the training of seamen boys, many boys in the Royal Navy and in the Mercantile Marine had begun their service in one of a number of wooden-walled training ships. An advertisement in a local evening paper would have offered the opportunity of training for the navy for 'boys of good character'. Application, a medical examination, an easy academic test and an interview might in due course lead to the signing of indenture papers. A twelve-year old boy destined for the Merchant Marine and signing such papers in the presence of his father or guardian voluntarily bound himself apprentice to the commander of the training ship and to his successors, until the age of eighteen had been reached. Among the regulations he accepted were that he would not 'damage the commander' nor 'frequent taverns or ale houses nor play at unlawful games'. In return for his obedient service, the apprentice would be taught 'the business of a seaman'. He would be lodged, fed and clothed and given medical and surgical assistance. For the Royal Navy, the minimum age of entry was just under sixteen.

As might be expected, training ship experience varied with the regime established by a particular commander and his officers. Victor Hayward in his book *HMS Tiger at Bay* wrote with affectionate recall of HMS *Impregnable* at Plymouth. There was much to which he had to adjust, not least an almost shaven haircut. Barefooted, there was sandstone block holy-stoning of the sanded decks and then, with a salt water hose playing on the deck, brooming away the sand and finally drying the surface off with rope swabs. Food was good and plentiful, the routine for a day, full, strict and rigid. From 5.30 a.m. to 9 p.m., in a sequence sanctified by tradition, the ship was cleaned, there was physical drill, rifle drill, inspection, prayers, instruction classes in practical and theoretical seamanship, more physical drill, evening quarters or roll call and a final period of free time. There were also shore-based exercises like those on the nearby rifle range and later on came heavy and smaller calibre gun drill.

Hayward pays tribute to the Royal Navy Sailor's Rest in Devonport where training ship boys were introduced to the welfare services provided by Dame Agnes Weston whose concern for the spiritual as well as the physical

2

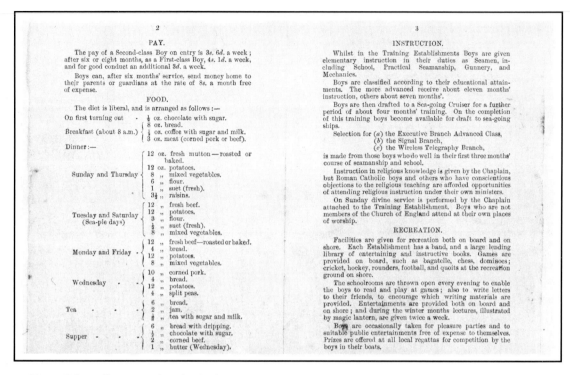

PAY.

The pay of a Second-class Boy on entry is 3*s*. 6*d*. a week; after six or eight months, as a First-class Boy, 4*s*. 1*d*. a week, and for good conduct an additional 3*d*. a week.

Boys can, after six months' service, send money home to their parents or guardians at the rate of 8*s*. a month free of expense.

FOOD.

The diet is liberal, and is arranged as follows:—

On first turning out -	½ oz. chocolate with sugar.
Breakfast (about 8 a.m.)	8 oz. bread. ½ oz. coffee with sugar and milk. 3 oz. meat (corned pork or beef).
Dinner:—	
Sunday and Thursday	12 oz. fresh mutton—roasted or baked. 12 oz. potatoes. 8 ,, mixed vegetables. 6 ,, flour. 1 ,, suet (fresh). 3½ ,, raisins.
Tuesday and Saturday (Sea-pie days)	12 ,, fresh beef. 12 ,, potatoes. 3 ,, flour. ½ ,, suet (fresh). 8 ,, mixed vegetables.
Monday and Friday -	12 ,, fresh beef—roasted or baked. 4 ,, bread. 12 ,, potatoes. 8 ,, mixed vegetables.
Wednesday - -	10 ,, corned pork. 4 ,, bread. 12 ,, potatoes. 4 ,, split peas.
Tea - - -	6 ,, bread. 2 ,, jam. ⅛ ,, tea with sugar and milk.
Supper - - -	6 ,, bread with dripping. ½ ,, chocolate with sugar. 2 ,, corned beef. 1 ,, butter (Wednesday).

3

INSTRUCTION.

Whilst in the Training Establishments Boys are given elementary instruction in their duties as Seamen, including School, Practical Seamanship, Gunnery, and Mechanics.

Boys are classified according to their educational attainments. The more advanced receive about eleven months' instruction, others about seven months'.

Boys are then drafted to a Sea-going Cruiser for a further period of about four months' training. On the completion of this training boys become available for draft to sea-going ships.

Selection for (*a*) the Executive Branch Advanced Class,
(*b*) the Signal Branch,
(*c*) the Wireless Telegraphy Branch,
is made from those boys who do well in their first three months' course of seamanship and school.

Instruction in religious knowledge is given by the Chaplain, but Roman Catholic boys and others who have conscientious objections to the religious teaching are afforded opportunities of attending religious instruction under their own ministers.

On Sunday divine service is performed by the Chaplain attached to the Training Establishment. Boys who are not members of the Church of England attend at their own places of worship.

RECREATION.

Facilities are given for recreation both on board and on shore. Each Establishment has a band, and a large lending library of entertaining and instructive books. Games are provided on board, such as bagatelle, chess, dominoes; cricket, hockey, rounders, football, and quoits at the recreation ground on shore.

The schoolrooms are thrown open every evening to enable the boys to read and play at games; also to write letters to their friends, to encourage which writing materials are provided. Entertainments are provided both on board and on shore; and during the winter months lectures, illustrated by magic lantern, are given twice a week.

Boys are occasionally taken for pleasure parties and to suitable public entertainments free of expense to themselves. Prizes are offered at all local regattas for competition by the boys in their boats.

Conditions of service for boys at the Royal Navy Training establishments, 1909. (F.W.H. Miller)

welfare of the sailor may give rise today to some wry amusement but performed then an appreciated as well as a useful function. Hayward recalled the boys' striking improvement in physique and in self-confidence. 'We could climb the masthead with the agility of monkeys and up through the "lubber's" hole and down the other side: we knew our knots and splices, could pull well in a fourteen-oared cutter, and knew quite a bit about sailing. We had learned very much about seamanship and gunnery.'[4] When the time came for their engagement as 2nd class boys in a cruiser calling at Plymouth to deliver her boys, now 1st class, after six-months sea training, he was supremely confident of preparedness for the next stage of his naval service.

That the training establishments could provide a harsh introduction to service life is attested by the flight of some boys from Shotley (HM Training Ship *Ganges*) but W.H. Campbell recalls no excessive bullying there and considered that the six weeks' course of seamanship and schooling helped him make the transition from civilian to service life. Harry Miller, however, was one lad who did suffer periods of homesickness at Devonport (HM Training Ship *Impregnable*) and remembers too the rope's end called a 'stonicky' and used to encourage the tardy or clumsy in many activities. His first acquaintance with this informal disciplining was occasioned by his difficulty in getting into and out of his hammock until he learned to use a steadying handgrasp of the beam above.

A choice of steak and eggs or cod and chips was the greeting of *Impregnable*'s Chief Cook to one small party of famished New Entries, their hunger being scarcely eased by the lump of corned beef and the hard loaf they were given to share after the Cook had deliberately waited to hear each boy's careful decision. F.G. Holvey adds to this chastening recollection that his next meal was aboard the hulk *Circe*—a basin of cocoa and some hard biscuits—after which the group was returned to *Impregnable* to witness an official caning for smoking. Seeing the weals appear through the duck pants the victim was wearing, the young Holvey resolved there and then that he had smoked his last cigarette. This particular new non smoker seems to have gained little spiritual comfort from The Sailor's Rest for his self-imposed nicotine deprivation. He has written of the couple of buns and a cup of tea he was given but added that he was 'made to sing hymns while a woman played the piano'.

The training for older recruits like those joining to be stokers at Chatham included an appropriate degree of specialism after the six weeks' field training and squad drill—for stokers it was six weeks' stoke hole training shovelling flints into a dummy boiler. After successfully proving himself at this, L.V. Bedford took a swimming test, had some time on the rifle range and was sent off in 1910 to his first ship as a 2nd Class Stoker.[5]

Entry into the service from the Training Ships and shore establishments did not supply sufficient seamen and a five-year term of entry was offered to men between eighteen and twenty-three. Following upon their full-time engagement, the men then served seven years in the Royal Fleet Reserve. Considerable numbers of RFR men had been stokers in naval service or were miners in civil life. It was these reservists and Royal Naval Reservists, usually in the Merchant Navy or fishermen and yachtsmen, who were called back to their depots from varied walks of life in that shrewd move by Churchill, the 1st Lord of the Admiralty in the July 1914 international crisis. Reservists would not be in top physical shape but their previous five-year service was good, if not ideal, preparation for the war.

Signalmen, telegraphists, writers, tradesmen like blacksmiths and carpenters, gunners and various types of artificer and stoker were among the special areas of service holding their own promotion ladders through to petty officers and indeed in some cases to warrant officer.[6] The revolution in so many aspects of technology demanded high levels of specialist skills. In the plain seaman, too, the new demands of his work

The information contained in this pamphlet is extracted from the various Regulations, which are liable to alteration; no person has any right to pay, pension, or other advantage on account of apparent eligibility under the rules as herein published. The terms and conditions under which Boys and Men accept service in the Royal Navy are given in the King's Regulations.

ROYAL NAVY.

BOYS AND YOUTHS UNDER TRAINING.

BOYS.

Boys, who are entered between 15¾ and 16¾ years of age, are trained at Shotley Training Establishment, Harwich, and on board H.M.S. "Impregnable," at Devonport.

Full information as to the pay and prospects of Boys and Youths is given in the pamphlet entitled "How to join the Royal Navy." The following particulars refer specially to the Harbour Training Establishments :—

CLOTHING.

A free outfit, including a set of bedding, is granted subject to certain conditions specified in the King's Regulations.

The outfit on entry comprises, amongst other articles of clothing :—

2 jerseys.	1 comforter.
2 pairs serge trousers.	3 serge jumpers.
2 pairs duck trousers.	2 duck jumpers.
2 shirts.	2 pairs woollen drawers.
3 flannel shirts.	2 collars.
2 pairs socks.	1 silk handkerchief.
2 caps and ribbons.	2 towels.
1 cap box.	1 bed, 1 blanket, 2 bed
1 pair boots.	covers, and other small
1 pair shoes.	articles.
1 knife and lanyards.	

The supply of clothes being in every way sufficient, the boys' friends are requested not to furnish them with clothes of any description.

The clothes in which a boy joins the service can be returned to his friends, or sold for his benefit.

x (12)2793. Wt. 18623—P. 772. 5000. 10/09. E. & S.

Free clothing issue for boys entering the Royal Navy Training establishments, 1909. (F.W.H. Miller)

'Sunday Morning Divisions'. Captain's inspection HMAS *Australia*. Men being inspected have their caps off. (G. Shearer)

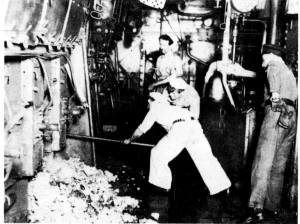

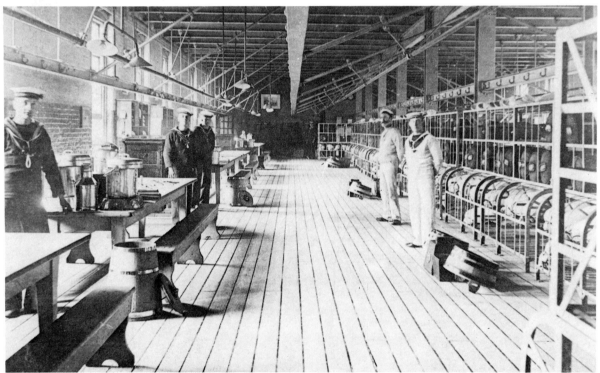

Top left
Coaling HMAS *Australia* (battle cruiser). Note the variety of headgear and clothing. (G. Shearer)

Top right
Stokers in Boiler Room HMAS *Australia*. (G. Shearer)

Centre
Mess Room, RN Barracks, Portsmouth. (F.W.H. Miller)

Left
Seamen arriving at Portsmouth with kit bags, ditty boxes and lashed hammocks for the Commissioning of the battle cruiser *New Zealand*. (Commander C.F. Laborde)

required considerable practical competence, achieved through intensive training and practical experience. An excellent account of the rigours of shore training for the wartime recruits is given in A. Trystan Edwards book: *British Bluejacket: 1915–40*. There was pride in donning the baggy trousers, tight jumper and dark blue collar with its three rows of tapes but my goodness how much better does the naval expression 'shaking-up' rather than the conventional civilian 'settling down', describe the adjustments needed to adapt to the new routine of service life.[7]

ROYAL MARINES

It had been the traditional role of the Royal Marines for over 300 years to reinforce the personnel of the Navy. Every large unit in the Navy had Marine Officers and a detachment of Marines.[8] Quite apart from the fact that the Marines normally manned several guns, they had by tradition certain security and ceremonial duties to perform. It was also usually the case that the Marines provided the servant or rather attendant for the Wardroom officers. The youthful Marine buglers, initially in their service, sounded on their instruments the timed activities of the day and then at eighteen years of age they became Marines or Marine bandsmen. Many bandsmen were recruited as such. They sometimes became Midshipmen's servants. Eighteen was the normal age of recruitment to both the Royal Marine Light Infantry (the Red Marines) and the Royal Marine Artillery (the Blue Marines). The RMLI depots were at Chatham, Gosport and Devonport and the RMA at Eastney. Basic training was carried out at Deal and from the start Marine discipline was a notch or two tighter than the already exacting standard expected of the sailor.

MOBILISATION

The General Test Mobilisation ordered for July 1914 had first been mooted by Churchill in October 1913. The mobilisation was timed to commence two days before the Spithead Review of the whole fleet on 17–18 July. Perhaps Professor Marder understates the case when he records that: 'It was a wonderful stroke of luck then that the whole fleet in home waters was practically on a war footing in the middle of July.'[9] Partial demobilisation did take place but was arrested when Prince Louis of Battenburg, The First Sea Lord, acted in Churchill's absence with shrewd judgement in cancelling demobilisation of the 3rd Fleet on receipt of the news of the Austrian ultimatum to Serbia. Churchill, returning from his sick wife's bedside, took the further step necessitated by the worsening of the diplomatic scene. The 1st Fleet was ordered to proceed towards its battle stations with its battleships at Scapa Flow and Cromarty and its battle cruisers at Rosyth. The 2nd Fleet assembled at Portland and the precipitate appointment of the experienced but relatively young Sir John Jellicoe as Commander in Chief of the Grand Fleet, placed a new man at the head of the colossal material resources of the navy.

There may well have been no clear understanding between the Admiralty and the Commander in Chief as to how the war was going to be fought, how German submarines were to be dealt with, how the British were to exercise our policy of blockade and how the anticipated decisive battle would develop. There were few if any in a position to forecast the capital ship's dangerous design fault under fire, the need for better deck and turret armour, for improved design of armour piercing shells or for the complete overall introduction of director firing to all ships of cruiser class and above. Some may have been concerned at the lack of advance in naval communications, the lack of training in engagement at night and the absence of any devolution of command responsibility and initiative and, instead, the stifling rigidity of adherence to inflexible tactical principles; but, whatever may be the case in these matters, the young officers and ratings were supremely confident. Geoffrey Bromet, a newly-appointed Royal Naval Air Service in-

To very few had it occurred that the test would never be decided in Trafalgar-like terms by reason of the dominant influence of the new technology upon policy and of the mine and torpedo upon risk in achieving battle. Just as a steadiness of nerve and a steely resolve to hold on were to be called for at the top level of command, so were they to be demanded in the Wardroom, the Gunroom and on the Mess decks. Together, officers and ratings were in the end to triumph. The final unglamorous but decisive proof of that triumph lay in the incapacity of the officers and men of the High Seas Fleet to pull together any longer in November 1918. There were nearly fifty-two months between the British mobilisation in 1914 and the internment of the High Seas Fleet in 1918. The British record in those months began inauspiciously, developed not always satisfactorily but concluded with a sense of remorseless, inexorable destiny.

WAR: 4 AUGUST 1914

The Admiralty Signal, 'Commence hostilities against Germany', went out to all ships and naval establishments at 11 p.m. on 4 August. The proving time had been reached. The journals compulsorily kept by Midshipmen vary considerably in the official but personal record they reveal of the last days of a tense peace. Keeping a journal was both a chore and a matter of pride. To some extent the information it contained and the way in which it would be expressed were influenced by the source of inspection as well as the inspiration of the writer. N.J.W. William-Powlett (Battleship: *Conqueror*) filled his pages with news of the international situation but A.G.D. Bagot (Battlecruiser: *Queen Mary*) gives a clearer impression of the impact of the crisis on the Grand Fleet.[11]

30 July 'Destination still unknown.'
31 July 'Making course for Scapa Flow. Arrived at same at 4 p.m. got torpedo nets out. Coaled all night finishing next day

With Britain not yet at war, a naval officer, Commander M.L. Goldsmith writes to his father of the Navy's readiness for action. Note that he underestimates the time for food in Germany to reach 'famine prices'. (Vice Admiral Sir Lennon Goldsmith)

telligence officer en route by train to his seaplane base at Westgate-on-Sea, expressed in his diary sentiments which ring as truly of the time and of the service as they sound discordant today.

'This is what we have been looking forward to and working up for, ever since we first put on the King's uniform – this is the real thing and thank God I've had the luck to be alive and in the Navy on "The Day". The average Englishman and certainly nine out of ten servicemen have no bitter feelings against Germany but Germany has sinned and must be made to pay for it and you can depend on the Navy of today to uphold the traditions of the British Navy and give them a good hiding in the straightforward, humane and thorough fashion that is one of the features of our race.'[10]

took in 2200 tons.'

1 *August* 'Landed all boats except P boats and motor launch. Still clearing for action.'

2 *August* 'Landed all furniture except which was necessary. Position of ammunition in turrets was gun loading cage waiting tray, main cage loaded, also auxiliary hoist.'

He recorded the new appointments of Beatty and Jellicoe on 3 August. 'V.A. Beatty came on board and gave a speech as regards the war. Was loudly cheered on leaving. 7.40 Signal to weigh. 1st B.C.S. sailed. General quarters, loaded. Heard firing at entrance. Turned out to be Territorials practising on shore. Out in search of two German transports. Manned the fore-guns day and night. 3 watches.'

The news of the British ultimatum was given on 4 August, then that war was to be declared at midnight, King George's message to the Royal Navy, which, incidentally, many midshipmen seemed to record in full, and then at 12 Midnight: 'War declared on Germany. Commence hostilities. I welcomed the news as I kept the first watch.' Thoughtfully, one of the first actions undertaken by HMS *Queen Mary* was to have a 'large piece of tin with "War with Germany" painted on it so as to show any fishing vessels that have not yet got the news.'

Just as Bagot was not to be in *Queen Mary* when she and her complement suffered their dreadful fate at Jutland, so did personal destiny save Keith Lawder from the terrible destruction of the cruiser *Defence* at Jutland. Lawder, in HMS *Defence* as Captain's Clerk in 1914, could scarcely exclude his excited wonder at all there was to record as *Defence* was ordered to Malta to ammunition and provision. 'All loose gear was bundled out of the ship into empty coal lighters. Officers and all hoisting the stuff out. It was quite heavy work lumping the sea chests about the place. There was no time to stow the lighters at all carefully so everything was just jumbled on pell mell . . .'[12]

It may be left to the very junior to provide the most strikingly hectic prelude to the war, one which gave rise then, as it does today, to a sense of concern at the wisdom of the Admiralty policy in its precipitation of boys of 14 and 15 into active service with the additional burden of bearing some responsibility too. Whatever may be subjective verdicts on this, I think it might be added that the responsibility should be seen as much as a sustenant to morale as a burden upon it. Plans had been made to cut short by a full year the education of the Blake Term of the Dartmouth cadets. Together with more senior cadets, they were to be sent to war appointments directly from college. Eric Bush in *Bless Our Ship* describes the interruption of a cricket match to set in motion the procedure previously notified to the college authorities, and Charles

1 August 1914: The threat of war. A Dartmouth cadet explains to his mother that he may not be coming home for the summer vacation. (Vice Admiral Sir Charles Hughes Hallett)

29

Hughes Hallett from the more senior Grenville Term vividly recalls the bulky sea chests being hurriedly moved from the dormitories by college servants and leaving unsightly but historic scars on the panelling of the staircases. Local farm carts were then commandeered to assist in getting the chests to the ferry across the Dart to Kingswear. Hughes Hallet himself was on the first train to leave as his ship was alleged to be at Chatham but after some sleep in the Royal Naval barracks at Chatham, he and others had to journey back westwards to Portland to join their appointed vessels.[13] There have to be exceptions to every rule and while naval mobilisation procedures were undeniably effective, for some cadets it may all have been as confusing as it was exciting. The sequence of events is laid out in Cadet A.W. Clarke's personal diary:[14] The Grenville Term would under normal conditions have continued college education until December 1914 but

Clarke's diary records the drama of personal involvement in national destiny.

Saturday 1 August 'Carried on with Exams as usual. Was in the middle of a cricket match when the General Recall was hoisted 3.50 p.m. Cadets were ready to leave college at 4.30 but we did not leave College until 7.00 p.m. We entrained in a special train. We went straight to Chatham dockyard arriving at 2.00 a.m. Got out and slept in the Gymnasium.'

Sunday 2 August 'Turned out at 8 a.m. went to officers' Wardroom and had breakfast. Afterwards we fell in and went to the dockyard church. We then returned and were served out with kit bags and hammocks from the store. We then went to the Wardroom to lunch. After lunch we returned to the Gymnasium and took things absolutely necessary out of our Sea Chests and placed them in our kit bags . . . Those cadets who belonged to the second fleet were mustered and their bags and hammocks placed in lorries to take them to the

Torpedoes being 'struck down below'. HMS *Prince of Wales*, Portland, 1914. (Commander H. Vetch)

Battleship HMS *Collingwood* coaling at Devonport in 1914. (Rear Admiral D.J. Hoare)

Ammunitioning ship: battleship HMS *Benbow*. (Commander H. Burrows)

station. Cadets followed. Arrived in town 4.49 went to Paddington and had tea. 5.30 left Paddington for Portland. Arrived there at 12.00 midnight.'

Monday 3 August 'Went on board *Implacable*[15] of Second Fleet at Portland. Slung our hammocks and turned in. Turned out at 7.30 a.m. and had breakfast in Midshipman's study. We were divided into watches. I took the third watch. I also took command of the 3rd division of seamen. The main top men. Each cadet received a gun. I got the fore turret. We then went to General Quarters after breakfast. Then to lunch. Then we went to Gunnery practice in a 6″ casement, Went to quarters at 4.00 p.m. I took command. Went to man and arm ship's stations at 6 p.m. and rigged search light gear. 10.00 p.m. turned in.'

Tuesday 4 August 'We started watch keeping. Had breakfast. Divisions.[16] After divisions went to general quarters for an hour, to the fore turret and worked the dumaresque.[17]

Loading apparatus was worked several times and orders were passed down from fore top as in action. All the methods of control were practised. Chipping paint-work commenced in officers cabins and wardrooms.[18] ·After lunch a lighter came alongside and we hoisted in 120 tons of coal. This took about 3 hours. The boy was slightly hurt by the winch coming back too smartly. No night defence stations. War declared by us on Germany at 11 p.m. this evening.'

It must all have seemed a far cry and not four days from the pleasant playing fields of Dartmouth. Eric Bush, reporting excitedly to the cruiser *Bacchante*, was not yet fifteen and, as has been mentioned, very small. *Bacchante*'s complement was largely reservist and, in consequence, was made up of men rather older than would normally have been the case. One wonders what the private thoughts of the fiercely moustached thirty-two years old S.J. Allen must have been when he clapped eyes on the diminutive Bush. Unfortunately, but not surprisingly, his diary records no such impressions.

THE ESCAPE OF *GOEBEN* AND *BRESLAU*: 4–10 AUGUST 1914

The last days of peace found the new German battle cruiser *Goeben* and her accompanying light cruiser *Breslau* in the Mediterranean. The British Commander in Chief Mediterranean, Sir Archibald Berkeley Milne, received somewhat equivocal orders for protecting French troop convoys from North Africa to Marseilles and for dealing with a ship which individually outmatched any units in his command. By well judged concentration, he and his second in command, Rear Admiral Troubridge, despite the problems raised by Italian neutrality, ought to have been able to block the exits to the Straits of Messina while *Goeben* coaled there after shelling two French Algerian ports. The failure to do this and the subsequent escape of the two

German ships to the Ottoman welcome of the Dardanelles, Marmora and Golden Horn had calamitous consequences. The escape clearly played a major part in bringing Turkey into the war on the side of the Central Powers. Court martialling Troubridge may have released a head of steam but smoke too was emitted. With Troubridge acquitted, the smoke was needed to hide a proper apportionment of blame between all the authorities concerned. Whether the court martial 'encouraged others', as a latter-day

Royal Naval Reservist S.J. Allen, HMS *Bacchante*. (S.J. Allen)

Voltaire might have observed, is difficult to judge. It is doubtful whether any force commander needed encouragement to seek action and if, as is hinted by Marder, Sir Christopher Cradock were to have had Troubridge in mind before seeking battle on disadvantageous terms off Coronel, then the two tragedies, one of caution, one of boldness, may possibly have been linked.

Flagship of Troubridge's 1st Cruiser Squadron was *Defence* and Keith Lawder was the Captain's clerk. Lawder's log unselfconsciously reports at the centre of the whole episode:

Monday 3 August 'Things seem to be getting pretty critical. Clearing ship for action in the forenoon. Plenty of decoding so we are working in three watches. Yesterday we were steaming west to try to catch the *Goeben* and *Breslau* who were reported to have left Messina to the westward. At about 5.30 p.m. we got orders to split up, the *Indom* and *Indefat*[19] going on west, while we turned back east to reinforce the destroyers who are watching the mouth of the Adriatic.'

Tuesday 4 August 'Watching the Adriatic all day. At about 7 p.m. we turned away and steamed South, so as to avoid any possible torpedo attack.'

For Wednesday, the log has details of the further preparation of the ship for action and the ditching of all moveable wood and the dismantling of the Captain's office, only the most important forms, books etc., being retained and stowed in a container which would sink. An alteration of course was made to avoid the trail of litter giving away *Defence*'s position. The battle cruisers were reported to have found *Goeben* and *Breslau* off Cape Bon, having chased them East but then losing them at night. Dispositions were made to catch them by closing both exits of the Straits of Messina. Then Lawder writes, still for 5 August:

The C in C in *Inflexible* was lying to the North of Malta, but for some reason joined up with the BC's [battle cruisers] instead of blocking the Southern Entrance, which we might have been fetched across to help in. In the night we ran across due West to cut them off if they ran for the Adriatic. Our only chance is to catch them at night as they outrange us by about 4,000 yards, as well as having about five knots speed on us. In the dark we might get within range of our 7.5 before being discovered. If we meet them in the day time we will run for the Greek Islands and try to make them engage us among them where we might be able to choose our own range. Unfortunately they didn't come out and so we have to go back again. The destroyers are getting very short of coal, the supply of colliers having been badly arranged by the C in C.'

On Thursday, the 6th, Lawder notes that the German ships left Messina at about 7 p.m. for the Adriatic and the chase began again, the cruiser *Gloucester* following, keeping just out of range, reporting half hourly the course and speed of the quarry. When *Goeben* and *Breslau* turned South, their high speed again enabled them to evade *Defence*'s attempt at interception. On Friday, he recorded: 'We could not have caught up with them until shortly after 6 p.m. when it would have been much too light for us to attack. We would have been sighted about 20 miles away so that they could either have run away from us or kept outside our range and hammered us. So we had to abandon the chase.'

Though *Gloucester* and *Dublin* were to press the pursuit at considerable hazard to themselves, the trap, such as it was, had failed.[20] Not merely was the whole affair to have dire consequences, it was on grounds of morale a poor start to the anticipated demonstration of British command of the seas.

2

North Sea Action and Naval Losses

Some soothing balm for the *Goeben* wound to national self-confidence and some slight reward for the public's understandable but, in fact, unwarranted anticipation of an early decisive naval victory, was brought by the first major naval action of the war. Commodore Roger Keyes, in command of the 8th Submarine Flotilla, hatched a plot with the Commander of the Harwich Force, Commodore Reginald Tyrwhitt, to raid enemy patrols in the Heligoland Bight and then to draw out major German vessels as targets for the British submarines. The Admiralty rejected Sir John Jellicoe's wish for a bigger scale Grand Fleet operation but accepted that Beatty's five battle cruisers and Commodore Goodenough's 1st Light Cruiser Squadron should take part.

In fact, lack of communication and coordination led to the development of alarming dangers not all posed by the threat of German shells. There was even a British submarine torpedo attack, fortunately unsuccessful, upon the light cruiser *Southampton*. The British light cruisers and destroyers became heavily engaged with German forces and Beatty decided to bring his battle cruisers to a rescue which placed his own vessels at alarming mine and torpedo hazard. In a dashing but uncoordinated and indifferently conducted action, the British suffered some casualties and sustained damage to four ships. The German losses were much heavier. Three light cruisers and a destroyer were sunk with 1,200 killed, wounded and missing. The victory was a boost for civilian and service morale but did not reflect the British mistakes made nor that the taking of such risks

had brought the Navy within reach of serious losses. That it had been a near run thing for the destroyers is made clear in Reginald Godsell's letter home written on the very day of the action.[1]

'How we got out of it alive I don't know, by right we should have been sunk by the Heligoland forts and the German cruisers. We had hoped to find the enemy out and get between them and the Heligoland forts and so cut off their retirement but as it happened we found them outside but not far enough to allow us to get between them, so we chased them in and fought them right under the Heligoland forts . . . while it lasted it was awful, looking back on it now one thought that one would never get out of it, and one was too busy looking after one's ship to worry. It was after it was all over that the reaction set in and made one feel sick.' Godsell described the four episodes of action in which his destroyer had taken part and wrote bitterly of a German cruiser firing on a destroyer whose boats were lowered to pick up Germans from the water. The men manning the boats had had to be left to providence which was fortunately at hand in the unlikely form of a British submarine. The submarine 'opened her hatch and popped in our sailors also three Germans as samples the Captain of the submarine told me.' The remaining Germans had been given a bag of biscuits and encouraged to row the three miles to Heligoland.

The danger of torpedo attack or mines does not seem to have occurred to Midshipman Bagot[2] in the battle cruiser *Queen Mary*. 'A splendid day, spirit of everyone extraordinary. All excitement. An impressive sight to see the 1st BCS [Battle Cruiser Squadron] steaming 27

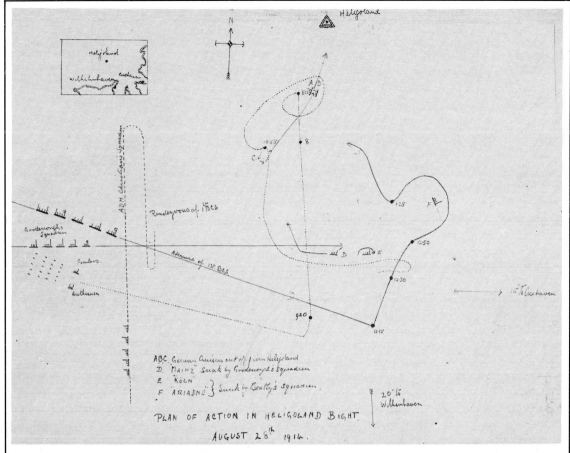

Within the sketch map:

Heligoland

N

Heligoland
Wilhelmshaven Cuxhaven

A/D
10·55
C/A
8
1·25
F
1·25
1·50
12·30
9·20
12·15
15′ to Cuxhaven

ADM Cleveland's Squadron

Rendezvous of 1BCs

Advance of 1st BCS

Goodenough's Squadron

Frontiers

Cuthmen

20′ to Wilhelmshaven

ABC. German Cruisers cut off from Heligoland
D. MAINZ Sunk by Goodenough's Squadron
E. KÖLN
F. ARIADNE } Sunk by Beatty's Squadron.

PLAN OF ACTION IN HELIGOLAND BIGHT.

AUGUST 28th 1914.

Battle of Heligoland Bight, 28 August 1914, sketched on
HMS *Queen Mary* notepaper. (Commander A.G. Bagot)

the bridge except the boxswain, who was badly
wounded, but nobly hung on to the wheel.
A shell burst in her foremost magazine,
which was fortunately empty — so the fore
part was merely flooded with water.
'Lysander' miraculously escaped absolutely untouched. With relief I saw our torpedo
plunge on its way, & put the helm over
to follow in Lysander's wake. Then a
great wave of stinging spray hit me in
the face & a deafening crack shook the
ship. I was watching the Mainz as I
gave the order — saw her broadside flash
out — & knew what was coming. One shell
burst in the water just below the bridge
— gave me my bath, wounded a man on
the f'x'le, & nearly cut the topmast in half.
Another entered the ship's side, burst inside
a boiler & scalded 4 men tending it: a
third went through the base of the centre
funnel & exploded on the other side,
killing 2 men, wounding a third, &

Heligoland Bight, August 1914: 'I knew what was
coming.' (Vice Admiral Sir Lennon Goldsmith)

kts cleared for action. Water on the decks. Everyone on top of the turrets looking for enemy, 11.30 closed up again, 11.45 loaded 13.5″ and brought to ready, chasing German cruisers. Two in number. 12.58 1st gun fired. Salvo commenced. 1.00 right gun out of action owing to lock jamming. 1.5 right gun alright again. 1.10 check fire. Shift target. One cruiser sunk. Passed *Mainz* in sinking condition on starboard side with destroyer in attendance. 1.18 Finished action. *Lion* just sunk second cruiser. A torpedo fired from submarine just missed our stern by about ten yards owing to manoeuvering of ship . . . We all came and stood on top of turret again and as we passed *Lion* and *P. Royal* we all cheered each other. We were not hit once but *Lion* was hit three times and *P. Royal* once. Submarine attack was successfully repulsed also avoided floating mines.'

The exhilaration and danger of the destroyer action are superbly evoked in Cdr Lennon Goldsmith's letter of 6 September. HMS *Laertes* (3rd Destroyer Flotilla) was one of the opponents of the big German cruiser *Mainz*. 'At 4,000 yards our good little guns were sending bursts of flame all over her, and I yelled down to stand by for a torpedo. Meanwhile she had our range to a yard, and her salvos came whistling about our heads in grand fashion. Her shooting was really admirable. As our leader, the *Laurel* turned having fired her torpedoes, she got a broadside, the main effect of which was to blow the centre gun's crew literally to bits – almost nothing was found of them. She lurched away in a dense cloud of black smoke, with her Captain wounded by splinters of brass bridge rail, and her main steam pipe in jeopardy of bursting. Next came the *Liberty* as she turned a salvo struck her. I saw her mast disappear and feared for Bartelot – he was killed together with everyone on the bridge except the Coxswain who was badly wounded but nobly hung on to the wheel . . . *Lysander* miraculously escaped absolutely untouched. With relief I saw our torpedo plunge on its way, and put the helm over to follow in *Lysander*'s wake. Then a great

Heligoland Bight, August 1914. The German light cruiser *Mainz* on fire after heavy punishment from British shells. She has struck her colours after gallant resistance and British boats are attempting to rescue the survivors of the action, many badly wounded. (Rear Admiral D.J. Hoare)

wave of stinging spray hit me in the face and a deafening crack shook the ship. I was watching the *Mainz* as I gave the order – saw her broadside flash out – and knew what was coming. One shell burst in the water just below the bridge – gave me my bath, wounded a man on the foc'sle and nearly cut the topmast in half. Another entered the ship's side, burst inside a boiler and scalded 4 men tending it. A third went through the base of the centre funnel and exploded on the other side, killing 2 men, wounding a third and shattering the two boats. The fourth entered and passed through my cabin, went on through two more bulkheads and exploded in the officers quarters. It blew the next bulkhead to bits and sent some spare parts through into the engine room bulkhead beyond, breaking and lacerating a man's arm. The hard tip shattered a dynamo fly wheel – a great solid casting and was found there lying. Meanwhile the ship had stopped. I looked at the *Mainz*, and saw a great explosion under her quarter – "our fish" I thought and felt happy.' *Fearless* took

Laertes in tow but the badly damaged ship managed to raise steam again and was able to return safely to Harwich. The destroyer commander concluded his letter: 'The men were splendid. I don't think we need to talk about deterioration yet. I've sent them all away to see their best girls – and took all on board to a nice service in the Dockyard Church this morning.'[3]

READINESS FOR ACTION AT SEA

Some qualification must be put on any attempt to describe in general terms the running of a ship at sea because of the differences in scale and specialisation appropriate to particular classes of ship. If, as representative, a destroyer, the maid of all work, were chosen, that still requires the qualification that a destroyer with the Grand Fleet was always ready for Gun action when at sea whereas a destroyer on convoy escort duties was not normally under a Gun action threat but had to be much more ready to deal with a submarine by depth charge attack. The significance of this is made clear by the fact that there were two stages of readiness for Action Stations, the second of which reflected a less critical situation during which men were allowed to fall out, a few at a time, for meals; then, for normal duties at sea, that is Defence Stations, the ship's company was divided into two or three watches with one watch always 'closed up' for action. A watch would be four hours on and four off, or four hours on and eight off, and when on watch men would man as much of the ship's armament as was within the capacity of the number on duty – usually enough men for one gun or to launch the depth charges. Engine room staff usually worked in three watches irrespective of the ship's state of readiness.

HMS *Hardy*, a 'K' class destroyer built just before the outbreak of war, had a complement of about ninety. When the ship was at Action Stations (first degree of readiness) there would be eight men to each of the three guns, at least ten on ammunition supply, three at Gunnery Control and eight with the torpedoes. On the bridge there would be four signalmen, in the wireless room three telegraphists and six ratings at the depth charge chutes and throwers. Twenty-five men would be required for engine room, boiler and fire party duties and two men, usually cooks or stewards, for first aid. On the bridge with the officers were the Quartermaster, Telegraph man and the messenger.

Of the officers, the Captain would be on the bridge with a sub-lieutenant as Torpedo Control Officer. The second in command, the First Lieutenant, known as Number One, would frequently be Gun Control Officer with his control position on the bridge too. This had a clear disadvantage in making the two senior officers vulnerable to the same enemy shell. The problem was answered by the presence of an extra officer in the 'V' class destroyer on service in large numbers later in the war, as the 'Number One' was thus freed from bridge duty. A torpedo gunner would be at the torpedo tubes and he took over the ship if the Captain and 1st Lieutenant were unable to fulfil their responsibilities. A midshipman would act as a Gun Officer of Quarters at the after end of the ship, again far from the bridge. If the ship were to carry a Doctor (a surgeon or surgeon probationer), he would be in the Wardroom preparing to receive casualties.

To move from the actuality or imminence of battle to a stage of no anticipated danger (Defence Stations at the third or fourth degree of readiness), the men off watch were employed in the mornings on ordinary ship's duties, cleaning ship in the main, but in the afternoons they would sleep or simply relax, having been on watch for four hours during the previous night and being faced by the prospect of another four hours on watch during the coming night.[4]

HOGUE, CRESSY AND *ABOUKIR*: 22 SEPTEMBER 1914

Less than a month after the action in Heligoland Bight, the Royal Navy suffered a triple loss which has remained a sad legend of the war. On 22 September, a U-boat successfully torpedoed

HMS *Hogue*: One of the three tragic sisters. (Commander G.C. Harris)

three old cruisers, *Aboukir, Hogue* and *Cressy* which were engaged without destroyer escort on slow patrol off the Dutch coast. The unsuitability of the vessels for this dangerous operation was compounded by the element of mystery concerning the agent of the first destruction, by the unwise call to the other cruisers for assistance and by the misplaced chivalry of the commanding officers of the second and third cruisers in stopping to render aid to their sisters in distress. What added especial poignancy to the losses was the death of numbers of the young lads so recently at Dartmouth from the Blake and Grenville Terms appointed from their foreshortened Dartmouth course directly to the ill-fated ships. In the resultant inquiry, the Admiralty was rightly blamed for the unnecessary hazarding and consequent loss of the old cruisers. The press attempted to counter the development of the public disquiet by stressing the overall picture of the superiority of British naval resources. Indeed, it was true that the loss of the ships was of no really damaging significance but nothing could disguise the fact that the loss of life was.

There were more disappointments or disasters to be faced in the first months of the war but little which seems to savour so much of Admiralty unpreparedness as the undignified nervous scurrying of the major units of the Grand Fleet from Scapa Flow to Loch Ewe, Loch Na Keal and to Lamlash Bay, denied security from U-boat attack in the designated base of the Orkneys. Neither Cromarty Firth nor the Firth of Forth were much better protected.[5] Despite makeshift measures, the insecurity of Scapa Flow had at first kept the Grand Fleet in expensive, continuous sea patrolling. When the battleships were temporarily moved to Loch Ewe, considered to be outside submarine range, the North Sea was being conceded to a fortunately unadventurous organiser of German maritime excursions.

Several sources recall the embarrassment of the consequence of shelling what was mistakenly judged to be a U-boat on foray into Cromarty Firth. The shelling damaged buildings in the tiny settlement of Jemimaville. Of course, a new derisive battle honour was generously offered to the ship concerned by those not engaged.

AUDACIOUS: 27 OCTOBER 1914

It was when the Grand Fleet had moved from Loch Ewe and Loch Na Keal to Lough Swilly in the North of Ireland that a really damaging blow was inflicted upon it. This time, it was a mine not the U-boat which put its explosive constraint upon British freedom of the seas. U-boats had already claimed the light cruiser *Hawke* as well as *Hogue, Aboukir* and *Cressy* but the mine claimed a far bigger prize.

T.G. Galbraith's[6] duty when submarine scares alerted the Grand Fleet at Scapa had been to go on picket boat patrol armed with a hammer to wield against the watching but presumably unwary eye of a U-boat's periscope. Even at the time he was aware of the futility of this protective aggression but he recalled in particular detail the disaster to *Audacious* on 27 October 1914 off the Irish Coast. He had had the forenoon watch, taking over at 8.30 a.m. Soon after this a bugler had sounded 'General Quarters', sending everyone to action stations. At the same time, the leading 'King George V' class battleship hoisted a signal for her three sister ships to turn 8 points to starboard in succession. *Audacious* was third in line. 'When we had almost completed the turn the bridge shuddered.' Galbraith's first thought was a collision at the stern but, checking this from the other end of the bridge, he saw the last battleship well clear. 'At that moment Captain Dampier came dashing up the bridge ladder in a great hurry and capless – as he came he asked who fired that gun. I answered no gun was fired and as I said it we were on our way to the standard compass – as we arrived there the ship suddenly rolled over to port with a rush at

which the Captain said, "Close all watertight doors." That order I repeated though we were at action stations and I assumed they were already closed.

'The Captain then ordered the signal bridge to hoist the signal: "I have received damage from mine or torpedo." At the same time he ordered me to bring the ship's head to the swell as with the sea more or less on our beam we were rolling some 15 degrees or so to Port then coming back slowly. It was a horrible feeling – one wondered if she were going to come back and felt a great desire to walk up to Starboard as she rolled to Port. The ship was perceptibly making less headway. Gradually we stopped and then one felt she was dying. Horrible feeling. All this time things were happening. Boats were being got ready for launching and the main derricks were getting ready to hoist out the boom boats and then the power failed and the main derrick took charge and as we rolled, kept swinging from side to side smashing into the superstructure, but was soon got under control again and lashed so it could not move. As the main engines had stopped it was obvious that we would have to be towed and all preparations were made to that end.'

Audacious was alone; the other seven battleships had vanished over the horizon, but 'all of a sudden, so it felt, an enormous liner came into sight – the *Olympic* and with her appearance four destroyers came in sight – the sun had appeared and coming towards us at full speed they really made a wonderful picture.' One of the destroyers took a 6½-inch wire hawser to *Olympic* and, with several shackles of cable attached to it, Olympic attempted to get *Audacious* moving. The wind on *Audacious*'s superstructure swung her round and the wire parted. Meanwhile, *Audacious* was being evacuated of all but the executive officers and forty seamen. Disembarkation was far from easy in the heavy swell. As dusk fell, *Audacious* wallowed deeply in the water, well down at the stern. Rafts had been constructed against the emergency of the ship foundering at night but it was then decided that all those still in the

Above
HMS *Audacious* slowly settling lower in the water after having been mined in October 1914, the first British Dreadnought battleship to be lost of only two in the war, the other from internal explosion. (Rear Admiral D.J. Hoare)

Below
The end approaches for a Dreadnought battleship HMS *Audacious*, October 1914. Note the men still on board. (Rear Admiral D.J. Hoare)

Above
The evacuation of all but a skeleton crew from HMS *Audacious*, October 1914. (Rear Admiral D.J. Hoare)

battleship would be taken off for the night to the destroyers and would return in the morning physically better able to secure hawsers to the tugs anticipated from Belfast.

'I personally with the Torpedo and Gunnery Lieutenants stepped into a destroyer's whaler from the upper deck abreast 'Q' turret. All the other boats had gone but the Commander was still on board *Audacious* and in the dim light could be seen as he was wearing a white sweater, wandering round the upper deck. Guns hailed him several times but he paid no attention to them. Finally we shoved off and started rowing away still shouting to the Commander until eventually he came to the ship's side and we returned, took him off, and were taken to a destroyer.'

At about 9 p.m., there was an explosion and the 23,000-ton battleship, commissioned just a year previously at Birkenhead where she had been launched in September 1912, was gone.[7] She was the first of the two Royal Naval post dreadnought battleships lost in the war and she provides a grim illustration of the error of underestimating the mine and its influence upon the course of the war at sea. German mining of the North Sea and the Channel, the frustration of the Navy's February and March 1915 attempt on the Dardanelles and the fact that the Germans laid 43,000 mines in all, suggest the need for a very different assessment. The British response to the threat of the mine was to devote sufficient material and human resources to build up a mine sweeping service of 726 vessels and this is before one even begins to consider the phenomenal statistics of allied mine laying.

The Antwerp Expedition

Unsung by reason of a lack of apparent high drama, it must be remembered that the first months of the war had seen a record of considerable naval success in vital areas of the war effort. The British Expeditionary Force had been securely transported across the Channel; its supplies were similarly reaching France without hindrance. A huge new task was completed as the German threat to France worsened, the transfer in the first fortnight of September of the main army bases at Rouen, Havre and Boulogne to La Rochelle, Bordeaux and then St Nazaire. In Antipodean waters, there was Australasian naval achievement too in taking Australian and New Zealand troops to the successful seizure of Rabaul and Samoa. A good deal of German commercial shipping at sea at the declaration of war had been snapped up and the single ship engagement between armed passenger liners had ended in victory for the British *Carmania* over the *Cap Trafalgar*.

It was no fault of naval transportation that the force conveyed to Antwerp had predictably come to grief. Naval involvement in this expedition was, however, fundamental. In response to the Belgian Government's request for a diversion, the War Council had despatched the Royal Marine Brigade and then, after a hurried personal inspection of the position in Belgium

Royal Marines preparing to disembark from HMS *Prince of Wales* at Ostend. Is the litter personal papers jettisoned for security reasons? (Commander H. Vetch)

by Winston Churchill, the First Lord of the Admiralty, two newly formed naval brigades were sent. With insufficient ships for the expanded numbers of naval personnel being recruited, Churchill had authorised the formation of a new force. It was to be comprised of naval volunteers, reservists and the Royal Naval Volunteer Reservists. These men, in four battalion brigades and with Royal Marines to stiffen them, were to form the new Royal Naval Division. Apart from the Royal Marines, the force had had a month's training and had only just been armed. For the particular purpose to which it was first addressed, it was too small and ill-equipped. As a force, it was too little trained and above all it was too late. The Marines were sent first and then the remainder of the division was landed at Dunkirk and brought up to Antwerp by train. Early on 6 October, the men were taking up defensive positions between the forts guarding the approaches to Antwerp. Their positions may be compared to the hastily erected seaside sandcastles which a family might prepare to defend an incautiously sited picnic from the oncoming tide.

The defending force was comprised of French as well as British personnel in support of the Belgian troops. Apart from battle casualty, the fate of the British varied: for some escape by foot and rail to the Belgian coast and so south westwards, for others, capture by the Germans or for one large group, a march north eastwards to Holland and consequent internment there. In all, 936 men were captured by the Germans and 1500 were interned in Holland.

Escape was secured under different circumstances by two Royal Marine officers, Tom Jameson[1] and Arthur Chater.[2] They were in action before the arrival of the main force and had seen Winston Churchill in the uniform of Trinity House as they marched up by road. When they took up position under artillery fire in open country, they had, according to Jameson, no transport, no rations and no means of digging in. 'I well remember seeing my men use their mess tins to improve any ditch to be found.' A retirement followed, being shelled by

day, withdrawing by night until trenches were reached between the forts. This was in a residential area and in the houses prepared meals had been left uneaten by fleeing householders. As the retirement continued into Antwerp, there were the signs of destruction and fire from heavy calibre German shelling. The only sign of life seemed to be stray cats. There was concern as to whether the vital bridge over the river which barred their further retirement would still be in position. It was still in place and was demolished by engineers after the Marines had crossed.

After a tiring continuation of the march on pavé roads to St Nicholas and beyond, they were able to board a train filled with refugees. The train came under small arms fire when it halted at an open station and level crossing. The fire was returned at German soldiers running along the road parallel to the track. 'Then we saw the two engine drivers leave their engines carrying lighted lamps and disappear into the darkness.' Investigation showed that the line ahead was out of order. In the confusion of firing and panic-stricken refugees, a Major French got the officers to form units to attack concentrations of German troops in and around the station. Interrogation of a German prisoner revealed that the enemy was an advance guard of a far larger body and the whole episode of the train had been a trap. Many of the Marines were desperately tired but only a swift determined move offered any prospect of escape. Only about 150 had the capacity to achieve it by moving on another eight miles to Selsaete. Here they entrained for Bruges and from thence again by train to Ostend.

For Chater, the circumstances of his escape were through being wounded in a stand made at Lierre. Taken to hospital in Antwerp, he was evacuated by car to Ostend. For him an awkward recall is not of his wound but of being asked his age by Churchill when all Chater's men in earshot could hear his embarrassed confession to a youthful eighteen years.

From the Royal Naval Division battalions whose men chose Dutch internment rather than

German captivity, one man recalls eating raw meat on the march and, after sleep in a field, the rasping sound of his frozen uniform as the escape attempt was resumed,[3] another the sight of the bodies of Belgians suspended from trees from which they had been hanged on spying charges by Belgian authorities.[4] J.D. Ewings wrote from Holland to his Walthamstow Unitarian Minister of the last stage of the Benbow battalion's stand: 'We decided to leave the fort (which was our last stand, after being in three lots of trenches) by the underground entrance and chance getting clear by dodging the enemy who had by this time completely surrounded us. We managed to get clear somehow and we heard the fort being shelled about a quarter hour later. Soon after this we lost our officer . . . What seemed the thing that kind of affected me most was when we made a last stand against an unexpected patrol in a ditch, a few moments before they came into range, the fellow next to me brought out a Bible and started reading it and saying his prayers. Until then I hadn't worried about death or anything but when I saw this fellow, I think I can say I felt rather frightened of what might happen if I got killed, . . . I thought I would just tell you about this but perhaps you cannot understand it.'[5]

To set against the gloom of failure at Antwerp, the embarrassment of a poor performance in a combined operations landing at Tanga in East Africa, the humiliation of the German shelling of Hartlepool, Whitby and Scarborough and the shock of the destruction from internal explosion of the old battleship *Bulwark*[6] moored in the Medway, there was also during these early months of the war an undoubted record of achievement. Several British and Commonwealth Expeditionary forces had been safely transported world wide to war stations or staging posts, the Australian cruiser *Sydney* had destroyed the German raider *Emden*, a second raider *Karlsruhe* had fallen to a fate similar to that of *Bulwark*, the *Konigsberg* had been bottled up in the Rufiji delta of German East Africa, and the navy had rendered considerable assistance to the allies in Flanders through bombardment of German coastal positions.

September 1914, off Manila Harbour, nothing to shoot at but sharks. Geoffrey Miles, lying down, watches a fellow officer at work. (Admiral Sir Geoffrey Miles)

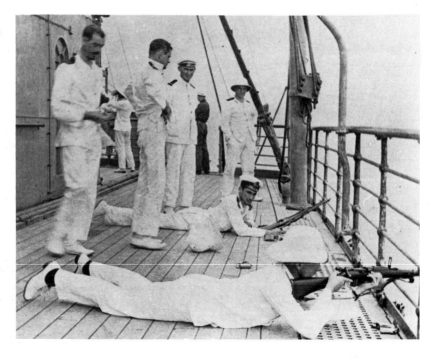

Emden destroyed. This photograph was taken the day after she was driven ashore. (Captain the Honourable H. Wyndham Quin)

Emden's bridge. (W. Shearer)

August 1914, Far East: a Jardine Mathieson steamer *Hang Sang* has been hurriedly adapted for mine laying. Its full speed was 9 knots! (Admiral Sir Geoffrey Miles)

4

Coronel and the Falklands

The circumstances which led to the battle of Coronel illustrate sadly that in fulfilling a naval role on so vast a scale, the Admiralty did not always get the distribution of British units appropriately spread in strength to widely separated vital areas. In those early months of the war there was still a German squadron at large and from a British point of view the result of policy error over this was to be tragic. In the longer term, British retribution was to bring consequences even more tragic to the German victors of the November battle.

The German China Squadron under Vice Admiral Count Von Spee was at large off the West coast of South America. It consisted of two armoured cruisers, *Scharnhorst* and *Gneisnau*, and three light cruisers, *Leipzig*, *Nurnberg* and *Dresden*. To oppose this modern force, Rear Admiral Sir Christopher Cradock had but two old cruisers, *Good Hope* and *Monmouth*, the light cruiser *Glasgow* and the armed merchant cruiser *Otranto*. The Admiralty sent only the powerfully armed but slow fifteen-year-old battleship *Canopus* to strengthen Cradock. The Admiral interpreted the instructions which reached him as a requirement that he must search for and engage the German ships threatening the trade routes. Accordingly, he sought battle before ensuring that if it were to develop, he would have whatever protection *Canopus* could offer. He must have been aware of his overwhelming disadvantage in his ship's speed, armour, armament and even crew training (his ships' companies were mainly reservists). Of the explanations offered for Sir Christopher's suicidally brave action, Professor

Marder inclines towards an intriguing link with Troubridge's *Goeben* dilemma. Marder quotes the navigating officer of *Glasgow*. This officer, Lt-Cdr P.B. Portman, wrote home in a letter dated 10 November 1914: 'He was as good as told he was skulking at Stanley? He was a very brave man and they were practically calling him a coward.'[1]

About fifty miles west of Coronel, as the sun set, Cradock's ships were clearly outlined in the afterglow. Von Spee skilfully avoided having his sighting obscured by the rays of the setting sun. In seas so heavy that *Good Hope*'s and *Monmouth*'s 6 inch guns were unusable, the engagement lasted an hour before *Good Hope* blew up two hours before disabled *Monmouth* was pounded at point blank range till she sank. Staff Officer (Intelligence), Lloyd Hirst who, but for fortunate circumstances, would have been with *Good Hope*, watched her torment from *Glasgow* before the latter, accompanied by *Otranto*, made her escape.

'*Good Hope* after three quarters of an hour in action, was keeping up a desultory firing from only a few of her guns. The fires on board were increasing their brilliance, and soon she dropped back more on our port bow and towards the enemy. At 7.50 p.m. there was a terrific explosion on board between the mainmast and her aftermost funnel, and the gush of flames, reaching a height of over 200 feet, lighted up a cloud of debris that was flung still higher in the air.

'Those that lived through the explosion must undoubtedly have been stunned; her fire then ceased, as did also that of *Scharnhorst* upon her and she lay between the lines a low black hull gutted of her upper works and only lighted by a dull red glare which shortly disappeared.

HMS *Good Hope*, lost with all hands at Coronel in November 1914. (Commander G.C. Harris)

Although no one in *Glasgow* actually saw her founder, she could not have survived such a shock many minutes.'[2]

Hirst's retrospective account of his feelings during the action is very good and he adds a sad little postscript of the dazed flutterings of Brazilian parrots bought by *Glasgow*'s ratings for an anticipated homeward journey but in futile sympathy released during the engagement.

Apart from *Glasgow* and *Otranto*'s escape, the only British compensation for the loss of 1600 men and two ships was the heavy consumption of irreplaceable German shells. This was to be a factor of some significance as the Admiralty moved swiftly to exert retribution.

THE BATTLE OF THE FALKLANDS: 8 DECEMBER 1914

The decisive speed of the British response to the defeat off Coronel makes a striking parallel with the 1982 crisis also off South American waters.

Septuagenarian Sir John Fisher, recalled to the Admiralty as First Sea Lord, ordered the immediate dispatch of two battle cruisers, *Inflexible* and *Invincible*. They were hurriedly prepared at Devonport for overseas service, their task to do more than reverse a naval defeat. They had to restore faith in the Navy and indeed the Government itself needed buttressing against the increasingly felt national bewilderment that neither on sea nor on land was the war effort progressing satisfactorily.

So precipitate was the departure from Devonport on 11 November that a number of naval dockyard workers had to remain aboard *Invincible* to complete refurbishing tasks. Off the South American coast, Von Spee was seriously short of ammunition. He planned merely to destroy the Falkland Islands Port Stanley wireless station before he risked the return to German home waters. On this occasion, however, the priceless advantage of time was to be seized by the British. *Inflexible* and *Invincible* with support ships reached Port Stanley on 7 December, twenty-one hours before Von

Spee's squadron appeared. By this narrow margin of time and because of German communicational incapacity to warn Von Spee, a shattering surprise awaited the latter at the Falkland Isles.

Nevertheless, the British Force Commander, Admiral Sir Doveton Sturdee, was himself nearly caught in Port Stanley without opportunity of using the superior fighting quality of his ships at sea. On 8 December, Von Spee's two leading vessels hove in sight of the harbour where the British were still coaling. The coaling battle cruisers were given an extra quarter of an hour's warning by the lighthouse keeper who

was the first to sight the German squadron and sent his wife on horseback to Port Stanley to give the alarm. (She was heavily pregnant and died as a result of the emergency ride.) Any possibility of the battle cruisers being trapped was fortunately averted by shelling from the concealed, camouflaged and deliberately grounded *Canopus*. The German ships sheered away from the shelling thus allowing the British vital time to clear the port entrance. The distinctive tripod masts of modern battle cruisers must have brought grim realisation to the Germans of their likely doom. With the battle cruisers were four heavy cruisers, two light cruisers and an armed merchant cruiser in 'General chase' of Von Spee's two armoured cruisers and three light cruisers.

Battle of the Falklands, 8 December 1914. The battle cruiser *Invincible* picking up survivors from *Gneisnau*, photographed from HMS *Inflexible*. (Commander C.F. Laborde)

To British superiority in materiél were joined the advantages of a calm sea, clear visibility and plenty of daylight for the chase. The three German light cruisers were ordered to scatter but two were swiftly hunted down and sunk, the third escaping this action but not her fate in due course (in March 1915). The British battle cruisers and the heavy cruiser *Carnarvon* hammered the German armoured cruisers *Scharnhorst* and *Gneisnau* to defeat but the German commanders, officers and men fought their last battle with superb courage.

E.W. Bullock,[3] one of *Inflexible*'s off-duty stokers, asleep on the engine room gratings where it was pleasantly warm, was roughly awakened to hectic activity on the sighting of the German ships approaching Port Stanley. He was ordered to get the coal shoots down at once. With this carried out he was able to join men on the deck pointing at five smudges of smoke on the horizon. When action stations was sounded it was with an accompanying order: 'Hands shift into clean underclothing', a pre-

caution against the contamination of wounds by fragments of dirty clothing. 'We all had a meal as it was to be a long chase and the cease fire had been given as the enemy had increased the distance between us. When we were nearly in range again action stations were again sounded and in this action I was in the fire party amidships. About 2 p.m. the fire started and clouds of coal dust were everywhere and at each salvo the ship shook and rattled. We had an undercover position but abandoned it now and again to clamber up the casing to have a look at what was going on. The first time I did this the hat I was wearing sailed away with the blast from a gun and I noticed that the deck was scattered with pieces of shrapnel.' Bullock was to see the *Gneisnau* suddenly turn on her side and slowly vanish leaving hundreds of men in the icy water. Rescue work from *Inflexible* was hampered by the damage caused by an enemy shell to the main derrick and the larger ship's boats.

HMS *Carnarvon* had a newly appointed midshipman, R.M. Dick.[4] He was doing signal duties and his letters home had a youthful awareness of the interest and excitement of distant travel. On 7 December, the day before the Battle of the Falklands, he wrote of having met in the last weeks: 'monkeys and natives and

Opposite top
Battle of the Falkland Isles: *Invincible* and the 'County' class cruiser *Kent* or *Cornwall* leaving Port Stanley, viewed from *Inflexible*. (Commander C.F. Laborde)

Opposite bottom
Battle of the Falklands: HMS *Inflexible*. (Commander J.G.D. Ouvry)

fire we go out in chase of 5 german ships + 3 or two Battle Cruisers engage two germans We watch the action for an hour. We are now doing 25 knots chasing the other three. They have ceased firing and they are too far away from us to see what have happened The Bristol captured two colliers We received a wireless message to say that the Invince and Inflex sunk the Scharn

horst and Gniesnau The Glasgow went into action about 3.30 and We sounded off action at 4.15 As soon as they sounded off a cheer went up and we opened fire at 4.30 Our Foe Turret and A and B Groups opening fire first. She was off our Port Bow and we were going at 25 knots a record for this ship We seen about 6.0 that she had caught afire aft on her quarterdeck soon after that we had started using Lyddite shell and a hour afterwards she burst out into flames fore

The flames were going up 9 or 10 ten feet high but she would not cease firing There was a lull in the firing afterwards We opened fire again on her and at times we got whole Broad sides into her and shell was pitching all around us and at 9.0 she sent up signals of distress We went as close as we dared and attempted to lower the boats only two was sea worthy the others being hit by german shell And before they could get over there we

Dec 9 Arrive Back at Falkland Island We are Pumping Water out of our bunker all night where we were hit We are listing heavily to hort We prepare again for coaling Kent & Kent sinks the Nurenberg It is raining and very cold We send a mail We have steamed 18171.2 miles up to Nov 22nd Dec 10th We coal ship 200 tons to give ship a list of 15 degrees and when we finished we found we were damage

Battle of the Falklands: the diary of a seaman aboard HMS *Cornwall*. (F.G. Holvey)

whales and wonderful butterflies and lizards and weird creepy crawly things.' But such travelogue memories were soon to be submerged. Three days later, he described the aftermath of the Falklands battle: 'Three of our boats, all we had, went to the rescue, I went away in charge of the fourth cutter . . . I was able to save one officer and fourteen men odd in my boat, then as we were rowing back to the ship the whaler, which was overloaded by the men in humanity, sank and we had an extra twelve men in our boat. We got alongside and had a most frightful time trying to get those half drowned wretches on board, but we managed it in the end, though one man was lost I regret to say . . . The horror of that two hours of rescue work will live with me for many a long day . . . It brought the ghastliness of war very very close to me.' From his account of the rescue work, Dick moved to the battle itself.

'I don't mind admitting freely that I was in the deuce of a funk when we sallied out. I hope I did not show it. But I got so excited that I soon forgot all about the purely personal view before we were an hour out of the harbour. I think these remarks apply to most people. The long wait was rather trying but once we got firing we had no time to think.' The midshipman was rightly proud of *Carnarvon*'s gunnery, stirred by the King's congratulatory message ('I am swelling 'wisibly' with pride'), but he returned again to the aftermath of battle. As *Gneisnau* vanished, she left 'a great mass of floating wreckage with funny black dots bobbing up and down seen as we reached the crest of the wave. I told my coxswain to steer towards the edge because being a small boat in a heavy sea, if we had gone to the middle we might have been swamped by a rush and I had to consider my own men. When we got to the spot, there was a huge quantity of wreckage: stools, hammocks, baulks of timber, life buoys and all sorts of things, all bearing a freight of men. Most of them could not climb into the boat and we had the most awful job to get them in.' Then, on having to take extra men in: 'They fought, and bit and held onto one's legs . . . one in particular who apparently took a dislike to me rose at me with a mad grip and eyes starting nearly out of their sockets. I said: "Sitten sie down" with great firmness in my best German but with little effect.'

Of the battle, Professor Marder observed that it had been 'fought out in the old style, the last such action between surface vessels alone in the war. Thereafter, torpedoes, mines, submarines and to some extent aircraft introduced complications unknown to Sturdee and Spee.'[5]

Marder might well have made still more of the battle's historical union with Coronel. By location, by time, by motivation, by materiél imbalance pre-determining the result and by tragically unavailing courage unsustained by any legitimate hope, the officers and men of Coronel and the Falklands are permanently bound together. 'Yes we all admire those Germans who fought so bravely against such vastly superior odds,' wrote Clerk C.F. Laborde to his father on 13 December. Laborde had thought *Gneisnau*'s sinking: 'a terrible and awful sight . . . so different from looking at a picture.' His account of the kindly hospitality offered by *Inflexible* to *Gneisnau*'s survivors reflects the traditional respect by the victor for the vanquished in naval action.[6]

Eastern Mediterranean

DARDANELLES SHELLING

Attention must now be drawn to 1914 naval operations of a distinctly different character from all that has been considered so far. On 3 November, in retaliation for the shelling of Russian Black Sea coast towns by a German/Turkish fleet led by Admiral Souchon in *Goeben*, the Admiralty had ordered the bombardment of the outer forts of the Dardanelles. The battle cruisers *Indefatigable* and *Indomitable* led the bombardment together with French ships. W.G. Cave,[1] a rating in the cruiser *Dublin*, was impressed by what he saw. 'It seemed to me to be a deliberate bombardment of practically every building in sight, care being taken not to hit the minaret. This would be because of its use for range finding and also perhaps because of a wish not to offend religious sensibilities. The main target was certainly the fort, which we made a mess of, culminating in a huge explosion. There had been sporadic return fire from several positions but we certainly weren't hit and it was all a most one-sided affair.' Ironically, this demonstration shelling was as effective as anything achieved in early 1915 in the serious attempt to destroy the forts protecting the minefields but it was not immediately followed up. It seems a curious instance of action preceding policy, an ill-advised procedure.

AKABA

A second operation was at Akaba to secure the southern outlet of the Suez waterway from the Mediterranean to the Red Sea. The light cruiser *Minerva* was used in operations well described in Lt H.K.L. Shaw's letters.[2] 'We arrived off the town on Sunday afternoon and sent in a boat to demand the surrender of the town which was refused so we promptly started to bombard forts, barracks etc., with 6″ lyddite and shrapnel and soon had the forts silenced. We could see all the enemy leaving the town and taking to the hills. It was terrible to see the effect of our shells huge buildings crashing down in a heap of smoking ruins and flames. We ceased our firing after about an hour's bombardment and lay off the town all night. In the morning we landed a large party from ship as follows; a Company of Marines under the Captain of Marines, a company of sailors with field gun, a company with maxims and the Gunnery Lieutenant and another company with rifles. I had charge of the last lot. It was most exciting work and I could not help thinking of the weird working of fate. Who would ever have imagined that I, a peaceful "Union Castle" officer would in a few months time be leading a company of blue jackets against a lot of wild Turks and Arabs but such was the case. I had a revolver and cutlass (not seeing the force of getting my swagger sword all ground up). It was just daylight when we left the ship in boats the ship covered our landing with a bombardment of shrapnel. Arriving on shore we advanced on town from three different places. We fired several volleys into the fort, barracks etc. then advanced taking cover where best we could, the few remaining soldiers in the place did not wait for us but firing wildly for a few moments took to the hills. It was my first experience of being under fire and was a very exciting experience. Well we then proceeded to set fire to fort, barracks, post office, also searched the town and burned all sorts of stores – all this time being sniped at from the hills. We had a great morning's work and soon had the place useless from a military point of view. We then returned to ship having no casualties.'

The following day, another party landed and advanced inland searching for any concentration of enemy troops:

'Sun beating down, not a bit of vegetation anywhere, huge eagles and vultures circling over our heads. We came across any amount of skeletons of men and camels picked clean by these brutes.' There were a few skirmishes on this venturesome foray but the main body of the enemy remained in concealment.

THE SYRIAN COAST

Operations not dissimilar to Akaba, but having an entrancing admixture of diplomacy and demolition, took place on the Syrian Coast and off the Gulf of Smyrna at this time too. HMS *Doris*, another light cruiser, was engaged in shelling and landing shore parties to demolish installations at Alexandretta. Midshipman Haldane's Christmas Day letter indicated the variety of the work.[3] 'Here we first bombarded some railway bridges and two trains. Then we sent an ultimatum to the town threatening to bombard it if they did not give us up their stores. They replied by threatening to kill an English prisoner at Damascus for every man killed during the bombardment. After much difficulty we compromised and destroyed the two engines . . . While we were at Alexandretta we sent a landing party to destroy a railway bridge' and later: 'we went to a bay near here to examine a German steamer which was supposed to be aground. As we were approaching it we were fired upon by a field gun ashore. Fortunately we were not hit and quickly silenced it by a few shots from our own guns which were far more powerful. The German ship proved to be a valuable steamer only built a year or two ago and in excellent order. We had not the time or means to salve her so after removing all that we could which was a good deal we blew her up and set her on fire, totally destroying her . . . I miss being at home very much. However I ought not to complain as we are getting a very

pleasant and exciting time here.'

The diary of Signal rating S.W. Brookes indicates similarly the interest and variety of the work.[4] 'The coastal telegraph line of five wires and the telephone to Damascus were carefully removed for a distance of 1200 yards. No time was wasted in its destruction. 44 poles were "downed" and sawn into three parts. A number of the inhabitants even stopped to converse with the party and the only soldier seen was a Turkish mounted gendarme who rode off at a furious speed for about 2 miles in the direction of Saida. The party all returned safely after discarding an elderly man of his fowling piece and at 1 p.m. the ship departed. Mention might be made of a number of tortoises and rare frogs which were also brought off.'

After describing a steel and concrete bridge which could not be 'fatally hurt' and a railway engine 'wounded in its vitals' Brookes described an incident which would seem to have been from Gilbert and Sullivan comic opera. A Turkish civilian official accepted an ultimatum that railway engines must be demolished but 'explained that he had no experience and asked that some dynamite might be lent to him. So at 2 p.m. Lt Edwards with a party of torpedomen specially selected on account of the size of their beards (it being a Moslem town) set off with gun cotton . . . However on reaching the town the Turks refused to allow anyone to land and the German engineer confessed he could not use the explosive.' The official sought a compromise in delay but this was not granted. The official then suggested that 'if our Torpedo Lieutenant were to lay the charges satisfactorily to himself, he could then proceed to fire them if he were lent for the purpose to the Ottoman navy in order that the actual explosion may be caused by an officer duly authorised to represent the Sultan.' Under the eye of the US Consul, the operations were duly carried out, the actual firing being done by a Turkish quarryman.

Reference must be made to a fourth operation, launched in the Persian Gulf, for it was what the Official History records as 'One of the

Top left
HMS *Doris* preparing to hoist out her Nieuport Seaplane. Note the derrick to the left. (Dr T.G.N. Haldane)

Below left
Engine failure? HMS *Doris*'s seaplane in tow. (Dr T.G.N. Haldane)

Below
Landing party from HMS *Doris* cutting down a telegraph pole in the Gulf of Smyrna! (Dr T.G.N. Haldane)

Above
German ship *Odessa* being destroyed by HMS *Doris* in Ayas Bay. (Dr T.G.N. Haldane)

Left
At least one man aboard HMS *Doris* had his washing done properly! Mohammed, servant to Mr Dupuis, the interpreter, hard at work. (Dr T.G.N. Haldane)

6-inch shell from HMS *Doris* hitting a building in Port Sahib, Gulf of Smyrna. (Dr T.G.N. Haldane)

shelling, were followed by a transfer of the force at Bahrein to Saniyeh on the Turkish bank of the river on 8 November. From Saniyeh the troops were in a position to prevent the launching of an attack on the refinery. A parallel to this successful coup was the operation at the mouth of the Red Sea on 9 November in which a commanding fort at the entrance was shelled and a nearby landing effected from which troops carried out further demolitions before reembarkation.

In the five months of war in 1914, there were some operations involving naval personnel to which no allusion has been made in this book. An outstanding example of this is the work of the Royal Naval Air Service (RNAS) armoured cars in Belgium but, subjectively, I have chosen to exclude such obviously land-based operations from this book. From a similar standpoint, RNAS flying operations will not receive what might be judged their due. This aspect of young officers' and ratings' service involved air support of the allies on the Western Front and, in particular, reconnaisance and offensive patrol work over the Belgian coast. For some time, the RNAS also held responsibility for the air defence of the United Kingdom by seaplanes, planes and airships. However, in excluding the flying work of naval personnel, some exception will have to be made in dealing with the essentially combined operations in the Dardanelles during 1915 and also, for example, in the part played by airships and seaplanes in convoy duty later in the war. There will be further brief exceptions. One incident demands inclusion because of its extraordinary sequel. On Christmas Day 1914, there was an attempted seaplane bombing of the Cuxhaven Zeppelin sheds. By superlative work, Lt-Cdr Nasmyth's submarine, *E11*, rescued the crews of three seaplanes which had not succeeded in returning to their mother ship. Despite being under Zeppelin attack during the episode, the rescue was carried out successfully and *E11* remained in the area until it was certain that the three aeroplanes had sunk and could not be salvaged by the Germans.

best managed combined operations of the war.' There was a worthwhile objective, skilled deception of the enemy, efficient cooperation between the army and navy, surprise and decisive action. Small wonder that success ensued. The first move was the landing of advance detachments of the VI Indian Division off the Island of Bahrein in the Shatt el Arab. From the place of landing the force was ready to prepare protection for Abadan, the island with its Anglo-Persian oil refinery and pipe line so vital to the navy's modern oil burning ships. (The fact that the troop transports arrived off Bahrein on 23 October, before the German Turkish attack on Russian Black Sea Ports, does seem to suggest that the British Government had given up all hope of keeping the Turks out of the war.) Well-judged naval and military dispositions from the 31st, the day after the Black Sea

6

Home Waters Again: The Battle of Dogger Bank

Though it took place in the month following Coronel, no event in 1914 so seriously damaged public confidence in the Navy as did the 'brazen effrontery' of the German North East Coast raid on 16 December 1914. An earlier demonstration off Gorleston at the beginning of November had been headed off by bold destroyer interference, though a strong German force had been able to lay mines near the East Coast. In December, however, German cruisers and battle cruisers without hindrance shelled Hartlepool in County Durham, Whitby and Scarborough in North East Yorkshire. They departed having laid mines, adding further potential injury to the insults and injuries inflicted. The whole episode might well have developed into a major action. Just as the Germans had hoped to lead the British battle cruisers onto the battleships of the High Seas Fleet, so might the British 2nd Battle Squadron, with its advance intelligence of German movement from their river roadstead bases, have trapped the German raiders. On the British side, bad weather, low visibility and a signalling error from Beatty's flagship were to blame for the East Coast's tribulation and the national humiliation. The successful coup of British secret naval intelligence had led not to battle on advantageous terms but to a sense of frustration felt on the Mess deck as well as in the Admiralty buildings.

A major result of the raid, quite apart from the damage and loss of life was that Beatty's battle cruisers on 20 December were ordered to move their base from Cromarty to Rosyth and, in consequence, were so much nearer the likely location of a similar German operation.

The last day of a year of mixed fortune for the navy added another item to the debit balance. The old battleship *Formidable*, while on exercises in the Channel, was torpedoed. Despite the severe damage caused by two torpedoes, she remained afloat in heavy seas while the dangerous work of bringing aid was attempted by the light cruisers *Topaze* and *Diamond*. There was heavy loss of life, thirty-five officers and five hundred and twelve men. Vice Admiral Sir Lewis Bayley, who had determined the straight course and slow speed of *Formidable* between the exercises he was conducting, was ordered to strike his flag for such hazarding of *Formidable* and the disastrous consequence. Today, however, if distance might be allowed charity as well as enchantment, we may note with stronger emphasis than was accorded at the time, that no submarine had been reported in the Channel for a month and the heavy seas had made U-boat operations seem most unlikely.

Just as certainly as the combination of new technology and geography introduced special constraint upon the exercise of naval initiative in the North Sea, so were there factors which made it desirable or worthwhile to risk confrontation, but on terms necessarily planned to be self-advantageous.

On 23 January, Admiralty intelligence re-

Dogger Bank: January 1915: the battle cruiser *Tiger* on the left, *Blucher*, sinking, on the right. (Commander P. Haig-Ferguson)

Dogger Bank: the end of *Blucher* recorded in Midshipman Ouvry's Journal. (Commander J.G.D. Ouvry)

H.M.S.
DATE.

fired her after guns at them. One of them the *Meteor* was hit and she was covered by a cloud of steam and smoke. She was not however very seriously hit. The destroyers drew off. meanwhile we poured salvo after salvo into her as did the remainder of the Ships, except the *Lion*. She was soon in a sorry plight. We manœuvred round her so as to discharge a torpedo at her. She fired two of hers at us, which passed one just ahead and the other just astern of us. Our first torpedo could not be followed, and the result is unknown. Later on we fired another. This one, I believe, hit, as there was an explosion shortly afterwards low down with the bows. By this time she had stopped and was little more than a wreck. She still discharged solitary guns at us, and soon she ceased fire altogether. One of our salvoes exploded by her A turret and the whole turret was blown over the side. Another blew away her Conning Tower and bridge; and a small shell exploded just above her top, and brought her topmast down with a crash. There was a ghastly explosion forward, and for about one minute her fo'c'sle was enveloped in a huge mass of brilliant flames. At noon she struck her colours. Just previously the *Arethusa* and some destroyers had approached & the *Arethusa* fired one torpedo into her. At 12.10 the *Blücher* sank, many survivors

ported that the German battle cruisers under Admiral Franz von Hipper had left their River Jade base. The German intention was not known but their area of intended operation was. In fact, they were making for the Dogger Bank in order to investigate the strength of British forces there and to attack ships on patrol in these waters. The Admiralty planned an interception. The two squadrons of Sir David Beatty's battle cruisers with an accompanying light cruiser squadron and with three light cruisers, submarines and destroyers of the Harwich Force were to be just North of the Dogger Bank awaiting the unsuspecting Germans. The Admiralty had made a vital mistake: it had failed to involve Jellicoe's battleships in what would then have been a trap of classic potential.

The British cruiser *Aurora*, heading a flotilla of fifteen Harwich destroyers, had made the first contact with a German light cruiser and her destroyers. At 7.15 a.m. on 24 January, *Aurora* was shelled and returned the fire. The German ships were ordered to concentrate and make high speed for their base. In the chase which followed it was the British battle cruisers led by Beatty's flagship *Lion* which opened fire at 9 a.m. at a range of considerably over eight miles. *Lion*, at 26,350 tons, had a main armament of

Above
Dogger Bank: a contemporary painting by a surgeon probationer J. Shaw, HMS *Druid*. (Dr J. Shaw)

Below
Dogger Bank: *Indomitable* towing the 'wounded' *Lion*, in a contemporary painting by a Surgeon Probationer James Shaw, HMS *Druid*. (Dr J. Shaw)

eight 13.5 inch guns. The leading British battle cruisers reached their designated maximum of 27 to 27½ knots and only the slower *New Zealand* and *Indomitable* were unable perceptibly to overhaul their opponents. *Lion* fired on *Blucher*, then *Moltke* and then *Seydlitz* but she was herself heavily hit as the three German ships directed their fire on the British van. Next in line, HMS *Tiger*, under the command of Captain Pelly, continued firing upon *Seydlitz*, conforming to a principle of General Fleet instructions to disable the enemy's van and misinterpreting Beatty's signal to engage opposite numbers.[1] The respite given to a consequently unengaged German ship was well used and further damage was inflicted on *Lion*. Beatty's flagship was so badly holed and damaged internally that she began to fall behind. Then, in a mistaken judgement of the presence of U-boats, Beatty ordered an alteration of course which put his ships at a disadvantage in the chase, that is fully astern of their quarry. With his wireless destroyed and some of his signalling halyards gone, Beatty's communication problem grew as the distance separating him from his other ships widened. Of two signals he made to continue the pursuit, one was ambiguous and mistakenly read and the other was not read at all.[2]

The British battle cruisers concentrated their attention upon the disabled, doomed but still combative *Blucher*. As a result of this time-taking sledge-hammering of the one unit which could not run, the heavily damaged *Seydlitz* and the other two German capital ships were able to escape. Beatty, leaving *Lion* by destroyer for *Princess Royal*, transferred his flag to her and attempted to renew the pursuit. It was too late and the need to provide a defensive destroyer screen for the crippled *Lion* properly became an over-riding consideration. The towing aid of *Indomitable* was needed to bring *Lion* home to safety.

Conditions aboard *Blucher* during her brave fight must have been appalling. The translation of a contemporary German personal experience report describes the terrific blast pressure resulting from explosions in a confined place. 'All loose or insecure fittings are transformed into moving instruments of destruction. Open doors bang to and jam. Closed doors bend outward like tin plates and through it all, the bodies of men are whirled about like dead leaves in a winter blast to be battered to death against the iron walls – men were swept from the deck like flies from a tablecloth. Everywhere blood trickled and flowed.'[3]

Midshipman Brian Schofield[4] of *Indomitable* wrote to his parents of his work in Q turret firing upon *Blucher*. 'In and out recoiled the guns as we pounded the enemy. Open goes the breach, bang comes the cage, in goes the shell, then the charge, down goes the cage, bang slams the breach. "Left gun ready" shouts a voice and 850 lbs of explosive ready to hurtle at the enemy – when the cease fire sounded, I jumped up on top of the turret . . . and made a rough sketch . . . It was a pathetic sight to see that huge ship a mere wreck lying helpless as we steamed by with our guns hot with the fury of battle and just waiting for her to go down . . . Well Dad this is our first taste of battle and I hope it won't be the last.'

Pride in *Queen Mary*'s gunnery is clearly evident in A.G. Bagot's log. 'Our 13.5 blew the *Blucher*'s turret clean over the side, ditto *Moltke*. At the finish both *Derfflinger* and *Moltke* were on fire, only one turret of *Moltke* and two of *Derfflinger* were left firing.'[5]

Commander Lennon Goldsmith of *Laertes* had been saddened to see *Lion* like a 'great wounded mammoth with water gushing from her wounds – for blood' as she was towed away and indignant at the interruption of rescue work for *Blucher*'s crew. 'An aeroplane flew over and dropped four bombs at us while we were fishing for the swimming Germans.'[6]

Dogger Bank had clearly been a victory for the Royal Navy. The Germans had fled and had lost a heavy armoured cruiser and nearly 1000 men killed and almost 200 as prisoners. The British had lost no ships and but eleven men killed. Nevertheless, it had been far from the decisive victory for which there had been reas-

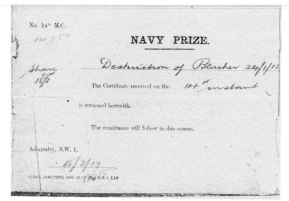

Dogger Bank: a surgeon probationer's 18 shilling share of the Prize Money. (Dr J. Shaw)

almost hull down. It was sad to see the mighty Kä... being towed slowly North and the "Indomitable" — she looked so like a great wounded mammoth with water gushing from her wounds — for blood. An aeroplane flew over us and dropped 4 bombs at *us when we were fishing for the swimming Germans! Very much love to you all from your very loving so*

Ken.

Dogger Bank, January 1915: a destroyer Captain writes of Beatty's Flagship, *Lion*. (Vice Admiral Sir Lennon Goldsmith)

onable expectation. Apart from the failure of the plan to involve the Battle Fleet, Beatty's signalling and the lack of professional intuition by Rear Admiral Sir Archibald Moore, in command of the 2nd Battle Cruiser Squadron, enabled the Germans to escape the full penalty of their incaution and the well-laid British trap. Moore had had a chance to defeat the German battle cruisers decisively and he had not taken it, choosing to bag a dying bird rather than the flight of plump pheasants. British gunnery too had been disappointing with *Tiger* in particular performing poorly. Above all, there was a very special profit and loss consequence of the battle. The Germans, aware of their nearness to losing *Seydlitz* through flash igniting cordite charges in a gun turret's working chamber, saw the danger of the destruction of a whole ship by a single shell. They took the necessary measures to secure against such a tragedy. The British, however, remained in ignorance of this design weakness in their own battle cruisers. A dreadful penalty was thus to await them at Jutland nearly a year and a half later.

7

The Dardanelles and the Gallipoli Peninsula

Any brief summary of the reasons for launching the Dardanelles venture, a venture which grew into the Gallipoli Campaign, runs the risk of exposing the writer to charges of superficiality or subjectivity. There is, however, clearly an obligation to paint an historical backcloth for the personal dramas revealed in the diaries, letters and recollections of men who played a part.

That the Turks might be knocked out of the war by the appearance of a British naval squadron off the Golden Horn was a Churchillian concept shared by Lt Colonel Hankey, the Secretary to the War Council. It was to be given an early chance of translation into action by a Russian request for assistance in diverting Turkish concentration away from their Caucasian focus of attack on Russia. Two factors assume great importance in any consideration of the form which the concept took in the process of being progressively translated into action. First, there is the way in which it was possible to build powerful arguments disarmingly to influence judgement that here at the Dardanelles lay immediate, mid-term and long-term potential advantages in the waging of the war. Secondly, there is the consideration or lack of consideration of the sufficiency and suitability of the means necessary to win success in this supposedly well-favoured location.[1]

For the historian, hypothesis and hindsight can be likened to the sword and battle-axe for the medieval knight, at one and the same time weapons of attack and against which to defend. To use one imprudently exposes an opening for adversarial use of the other. Why did the War Council not weigh more carefully the resources needed for success at the Dardanelles? The answer may lie in the urgency of the Russian request and the readiness of Churchill's response. There is ample evidence in their deliberations of an awareness that troops, many troops, would be needed at some stage. That this awareness took no form in an alternative proposal for Dardanelles action is a tragedy from the point of view of those who see the idea as a strategic conception surpassing all others and also from the point of view of those who see the whole venture as a tragic waste.

There are powerful arguments that success would have resulted from a major combined operation benefiting from such elements of surprise which still might have been secured by eschewing further bombardment after the ill-advised shelling of 3 November 1914. In the 8 January War Council Meeting, Kitchener had stated that: 'The Dardanelles seemed to be the most suitable objective as an attack here could be made in co-operation with the fleet' – 150,000 men would be sufficient for the capture of the Dardanelles but he reserved his final decision until a closer study had been made.[2] Hankey had prepared a celebrated paper advocating an assault by a French, British, Russian, Greek and Bulgarian force but no serious study was made of what was needed and what could be assembled. In fact, Churchill was to captivate his British colleagues and French counterparts with the economy of his plan for the navy alone progressively to force a passage through the Dardanelles and thus to exert British naval power off Constantinople itself. By a process of depressing logic, the naval endeavours in February and March led to a delayed combined operation, destroying en route the surprise elements which might have assisted the combined operation to victory. Just half the numbers of Kitchener's January estimate were used on 25 April, the day of the landings and an attempt to maintain at one and the same time offensives on the Western Front and a major military endeavour elsewhere, was surely rooted in infertile ground.

In view of the frustration which attended naval endeavour at the Dardanelles, it is a little ironic that high achievement should result from one of the earliest and most hazardous attempts aggressively to enter those waters, whose main South Westerly current runs at up to five knots. The eight-year-old Submarine *B11*, with a crew of twelve or thirteen, successfully found its underwater way into the Narrows accepting the challenge of varying depths, the strong current, the mine fields, shore batteries, searchlights, shore-based torpedoes and patrol boats. *B11*'s Commander, Norman Holbrook, has described the successful stalking which followed his dive to 60 feet at the Narrows. 'I came up to periscope depth and saw on the starboard quarter a large old Turkish battleship. We went down again but the tide got up and swept us into Sari Siglar Bay and now the ship was on our Port bow. I altered course and it needed full speed to combat the current and get into position for a shot. I fired one torpedo and then had to reduce speed because the lights were getting low and obviously our batteries were failing. We then found ourselves aground stern first and I could see the ship down by the stern and smoke from the shore suggesting that fire was being directed at us. By using full revs we got off but I couldn't see the way out of the bay. I looked for the farthest bit of land through the periscope but the Coxswain said the spirit compass lenses had packed up and all he could see was black spots. I told him to follow them and at full (submerged) speed in twenty minutes a sea horizon appeared on our Port bow. We made for it and were more or less swept out of the Straits having dived of course through the Narrows. We had been under water

for nine hours. What a wonderful crew – each a first class man – but we had been very lucky.'[3]

The date was Friday the 13th of December 1914. The battleship *Messudieh* had been sunk and Holbrook had earned the first gazetted naval VC of the war. Every member of his crew was to receive an award. It was the first triumph of a truly astonishing British submarine record in these waters. Turkish sea communications and, more remarkably still, as will be seen, land communications too were put at such risk by submarines that the Turkish supply of munitions for defence of the Peninsula was reduced to dangerously low proportions. The Sea of Marmora constantly held one or more marauding submarines from 25 April and men were landed to blow up viaducts and railway lines. *E11* and *E14* were to operate successfully even off Constantinople and in one twenty-nine day patrol in August, *E11* destroyed a battleship, a gunboat, six transports, an armed steamer and twenty-three sailing ships. The total submarine bag for these waters in 1915 was two battleships, one destroyer, five gunboats, nine transports, over thirty steamers, seven ammunition and store ships and 188 sailing vessels.

Just how varied was the submarine work in these waters is made clear in the diary entries for August of a Petty Officer serving in *E2*.[4] (It is worth recording that three British and four French submarines were lost in operations such as those described in the diary.) After the crew had checked torpedoes, embarked ammunition and charged up the batteries on 13 August 1915, the submarine dived at 3.55 a.m. 'We dived and proceeded through the Straits at an average depth of 80 feet. Got caught in nets about 6.25 but the Captain managed to clear them in about ten minutes, going to a depth of 140 feet to do so. While in the nets they must have fired at a mine for we heard the explosion but was too far off to do us any harm. Through the nets we proceeded on our way till about 12.30. Looked round several times and found a destroyer following us up. Went to the bottom about 1.00 p.m. had dinner and a rest. Came to surface at 3.15 p.m. and started charging battery which had dropped well down on our run through. About 6.30 our friend the destroyer appeared again so went down to 50 feet for the night. Came up on the 14th at 5 a.m. Coast clear so ran on gas engine to Sea of Marmora. After about an hour we sighted a gunboat. Dived and attacked her and soon disposed of her with a torpedo from our starboard beam tube. One way of announcing our arrival. Proceeded under engines and picked up a dhow taking six Turks out of her. Carried on till a sea plane made us a visit. This sent us under quick enough to dodge the bomb she dropped for we heard it explode when we were under. After she had gone we rose and proceeded to our rendezvous with E11. Picked her up about 2 o'clock and transferred ammunition to her. She gave us a bag of apples.'

On the following day another dhow was sunk and her crew and the six captured Turks, were put in the Dhow's equivalent of a life boat. E2 was unable to sink a steamer now sighted because the submarine's gun came loose on its mounting and, perhaps for reason of torpedo scarcity, the underwater weapon was not used. On 16 August after avoiding a destroyer and burning two more dhows, shelling from the shore forced E2 to dive and she later in that day played cat and mouse with a gunboat. It was not until the afternoon of the 20th that the submarine settled this account by torpedoing the gunboat which had seemed unaware that she was still being stalked. Twice, sighted steamers had to be left to their devices as they proved on close examination to be hospital ships but a large transport ship was torpedoed on the 22nd. Several harbours were visited but it appeared that E11 had bagged all the potential targets. On Thursday, 26 August, E2 fired at a gunboat zigzagging with a destroyer; the latter was hit and sunk. Ammunition works at Mudania were shelled as was a railway track, more dhows were burned (sixteen in one day). Then approaching Constantinople on 7 September:

'Prepared a gun cotton charge for our 1st Lieutenant to take ashore to damage the railway. We got on the move at 2 a.m. and made our

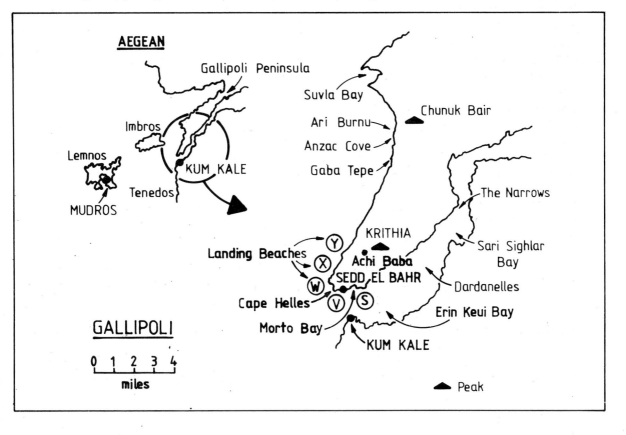

way nearer in shore till we reached 20 ft. First Lieutenant went off with his charge about 3 a.m. Since then we haven't seen him. Should very much like to see him back again for he was too good to lose. We waited on the beach till well after daylight with our conning tower awash but had to clear out as there were destroyers about . . .' The Lieutenant had been captured or killed, fuel was low and the equilibrium or trim of the boat had to be restored by what Stephens calls a "thorough reorganisation of the water in different tanks". One result of this return to an even keel was that meals were easier to take. However, on 12 September: 'at 2 a.m. the boat decided to come up on her own no doubt due to water leaking in aft and upsetting the trim.' This had to be seen to but they were then to hear by wireless from their mother ship that *E7* had been sunk. There was now an absolute dearth of targets in the Sea of Marmora and *E2* proceeded down to the Narrows, dived through but surfaced too early only to be shelled into a further dive and safe emergence in the afternoon of 14 August. Stephens, whose diary makes nothing of the dangers faced and the discomforts endured, laconically records the cheers and band reception and official photograph at Imbros but added: 'nobody thought to ask us if we would like a few loaves of bread which would have been very acceptable.'

Stephens' diary bears witness to the constant aggression of the submarines in the Eastern Mediterranean, the disciplined kinship of the crews and the leadership of the commanders. In the role the navy was required to play after the failure of the great attempt at close range bombardment of the Narrows on 18 March, there lies one of the paradoxes of the Dardanelles that from this date the surface ships were simply to play a supporting role to the army and no longer to strive to force the Narrows, thus doubling the Turkish anxieties even if straining the navy's available resources.

On 19 February 1915, in accordance with Churchill's plan, the Eastern Mediterranean squadron had commenced the shelling of the outer forts of the Dardanelles. Shelling from three old French battleships supplemented the British fire. In addition to spotting fire for each other, the accuracy of the shelling was assisted from the air by a seaplane from the seaplane carrier *Ark Royal*. Midshipman William Powlett, doing spotting work from HMS *Vengeance*, noted in his journal that a 'waterplane' was being fired at by the Turks.[5] Such a 'waterplane' was piloted by Royal Naval Air Service Lieutenant G.R. Bromet (*Ark Royal*).

Bromet's diary is as attractive as it is informative, relating the details of a seaplane pilot's support of the Dardanelles campaign. He comments with insight on so many aspects of the endeavour. The need to husband carefully the small number of fragile seaplanes is clearly revealed. The problems of wind and sea conditions for successful take-off and operating effectively, engine failure and slowness in climbing to ever unimpressive ceilings, all this is in the diary as is an account of a fearful spiralling dive into the sea by one seaplane. The pilot, Flight Lieutenant Garnett, just managed to keep the head of his scarcely conscious and injured observer above the water. In rescuing this man, Garnett had also rescued an idea, as it was his observer, Flight Commander Williamson who conceived and advocated the island-type configuration for aircraft carrier flight decks, an idea only belatedly accepted by the Admiralty.

HM Special Service ships were noted on their arrival off the Dardanelles in early March. They were merchant ships with wooden, skilfully copied battle cruiser superstructure. 'From a distance *Tiger* completely hoodwinked the majority of us', Bromet recorded. Closer inspection, however, showed that she was much too high in the water, had a merchant ship's stern and dubious funnels. The Turks may well have got a surprise when they torpedoed one of these 'battle cruisers' and the wooden turrets floated away!

Professional judgement runs cheek by jowl with more intimate personal observations in the Bromet diary. The Air Department came in for stricture for so belatedly favouring the supply

Sopwith 225 Sunbeam seaplane No. 857 aboard HMS *Ark Royal*, in the Dardanelles in 1915. (Air Vice Marshal Sir G.R. Bromet)

and support aeroplane work from the Island of Imbros rather than developing the meagre seaplane resources. Ashmead Bartlett, the War Correspondent, also drew Bromet's scorn, as did the national newspapers, though nothing so trenchantly as Churchill for his Dundee speech which minimised the naval losses sustained in the Dardanelles and the difficulties still to be faced in bringing the campaign to a successful conclusion. 'Apparently those who govern the country and draw large salaries for doing it, think there is nothing wrong in hoodwinking the public. To a serviceman this sort of thing is bewildering.'

Bromet expressed some concern about the quality of the 'hostilities only', 'civilian-dominated' Royal Naval Division and whether it would uphold the navy's reputation which was in its care when the nation's cause was being served but he also wrote of an RNAS officer posted to another appointment that he had been: 'Lacking in warlike guts and I think school work or some quiet seaside station would suit him better than knocking about in a ship in the Dardanelles.'

For praise, Bromet singled out the submariners and also the French naval officers who were 'always very polite'. The French officers were well liked by their British counterparts. RNAS ratings are paid a warm tribute by Bromet's naming of individual air mechanics who serviced the seaplanes. On one occasion in April: 'C.P.O. Finbow worked solidly on difficult and annoying work for 16 hours and I cannot praise him or A.M. [Air Mechanic] Somner too highly for their painstaking and successful work and for their cheery optimism throughout.' Bromet generously praised his fellow pilots, men who battled to reach and maintain a height for effective operations though frequently 'bumped' down to a very vulnerable altitude by turbulence in the air.

The diary reveals Bromet as a man with a capacity for shrewd appraisal of the historic scene upon which he played a limited role but it also shows him as a man of sensitivity. Nowhere

Above
Gunroom officers of HMS *London* in 1915 in the
Dardanelles. Note Charles Drage, third from the left in
the middle row, whose North Russian experiences are
included in this book, and the youthful faces of the two
seated in the front. (Captain C.F.H. Churchill)

Below
Ship's Divisions at Morning Exercises aboard the battle
cruiser HMS *Inflexible*, the crew running round the deck
with the encouragement of a band. Note the officers taking
part, bottom left. (Commander C.F. Laborde)

is this more clearly in evidence than in his recording of the tragic death of RNAS aeroplane pilot Flight Commander Collet. Having taken off from Imbros, Collet's machine suffered engine failure and crashed from a height of 180 feet. 'The wind was strong and the gusts were very bad over the Kephalo Cliffs and, when making a turn to land again he lost control of the machine and came to earth with a fearful crash as the result of a nose dive and side slip. The machine caught fire and before the pilot could be rescued he had been burned beyond recognition. Death resulted half an hour afterwards.' Bromet had admired him sincerely. 'To do his damnedest for his country was his only consideration' and that he should die so shocking a death as a result of an accident rather than in enemy action depressed the seaplane pilot, forcing him away from what he called his normally callous acceptance of the reality of war into a preoccupation with 'the sad thoughts that go hand in hand with the loss of a dear friend, or much admired brother officer.'[6]

To return to the development of the naval attack, the forts had to be destroyed as they protected the minefields, the real obstacle to allied progress. The low profile of the forts and the unsuitably shallow trajectory of naval shells for such a target as well as the difficulty of firing from a moving platform, resulted in far less damage being wrought than the smoke, dust and showers of earth might have suggested to observers.

'We did a lot of damage', wrote Charles Hughes Hallet (HMS *Vengeance*) to his mother, 'but the next three days were such windy ones that we could not continue.'[7] Operations were resumed on the 25th. 'We began again', reported Hughes Hallet; 'after lunch we and the *Cornwallis* ran in to 3,000 yards firing at most of the four forts.' Four more ships took turns on the same targets 'smashing up everything. That night we lay outside all night. Houses were blazing all over the place ashore. Several times one of the magazines would blow up with a most awful noise. All the night the minesweepers were working up and down sweeping for mines.'

The battleship *Queen Elizabeth* had joined the force and had commenced shelling with her 15 inch guns. Turkish batteries and ammunition dumps on both sides of the entrance to the Straits were hit but it was now clear that complete, irreparable destruction of the defences could only be achieved by landing demolition parties. The first was landed on 26 February. HMS *Irresistible* provided a naval demolition party and a covering Marine party

Ship's cat Jane on 15 inch guns of *Queen Elizabeth*'s Y Turret, Mudros, April 1915. (Admiral Sir T.H. Binney)

for the guns at Seddul Bahr on the European shore. From *Vengeance* similar parties landed at Kum Kale on the Asiatic shore. The first casualties were at Kum Kale where the Turks counter-attacked the Marines, killing a sergeant and wounding three of the party. Further demolition parties were landed on subsequent days.

The task of a junior signal rating with a landing party from *Irresistible* at Kum Kale is made clear in that rating's subsequent account. Signalman Peacock was laden with a service revolver, ammunition and a cutlass, two semaphore flags, a brass signalling lamp and candles. He had to remain near the officer commanding the party. Coming under sniping fire the party split up at a cemetery wall. Moving to left and right under cover of the wall the two parties charged cheering around their respective corner only to find themselves facing each other. A somewhat undignified retreat to the whalers ensued. When Peacock was safely aboard *Irresistible* he found that there were empty cartridges in his revolver but he had no recall of the targets at which he had fired.

The demolition work itself was laborious. Three lots of 30 pounds of wet gun cotton held in a canvas hose were used for each gun to be destroyed. On the spot, dry gun cotton was inserted into a thin tube as a primer. Firing was by means of either an electrical detonator or a time fuse and detonator.

Turkish opposition to the landing parties varied in strength. Good work was carried out on 27 February and 1 March so that with naval bombardment too, the slow work of mine sweeping was progressing satisfactorily. However, on 4 March, a severe check to further shore landing parties was administered by much stronger resistance.[8] An indifferent British performance under admittedly trying cir-

Queen Elizabeth inside the Dardanelles under fire from the forts of the Narrows on 18 March 1915. Above her foretop is the seemingly insignificant hill, Achi Baba. (Admiral Sir T.H. Binney)

cumstances at Kum Kale was a sobering experience for all who survived this particular affair. More seriously still there was an under estimation of the lines of mines and the numbers of mines to be cleared. The Royal Navy, rather than French ships, was undertaking the bulk of the mine clearance work but the twenty-one commandeered North Sea trawlers were quite unable to do the work required, such was the strength of the current.[9] In night work, there was the menace of searchlights picking up the scarcely moving boats as easy targets, despite naval covering fire. On occasion, trawlers were sunk or heavily damaged and even confused into colliding under the fire from the Turkish batteries. On one occasion, they turned tail without even commencing their dangerous work. A support light cruiser, *Amethyst*, was also repeatedly hit. Where the waters were narrow, escape from defensive fire was difficult; where the waters were broader, the mines more easily escaped attention.

Clearly, the forts had to be put out of action completely for the sweeping to continue. On 18 March, a concentrated attack was launched by the long range and close range bombardment of British and French ships. The battleships moved in for their work in a carefully worked out sequence. *Queen Elizabeth* was to fire 170 15-inch shells while in action. Well within the entrance of the Straits, her station and track were not to lie off the Asiatic shore, where tragedy awaited successive ships as they turned for their passage out of the Narrows. In these sheltered waters of Eren Keui Bay, a line of unswept mines claimed the British pre Dreadnought battleships *Ocean* and *Irresistible* and the French battleship *Bouvet*. The battle cruiser *Inflexible*, like the French *Gaulois* was severely damaged too. The confined arena of the Dardanelles had been the scene of high drama, described by many intimately involved. The performance of their varied duties, the fate of their particular ships, the opportunities afforded to watch happenings immediately nearby, ensured that there was much about which to write.

A midshipman in the battleship *Agamemnon*

HMS *Inflexible* after being mined on 18 March 1915 in the Dardanelles. An attempt is being made to position a collision mat over the hole but this did not prove effective. *Inflexible* survived the experience. (Commander C.F. Laborde)

Dardanelles, 18th March 1915: tripod mast of HMS *Inflexible*. 'Not under Control' signal hoisted after being mined. (Commander C.F. Laborde)

Above
Dardanelles, 18 March 1915: Purposeful activity and calm supervision. HMS *Inflexible*, having been mined, is taking a list to Port. The sailors manning the capstan are manoeuvring the collision mat into position. Two seamen with fiddles are apparently setting a tempo for the effort required. (Rear Admiral B. Sebastian)

Above right
Dardanelles, 18 March 1915: Some of *Inflexible*'s casualties being evacuated in the cutter. (Commander C.F. Laborde)

Right
Dardanelles, 18 March 1915: HMS *Inflexible*. Standing by to abandon ship, a stage which in fact was not reached. (Commander C.F. Laborde)

kept a personal diary which from his vantage point well describes the fortunes of the day. Humphrey Banks nicely juxtaposes such details as the provision of sandwiches to be taken to action stations and the Senior Gunnery Officer giving all the officers an indication of the overall plan of operations. 'The *Queen Elizabeth*, *Inflexible*, *Lord Nelson* and ourselves are to go up to within a range of about 14,000 and deliberately bombard the forts at the Narrows, fort 13 falling to our share among others. When the forts seem to be sufficiently silenced the four French ships were to pass through the 1st Division which formed line A and go up to 8,000 yards from the forts, the two outside ships being detailed to locate and destroy torpedo tubes which are supposed to exist on the European and Asiatic shores. The French ships were to be relieved by the *Ocean*, *Irresistible*, *Albion* and *Vengeance* (Line C). Action was sounded at 10.30. At 11 a.m. we came under the fire of howitzers and field guns and shortly afterwards we opened on No. 13 with the fore turret after first firing a few rounds from P1. Our shooting in the fore turret was very good and the Captain complimented the turret on it. The *Q.E.* was nearest the European side, then came the *L.N.* then us, then the *Inflex.* 12.15 French Squadron commenced to close in and passed through Line A who kept up a steady and deliberate fire on forts, single shots. No reply from the forts but concealed howitzer batteries firing. French ships closed to 10,000. 1.55 French ships returning. *Bouvet* was struck by shell[10] in magazine at 2 p.m. and sank in 1½ minutes. No explosion was seen, but she was coming down Straits at full speed, gradually listing more and more to starboard eventually

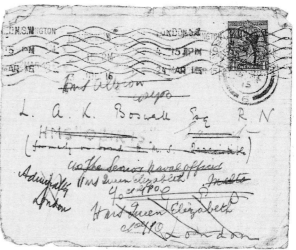

Losses and damage to British ships in the Dardanelles on 18 March 1915: a Seaman's diary. (G.E. Keeler)

turning turtle and going down stern first. Destroyers and picket boats went to save life immediately, but only a few survivors. They state that the magazine blew up. 4.11 *Inflexible* struck a floating mine and proceeded out of action with a slight list to starboard. 4.13 *Irresistible* struck a floating mine and took a heavy list to starboard and was down by bow. She went in towards Asiatic shore under Aren Kioi Village. 4.30 Destroyers closed *Irresistible* destroyer *Wear* going alongside and taking off crew. *Irresistible* was under fire from concealed howitzer at this time. *Ocean* then stood in to tow off *Irresistible*. The General Recall was hoisted at 6.5. 6.30 *Ocean* was struck on the starboard side in the engine room by a torpedo or mine.[11] The engine room was flooded and the helm jammed hard aport, so she could only move in circles. She listed about 15° to starboard and destroyers went alongside and took off all her crew. *Chelmer* was hit amidships as she was pushing off. 8.15 Remainder of fleet anchored off (island of) Tenedos. 9.0 Picket boat returned

The envelopes of a letter addressed to a midshipman of HMS *Irresistible*, sunk on 18 March 1915. (Captain L.A.K. Boswell)

and reported *Gaulois* had been hit by a shell.' (She had to be beached for temporary repair on Rabbit Island at the mouth of the Dardanelles). Banks recorded the following day that among the slightly injured were twelve from *Ocean*, 'mostly old men who had jumped off onto the destroyer too quick and sprained their ankles.' It would be interesting to know just how far they had had to jump. It may well have been a daunting prospect. There is a much grimmer reference too concerning *Inflexible*: 'Her fore torpedo flat, fore air compressor flat and fore shell room were flooded and 40 men drowned in them. She was also struck in the foretop and the officers in it including her gunnery commander were mortally wounded. They died last night.'[12]

Censorship strongly influenced letters in a way strikingly different from diaries and logs. Hughes Hallett's letter of 19 March 1915 reads in its entirety: 'No news: I am quite well and safe'. There was, however, frustration at newspaper reports of the action.[13] A consciousness of the importance of their operations and a determination to show proper optimism are revealed in T.S. Fox-Pitt's letters written from *Lord Nelson*. On 19 March 1915, he wrote: 'I wish I could tell you all about it as it is fearfully interesting. I should think it is one of the most interesting affairs in the war and it will be most important when we succeed.' On 22 March, he wrote that the loss of the allied ships 'makes very little difference as they were remarkably ancient, especially the French ship. On the whole things are going on very well here, though from what we see in the papers we get they are talking an awful lot of rot, and the pictures of the forts are marvellous, I didn't realise journalists had such wonderful imaginations.'[14]

For years it remained on the conscience of Cdr R.J. Hayward that as a Paymaster Sub Lieutenant in HMS *Irresistible* he had not done 'anything useful after we struck the mine.' With hindsight, he regrets that no responsibilities had been allocated for the emergency of the ship being reduced to a sinking condition. 'Action stations duties seemed no longer to obtain.' After lyddite shells struck the mined and listing ship, the order came to abandon ship. 'A considerable number of the ship's company jumped overboard intending to swim to a destroyer lying close at hand. This was unfortunate as the destroyer was about to come alongside to take off survivors but was prevented from doing so by all the live bodies in the water and increasing all the time. I decided that the point had come to join them. I inflated my life saving waistcoat jumped in and took off.'[15]

One survivor at least of *Irresistible*, Edward Grayken, was to have the unsought distinction of a second abandoning of his ship as *Ocean*, to which he had been transferred, was the next to strike a mine and sink.[16] A rating in *Irresistible*'s foretop, E.M. Peacock, was fully occupied with control work when there was 'an awful crunch, the ship shuddered and began to list to starboard. There was a complete silence for a few seconds and then the Gunnery Officer ordered "Everyone out of the top." One by one the crew went down the ladder leaving myself and two officers to follow when the Gunnery Officer said "off you go, lad" and down the ladder I went. Then just before I reached the lower rung a lyddite shell hit the foremost funnel and I let go the rungs on the mast and fell into the top (not many feet) and onto a number of gym mats which had been stored there.' When he got to the deck and had moved over to the guard rails, such was the list of the ship that it only needed a push from someone behind and he was in the water, losing new boots which had been slung round his neck but soon being picked up by the destroyer *Wear*.[17]

Whether the Turks, after what they quite reasonably term their victory of 18 March, were almost exhausted of ammunition supply and whether there were revolutionary ferment in Constantinople are not questions to be considered here. Rough sea conditions in any case arrested the British naval operations. On 22 March, the naval Commander in Chief, Vice Admiral J.M. de Robeck, and the newly arrived Commander in Chief of the military force being brought together, General Sir Ian Hamilton, held a conference aboard the *Queen Elizabeth* which resulted in a decision to prepare for the combined operation of landing troops against positions now certain to be defended.

Above all, it must be understood that the landing of troops was to facilitate the operations of the fleet in getting through the Narrows and on to Constantinople. This explains quite reasonably Hamilton's choice of beaches at the tip of the Peninsula and a major landing further North East where it narrowed and held commanding heights overlooking the Dardanelles. Capture and control of the Peninsula would

Sailors and soldiers in training for the Gallipoli Landings at Mudros Harbour, April 1915. (Captain L.A.K. Boswell)

neutralise Turkish defence of the European shores of the great waterway and make much less dangerous the minesweeping and any necessary bombardment of the Asiatic coast. To this end, diversionary landings and feints were planned to prevent the appropriate concentration of Turkish defence.

There was much to be done in the planning of the landings, correcting the stowage of the transports and training the officers and men of the Mediterranean Expeditionary Force in disembarkation, small boat work and beach landing. That mistakes were made is scarcely to be wondered at; that the operation was launched a month after the *Queen Elizabeth* conference is nothing short of remarkable no matter how regrettable that circumstances beyond the control of the planner had donated precious time to the Turks for the reinforcement of their defences.

A worrying illustration of the problems which could attend soldiers and sailors faced with the sudden need for swift cooperation in a crisis was provided by the troopship *Manitou* incident where men were drowned attempting to escape from a ship under attack but in fact not hit by the torpedoes aimed at her.[18] There was to be, in fact, far better cooperation by all concerned on the day of the landings despite the level of opposition which fully justified the 29th Divisional Commander's awesome note to all his men that there would be 'heavy losses by bullets, by shells ... by mines and by drowning.'

Bearing a more particular burden of responsibility than at any stage of the war hitherto, were the young midshipmen who were to be in command of picket boats and pinnaces towing in the strings of cutters and whalers to the selected landing beaches. A great armada of ships was secure in the haven of Mudros on the Island of Lemnos. The hugely impressive hulls, the music of bands, the route marches, the disembarking exercises, the ubiquitous evidence of preparation for a cooperative endeavour, all combined to sustain collective and individual confidence but many in blue or khaki must have wondered how they would perform their command responsibilities under fire and in front of their men. While at Mudros on 20 April D.S.E. Thompson (*Implacable*) wrote: 'Had to go and bring 1,000 soldiers off the beach in evening, it was the deuce of a job. They didn't know the bows from the stern or anything else. We had to do it all on our own. We had no matelots [sailors] to help us.' On the eve of the landing he 'discovered I was Senior Officer in our tow so went to picket boat to direct operations. Got no sleep all night of course.'[19]

An army padre, Oswyn Creighton, wrote of being saddened to see midshipmen at a ship's concert: 'Some only sixteen, drinking a good deal of whisky and smoking many cigarettes during the evening.'[20] This entry in his published diary was for 19 April. There was less than a week before some of these midshipmen would have to prove that they were men. In fact, they would do this even before sceptical Australians, not renowned for acknowledging anyone's endeavour other than their own. Ferrying troops onto the beaches under fire, bringing off wounded and in so many other ways on the day of the landings, the midshipmen would exercise command, show presence of mind and demonstrate resilient courage to the admiration of all.

In looking at naval support service in the Gallipoli Campaign two factors, however obvious, deserve reemphasis. Not only did naval officers and ratings work their small boats from ship to shore and also served on the beaches, all the time under potential or actual fire, but whole ship's complements shared some of the hazards of the soldiers of the Mediterranean Expeditionary Force. As the ships so frequently were close in shore they were even within small arms fire. The second and contrasting factor is that a proper bunk or a similar hammock and a hot, nourishing and by no means unappetising meal awaited the sailor at the end of his spell of duty. Such were not the conditions of service for soldiers on the Peninsula. Some of the related differences – fresh water untainted by petrol tin containers, proper latrines, rest, re-laxation and medical attention under good conditions – are perhaps brought together effectively by the evil smell of dirt and putrefaction which hung over the Peninsula: for the sailor it was unpleasant, briefly to be endured at close hand or when wafted aboard by an off-shore breeze; for the soldier it was so all-pervasive as to be accepted without comment, simply as part of his lot.

By just about two hours, the first landings made on the Peninsula were of Australians of the Australian and New Zealand Army Corps. They were landed about one and a half miles north of the intended beach. Explanations for this and the consequence of it have occasioned a continuing debate. Interesting theories have been put forward. It seems most likely that the current drifted the small boats north of their designated course and that in the half light and under the enormous stress of the occasion, a naval lieutenant mistakenly identified a headland as the correct one for their course.[21] The troops had been brought in to a small bay backed by three successive lines of broken ridges, severe slopes and precipices altogether different from the wider beach and more gentle slope inland of the terrain of their intended landing area. Part of the continuing debate is whether the dash of the Anzacs might have secured victory just north of the Gaba Tepe headland for which the landing was planned, in contrast to the frustration they endured at the small Ari Burnu promontory. Undeniably, the intended landing area would have been dominated and enfiladed by the higher ground of Gaba Tepe and from the greater height further North of the same ridges they had from their actual starting point to cross.

The Australians and then the New Zealanders were brought in by lines of towed small boats, first from battleships, then destroyer and finally from transports. All accounts evoke stirringly the coiled tension of the early morning as the battleships, *Queen*, *London* and *Prince of Wales* each slowly towed four lines of small boats towards the coast. Each line was headed by a steam picket or pinnace towing three

Australians embarking on HMS *London* on 24 April 1915 for the 'Anzac' Gallipoli landing on the following day. Note the naval padre in mortarboard. (Captain C.F.H. Churchill)

whalers or cutters. There was a midshipman with every steam boat and its small working complement. Three more senior naval officers were located separately in one of the twelve steam boats. Each boat to be rowed had five sailors for this purpose, with about forty heavily burdened Australian troops crammed in with them.[22]

The battleships stopped less than three miles from the coast and the picket boats stole in towards the beaches with their laden tows. From within a hundred yards of the shore the tows were cast off to be rowed in independently. A long, dark night of mounting, silent stress was being gradually illuminated by dawn, exposing the enterprise, when the sound of the picket boats' engines or propellers, flame from a funnel, the creak and wash of muffled oars or the shadowy outlines of the approaching boats alerted the defenders. A single shot and then a fusilade rang out from the land ahead. As Charles Drage, a midshipman (HMS *London*), had written in his diary for 24 April, it was going to be 'no picnic'.[23] Two midshipmen from the cruiser *Bacchante* were with the tows. Eric Bush was not yet sixteen but his gallantry on this day was noted in *Bacchante*'s official

Report of Proceedings. He and midshipman Dixon had been seen 'repeatedly doing good work'.[24] Bush in *Bless our Ship* has attempted to recreate the scene.[25] His picket boat had a crew of eight in all and they towed a launch, a cutter and a ship's lifeboat. One hundred and sixty soldiers and perhaps twenty-one seamen and a Petty Officer were under his command. Just after they had slipped their tow, Bush heard a bugle call. A Very light and a star shell followed and then a rain of bullets. It was dark enough for the flashes of the firing to be seen clearly but light enough to see Turks moving on the shore. First, the launch had to be picked up, wounded men in her having to wait attention until the other two boats were secured and more troops taken ashore. These troops had clambered down into the launch from a destroyer thus preventing the discharge of the wounded. A seaman from the picket boat was mortally wounded but the work had to go on to clear the troop transports now that the battleships and destroyers had discharged their human cargo. All morning, afternoon and into the night under shell and small arms fire, Bush's picket boat ferried troops in and wounded out. When eventually his stint was completed just before midnight he and his men were utterly weary and the young midshipman slept the clock around.

An Australian soldier wounded at the landing

75

SS *River Clyde* approaching 'V' Beach five minutes before beaching at 0610 hours on 25 April 1915. (Captain L.A.K. Boswell)

Gallipoli: The 'W' Beach landing on 25 April 1915 – six VCs before breakfast. (Captain H. Wilson)

wrote just over a week later that the hospitality and kindness he had received aboard *Prince of Wales* was unforgettable. 'If I ever have the chance to help any British sailor I shall do so.[26] Much less convinced of the adequacy of medical arrangement for the heavy casualties was Eric Longley Cook a midshipman of *Prince of Wales*. He had taken a load of wounded to ship after ship, only to be waved away as they were full. 'Finally I took them to my own ship, *Prince of Wales*, and risking a beating for insolence secured alongside and went up to the officer of the watch, told him what had happened and that

he must take them. All was well, the wounded were taken aboard and I returned to the beach.'[27] In fact, this anecdote provides a true reflection of the insufficient provision of casualty arrangements, one of the saddest and most reprehensible tragedies of 25 April at both Anzac and Cape Helles, where the British 29th Division was landed. The young naval officers at Anzac, exhausted as they must have been, were fortunately unaware of the alarming prospect raised by the Brigade commanders who wanted their men evacuated that night from the hard-pressed beach head which they had stormed at first light. Admiral Thursby, in naval command off Anzac, and Sir Ian Hamilton himself, with his resolute exhortation to dig, dig and dig, forstalled any further thought of reembarkation. Anzac beach was to be held.

At Helles, naval personnel conducted troops to five separate beaches. At one of these beaches, 'V', a collier, *River Clyde*, was run ashore in an attempt to throw 2000 men swiftly into the assault. Under heavy fire, Captain Unwin RN, with a midshipman and seamen, manhandled, lashed and held together lighters at the *River Clyde*'s bows to serve as a bridge to the shingle. Their courage was of the highest order. It seemed to make possible what, in fact, was virtually impossible – a safe passage ashore from the apertures cut in the steamer's sides. From these apertures specially prepared gangways offered a path to the lighters and so, ideally, would have avoided the hazards of heavily equipped men wading ashore up the sloping uncertainty of shallows and undertow. What happened was that the Turkish defenders emerged Phoenix-like from the dust and smoke of their shelled but undestroyed positions. Their withering fire caught the lines of men silhouetted against the sides of the ship. Killed and wounded toppled into the sea or onto the lighters. The wounded in the water floundered, their sodden uniforms and equipment dragging them down against whatever strength they had to try for the beach. There, survivors faced further hazards of wire, mines and continuous fire. Numbers pathetically sought shelter against a bank of shingle, their plight immortalised in a celebrated photograph.

Tows brought more troops in to 'V' Beach as they did to the other chosen landing spots. From the cruiser *Euralyus*,[28] Lancashire Fusiliers and a platoon of the Royal Naval Division Anson Battalion were landed at 'W' Beach adjacent to the North. They were joined later in their grim enterprise by men from other units. A superb account of this landing survives in the letter from Midshipman H. Wilson, in command of the picket boat of the sixth tow from *Euralyus*. 'As it was misty it was very hard to say what W Beach was like and where exactly it was. We had only rough maps of the place and as we approached it from a totally different direction we expected, you couldn't predict what sort of reception you were going to get. We slipped about 30 yards from the beach but my boat was closer as we had come round the corner. We were nearly on the rocks and only just slipped in time. All the tows slipped alright and pulled in without fouling each other. There were two rows of barbed wire the whole length of the beach. The Turks opened fire with maxims, pompoms, rifles, just as we slipped. You could see them standing up in the trenches, which obviously had not been properly shelled. They were pouring a terrific fire down on us and it is a most extraordinary thing how any of the cutters which were open and absolutely unprotected and crammed with men survived it. The soldiers had to jump out into three feet of water and it was a most awful sight seeing them being shot down as soon as they got into the water and the wounded must have drowned. When they got onto the beach they were held up by the barbed wire and got a tremendous lot more casualties as the Turks practically mowed them down as they moved through the gaps in the wire which they had cut.'[29] Wilson's log clearly indicates that the naval support work did not stop with landing the troops and shelling the Turks. 'About 11 p.m. the Turks counter attacked in some force very heavy rifle and machine gun fire was heard and it was necessary at W beach for the beach parties to reinforce our troops in the trenches.'[30]

Of special significance in the overall picture at Cape Helles was to be the fate of the 'Y' beach landing, the most northerly. It was in a position from which principal objectives might have been outflanked. Inland of Y Beach lay the village of Krithia nestling at the bottom of the gradual slope up to the dominant 700-foot hill, Achi Baba. The navy's connection with events there lay not merely in landing operations but in the fact that half the landing force was of Plymouth Marines.

The landing was unopposed but not pressed

forward with determination. There was uncertainty over seniority between Colonel Matthews of the Marines and Colonel Koe of the King's Own Scottish Borderers.[31] Matthews chose to entrench his clifftop hold on the beach head. The Turks took advantage of both Matthews' decision and the failure of the British Divisional Commander to reinforce 'Y' beach with troops unable to land at 'W' and 'V' beaches. All the troops fought well when the Turks came up in strength for counter-attack but the landing force was withdrawn later in the morning of 26 April. A considerable opportunity had been lost.

D.S.E. Thompson's diary acknowledged that the whistling of bullets is 'disturbing at first but you soon get used to them.' This was just as well as 25 April saw him busy with picket boat work at 'X' beach, then 'W' beach. At 2 a.m. on the 26th he was called to evacuate wounded from 'Y' beach. The cliffs are exceptionally steep there and the pathway up was difficult to find in the dark. 'This was the devil of a job – our

people were in an awful plight just got the beach they stand on and nearly out of ammunition. There was a shower of bullets falling around us the whole time. Its much the most ticklish job I've had so far.'[32]

Apart from 'Y' beach, all the landings had been successfully established though not developed – even Kum Kale on the Asiatic shore, merely taken to hold Turkish reinforcements on that shore, was held securely until it was judged that its particular purpose had been fulfilled. While the navy pounded the Turkish positions and once, in the case of a single 15-inch shrapnel shell from Queen Elizabeth, dramatically destroyed a Turkish counter-attack, no concerted effort was ordered at clearing the Narrows and forcing a surface passage to the Sea of Marmora. Of course, the army needed close support but

Gallipoli, 25 April 1915. Midshipman D.S.E. Thompson's diary of the Cape Helles, Gallipoli landings. It is scarcely surprising that the experiences of the day led him to identify wrongly the unit of the troops he took into 'W' Beach. (Commander D.S.E. Thompson)

Midshipman Tate of *Implacable*, serving as 'Doggie' to the Beachmaster of 'W' Beach, Cape Helles, Gallipoli, on 25 April 1915. (Captain A.W. Clarke)

1915. A U-boat has torpedoed a French Ammunition Ship, *Carthage*, near Cape Helles; it is about to take the final plunge, at left. The destroyer *Raccoon* is searching for the submarine. (Captain H.M. Denham)

the choice of the naval authorities to eschew any independent role gave the Germans and Turks an opportunity decisively to prevent second thoughts on the matter.

On the night of 12–13 May, a Turkish torpedo-boat destroyer with a German commander and a German-reinforced crew, skilfully used fog to approach and torpedo the pre dreadnought battleship *Goliath* in Morto Bay. In the warm weather the midshipmen had their hammocks laid out just below the gangway onto the quarter deck. In the few minutes *Goliath* kept afloat, Rupert Westall chose not to race for the deck and so overboard. He went below for his Gieves safety waistcoat. In consequence, *Goliath* was on her way down as he reached the upper deck. 'I simply went down with her.' He bobbed to the surface of the cold water and managed to puff some air into his waistcoat. He found some wreckage for further buoyancy. Westall recalls being impelled by a sense of duty as an officer to encourage others in the water. He shouted slogans and even sang, acknowledging years later in his retirement a sense of pride that he was 'very brave for a little boy.' In the darkness, feeling the pull of a strong current and with danger from collisions with heavy floating wreckage, it must have been an unnerving experience. Approximately an hour after the torpedoes struck, he was picked up by a boat from the *River Clyde*.[33]

About 570 men were lost. This was the first nail in the coffin; the second and third followed in the same month. Off Anzac on 25 May, HMS *Triumph*, also a pre dreadnought, was torpedoed by the German *U-21*. *Goliath*'s loss had been at night but *Triumph* sank in full view of thousands of troops at Anzac. It was a damaging blow but good discipline aboard *Triumph* and the skilful handling of the destroyer *Chelmer* made possible the rescue of all but seventy-three of the crew. Little vignettes from the nine or so minutes *Triumph* remained afloat personalise a dark occasion: a bugler obviously off duty reporting naked but for the bugle and its lanyard, completing his emergency bugle call before flinging his instrument into the sea and diving after it; a Chinese steward clinging to a slowly turning propeller when the ship turned turtle.[34]

Three days later, close inshore of 'W' beach, the old battleship *Majestic* followed her sisters, three scalps for *U-21* of greater weight in every sense than *Hogue*, *Aboukir* and *Cressy*. *U-21* was chased by *Bacchante* but escaped to hide in the Gulf of Cos. A fourth addition to the debit balance was narrowly avoided when the battleship *Albion*, which had run aground near Gaba Tepe, was hauled off by *Canopus*, destroyers and her own endeavours whilst under heavy fire.

There is no doubt that the necessary withdrawal of the big ships from close support of the Peninsula cast a gloom over the soldiers. Somehow even the well-publicised submarine achievements could not make up for the absence of the great grey silhouettes with their proudly encouraging white ensigns. Blister-protected shallow-draft monitors did come with their huge guns methodically to harass the Turks. At Malta, Paymaster Longden Griffiths from one monitor, HMS *Roberts*, met some of the naval officers who had recently arrived from the Dardanelles. They 'were extremely pessimistic and discouraging, saying that sometimes shrap-

Assistant Naval Paymaster and two RNAS warrant officers at sea off Gibraltar 1915. (Squadron Leader J.C. Andrews)

nel burst for hours over a battleship and the work really was hopeless, the Dardanelles is impregnable! This is rather happy news for us who, in company with other monitors are going to relieve nearly all of our fleet at present operating in the Straits.[35] However exaggerated were these reports, HMS *Lord Roberts*'s work

Crew of an anti-aircraft gun mounted on the kite balloon ship *Manica* in the Dardanelles in 1915. (G. Kingsmith)

The monitor HMS *Roberts* supports the attempted advance at Suvla Bay, Gallipoli in August 1915. (Commander C.H. Longden-Griffiths)

was affected by both aerial bombing and Turkish shells. In the foretop: 'As soon as we heard the report from the shore we ducked and could hear the shell whistling as it approached us; and especially annoying did this whistling sound when the projectile passed between us and the deck and fell into the sea on the starboard side.' HMS *Roberts* used balloon ship support for observation of the effectiveness of her shelling but she also had a seaplane detached from *Ark Royal* for this purpose. Longden Griffiths was able to celebrate an achievement secured by this seaplane and its RNAS pilot observer: '12th August. News has come through that Flight Lieutenant Dacre piloted his seaplane over the neck of the Peninsula and torpedoed a Turkish transport – 5,000 tons. This is the first time that a torpedo has been launched to advantage from a seaplane, in the world's history. The feat was performed in the entrance to the sea of Marmora.'

The monitors spectacularly supported the August landing at Suvla Bay, part of a great design to outflank the Turkish heights. 'Great upheavals of sand and columns of grey and brown smoke grew into huge grotesque figures on the whole face of the Peninsula. Thicker and thicker becomes the air and darker the smoke: shrapnel is bursting, like white puffs of wadding over the dark sea of fumes below.' Such was Longden Griffiths' description of Cape Helles. *Bacchante*, the old favourite, was off Suvla Bay, engaged not least in the incredibly difficult task of targetting accurately on Turkish held positions in the close fighting for the heights above Anzac. It may or may not have been *Bacchante*'s shells which disastrously ended New Zealand tenure of their bravely earned command of Chunuk Bair, a key position dominating the slopes of both sides of the Peninsula. If such a responsibility were incontestably proven, no one familiar with the terrain at Anzac would lay more than a charge of *Bacchante* having been the instrument of tragedy.

On the night of 6/7 August, thirteen recently-built motor lighters carried up to 500 men, protected by bullet proof decking, towards the Suvla beaches. Named K-boats and nicknamed beetles from the antennae-like supports for the lowering of a landing ramp, they could bring

It is rather fine to sit on deck all day & see a battle going on & no one firing at you but it hurts a bit seeing these poor devils on the beach being shot down. Also it is the uncertainty, if one only knew what was happening every four hours, instead of not knowing anything. We are to attack again this afternoon but so far there has been little firing except on the Imb's hills where it is incessant

You say in your letter you *wish* you knew where I was. Surely you know from all the hints I have dropped – Norah certainly knows

Mail just going
nothing fresh   Love J.

An official war artist, Norman Wilkinson, painting the Gallipoli, Suvla Bay operations in August 1915. Note the shells to the right of the photograph. The diary of Midshipman A.W. Clarke shows that he went to see the Wilkinson paintings exhibited in the New Art Gallery while he was on leave in London in April 1916. (F. Jaques)

A letter and sketch describe in some detail but do not name the location of naval support to the August 1915 offensive at Suvla Bay, Gallipoli. (F. Jaques)

their human cargo right to the shore, secure except from shelling. The light cruiser *Talbot* was to be stationed in support of this landing. Seaman Falconer describes well the ensuing drama. '6th August: 11 p.m. We have taken up our position. The night is rather dark. You could hardly discern the boats as they passed you making their way shorewards. 7th August: Off Suvla Point. Everything going with a swing and practically with no opposition until a field gun battery opened fire. It soon became clear that our flat trajectory would not permit of us reaching them.' *Talbot* took up a new station and fired 427 rounds during the day according to Falconer. It seemed to him that all was going well as Turkish batteries were silenced and British troops on the morning of the 8th seemed clearly 'in possession of several ridges facing the bay. The troops are quite at ease and settled down to their task. Some of the reserves have their usual dip all day long on the beach which is very well adapted for the purpose.'[36] At this stage, Falconer had no idea of the devastating significance of this observation. It was the very failure of Corps and Divisional and Brigade leadership to order the troops into determined progress which frittered away any chance of striking success at Suvla. Viewed from those involved in the demanding climbing and fierce fighting on the Anzac heights, Suvla's inertia was bitterly resented.

The new landing at Suvla and the attempt to break out of the Anzac position ended in stagnation. The campaign which had opened with such high hopes was doomed. There remained for the navy, apart from riding out the fierce storm in November which caused such suffering on the Peninsula, the major combined operational task of evacuating the troops. This was planned and executed brilliantly. Successfully evacuating Suvla and Anzac in December was a great achievement by all concerned but to cap this in the following month at Helles under the real threat of a major Turkish attack was little short of incredible.

Something of the sailor-soldier kinship forged by the shared Dardanelles experience is expressed by Charles Longden Griffiths, watching the Australians arriving at the island of Mudros from the Anzac evacuation in December, when he wrote: 'It is a sad sight to see them all, with just what kit they could save, strapped to their backs, getting into line and marching wearily up the road to a camp prepared for them – thousands of them marching – plodding along the dusty sandy road – they are trying to fight with undaunted courage against overwhelming odds at Anzac. And to what purpose? Having lost thousands and thousands and suffered privation and hardships untold they come back having accom-

The final evacuation of the Gallipoli Peninsula as observed from the monitor HMS *Roberts*. (Commander C.H. Longden-Griffiths)

At Rabbit Islands firing at the Asiatic batteries which seem to be growing daily in number and activity.
For the night we have returned to Mavro.
M.17 (92) has come here again.
After dark, Picton has opened fire again.
Saturday 8th Jan.
Early this morning M.17 & Picton opened fire & one or other has been firing nearly all day. We landed monitors & a marine on Mavro to assist in observing & signalling corrections from the observation Station, & proceeded to LoneyBank at 9.5 am. This afternoon we fired 9 rounds to register on 168 & 174; now we are ready for any emergency. All night the Turret's crew will be closed up & shall be ready to fire. Of course we are firing by angle - the light on Tenedos & a mound on the Asiatic shore (which at night will be played on by a destroyer's flash search light when we want to fire) being the aiming points.
Midnight. The evacuation is taking place; & considering the magnitude of the operation the ... seems particularly quiet. Guns are flashing but occasionally, & star shells are bursting at long intervals. Asia is particularly quiet & the batteries we (the Roberts) have to deal with have not yet caused any annoyance tonight. The 'Picton' has not fired half a dozen rounds at Asia from Rabbit Island

plished nothing, won nothing but the admiration of us all.'[37]

The same diarist was closer at hand with HMS *Roberts* covering the evacuation of Helles. On 8 January, he wrote: 'This afternoon we fired 9 rounds and now we are ready for any emergency. All night the turret's crew will be closed up and we shall be ready to fire. Of course we are firing by angle – the light on Tenedos and a mound on the Asiatic shore (which at night will be played on by a destroyer's searchlight when we want to fire) being the aiming points. Midnight: The evacuation is taking place and considering the magnitude of the operation the theatre seems particularly quiet. Guns are flashing but occasionally, the star shells are bursting at long intervals. Asia is particularly quiet and the batteries we have to deal with have not yet caused any annoyance tonight.

'4 a.m. The fires ashore have started – one after another they flare up and grow. Huge roaring boiling fires. They are consuming all that we left as we withdrew – provisions, ammunition, mines and gear of all kinds.'[38] A submarine scare alerts the writer; then as dawn breaks HMS *Lord Roberts* commences the shelling of the vacated beachhead at Seddul Bahr.

In *Lord Nelson*, also supporting at Cape Helles, George Keeler wrote more mundanely in his seaman's diary: 'We were told to stand by to turn out at any time during the night. At about 8 a.m. the *Lydiard*, a destroyer, came alongside and we took from her 1200 soldiers. They were just about finished as they had had no sleep for a long while. We got them some cocoa and I made a fanny of porridge for them or at least some of them. A lovely bonfire was burning on the beach. Blinker was on his beam-ends as to how he could catch the routine up.'[39]

Less concerned about routine was Midshipman Tom Traill, also of *Lord Nelson*, for he was prowling the beaches looking for stragglers. With remarkable luck, his cutter had bumped into an empty carpetted Turkish pleasure punt. The flat-bottomed, 10-feet long punt, held on a line from the cutter, had enabled him, dry shod to land at Morto Bay. Revolver in hand he had wandered along the beach calling 'Anybody about', relieved to hear no response in Turkish. Seeing not a soul and encouraged by the colossal explosion of the ammunition dump at the very tip of the Peninsula, he conducted his own evacuation.[40] In so doing, he may well have removed the single remaining Gallipoli-based allied threat to Constantinople, the focus of so much endeavour for so many months.

While affairs at the Dardanelles had remained the main area of concentrated naval effort beyond the North Sea after the avenging of Coronel, there had been both major and minor naval involvement in what became essentially land operations. In February 1915, defence of the Suez Canal against Turkish attack had involved a number of ships, including the pre dreadnought class battleship *Swiftsure*.

In October of the same year, the navy commenced the fulfilment of a heavy commitment to the allied forces landed at Salonika. The pre dreadnought class battleship *Agamemnon*, after fine service off the Gallipoli Peninsula, was at Salonika to earn a further and this time exceptional distinction in the shooting down of a Zeppelin, *LZ 85*, on 5 May 1916. It had been the Zeppelin's third raid on Salonika and her dispatch encouraged the morale of troops and local labour alike.

8

The Mesopotamian River War

Quite the most extraordinary cooperation given by the navy to land operations was in Mesopotamia. As long as the danger of the drama is not minimised, the events well deserve the delightful soubriquet of 'Townshend's Regatta'. To set the scene briefly, the Persian Gulf and its hinterland were of the utmost strategic significance in view of the increasing naval need for oil and the related needs for petrol and oil for internal combustion engined vehicles, aeroplanes and industry. German influence had spread through the medium of the Berlin–Baghdad railway, commercial activity and secret agents. Turkish entry into the war had greatly enhanced their hopes, not least through the fermenting of Teutonic advantage from trouble stimulated in the Arab world. British Government and India Office designs on the area counterbalanced those of the Germans.

In the Autumn of 1914, the expeditionary force had been landed as has been described and disposed in such a way as to protect British oil interests. Turkish military resistance to the British presence was overcome, Basra was occupied and by natural consequence an advance upon Baghdad came under consideration. Advance as far as Kurna, at the Tigris–Euphrates junction, was sanctioned and effected.

It had not been without difficulties. HMS *Miner*, one of the armed launches involved, fell temporarily a victim to both enemy fire and navigational hazards in the first attempt. 3 December: 'There was a perfect hail of shrapnel and [rifle] bullets and our twelve pounder went out of action . . . a shot got us in the engine room just below waterline and burst half in coal bunker and half in Engine room, severely wounding Stoker P.O. Jones and Stoker Lacy.

Ship immediately began to fill. About same time another shell cut the after fall of starboard boat and burst, several chunks coming off into the cabin. Apparently one or two other shells hit the side but bounced off without bursting, there was such a hail of bullets and bits and such a beastly row the whole time, added to which we only had about six inches of water to spare that it was difficult to know exactly what was happening. Finally we got back and beached her ahead of the *Espiegle* who temporarily repaired the leak. Stoker P.O. Jones did very well by sticking to the engines and finally drew fires.'

After repair, *Miner* suffered more damage in the next attempt on Kurna and when this diary is continued on 9 December and the author, Heath-Caldwell, was able to inspect the defences of the surrendered town, he wrote: 'It seems nothing short of a miracle that we are alive.'[1]

There were differing views on the advisability of proceeding further and indeed on the direction of any such move. However, both military and naval reinforcements made possible the bold amphibious plans of the Divisional Commander concerned, Major General Sir Charles Townshend, to pursue the Turks up the Tigris.[2]

It was the time of seasonal flooding for the Tigris. Water covered the area beyond the river banks to a depth of only two feet, but irrigation channels and nullahs offered problems to wading infantry. In the river itself, shallow-draught sloops, the *Espiegle*, *Clio* and *Odin*, and the mine sweeping launches *Shaitan* and *Sumana* could plough their way against the muddy current. They were supported by other naval vessels. On the flood plain, long narrow native boats, *bellums*, propelled in deep water by oar and

paddle, could be punted and, of course, almost hidden by the high reeds rising to six feet in profusion, aiding concealment. Soldiers learned to punt and their protection in action was made more secure by the provision of steel plates rising above the thwarts of their boat. Innovatively, 4.7 inch guns were mounted on barges and light mountain guns on a sort of double canoe. The instability of these firing platforms and the impossibility of seeing a target from so low a position naturally limited the effectiveness of the fire, though not of the impressive morale-influencing noise.

The sloops and launches breasting the flood were to fire on the Turkish defensive gun enplacements on the hillocks and sand dunes above Kurna, while the infantry in their *bellums* successfully stormed enemy entrenchments which themselves had been shelled by the naval vessels. The regatta parade was led by two armed launches jointly towing a mine sweeping hawser. Once early success had been achieved, the infantry transferred to a stern-wheeler paddle steamer looking like a 'two storied wooden house with an old hay-making machine at the stern, kicking up the water high into the air with as much grunting and groaning as though a spavined horse was setting the wheel in motion.'[3]

There were other paddle steamers, river tugs, steel barges, motor boats and native boats called *mahelas* converted into floating field hospitals. Mines had been a great danger but the capture and use of the Turkish officer responsible for the mines, helped in evading their hazard.

Above Abu Aran in extremes of heat the naval vessels alone continued the pursuit until Amara was reached. In the chase numerous Turkish

Mesopotamia: the stern wheeler, 'a two storied wooden house with an old hay making machine at the stern'. Note the gun mounted on the barge alongside. (Captain C.H. Heath-Caldwell)

small vessels had been sunk or captured and their main gunboat had emulated the *Dresden* in self-destruction. For trifling loss, the eighty-mile river chase had resulted in the capture of more than 3000 Turks and of all the small British warships none had distinguished herself more than *Shaitan*, the daring of whose commander, Lieutenant Singleton, and crew of eight sailors, had forced the flight of over 2000 troops and the capture of eleven officers and 250 men.

An unpublished personal account of the whole episode was written by Captain P.L. Gunn,[4] then an able seaman aboard a steam launch which had a square-cornered horse boat lashed on either side. The horse boats had guns mounted on them and the boats were to be slipped and secured to the river banks for artillery support fire. Attempting to sleep on a mattress laid upon lockers, stifling within the essential protection of a mosquito net, Gunn endured the humid heat. Before they got on the move, sleep and work fought losing battles against mosquitoes and flies. To awaken from sleep brought a fearful sense of suffocation under a blanket clutched over the head against the marauders.

The oppressive heat actually reduced Gunn

Opposite top
Mesopotamia: the armed launch HMS *Miner* photographed before the war. (Captain C.H. Heath-Caldwell)

Opposite bottom
Mesopotamia: HMS *Miner* nudges up against a barge on which a gun has been mounted. (Captain C.H. Heath-Caldwell)

to near despair until the flotilla left the lower reaches of the river. With Kurna and then Amara captured, the force forged up the Tigris. The steel protection plates on the small launches had been ditched as they had rendered the vessels unstable and the equilibrium of the four Moslem crew members of Gunn's launch had also been secured by the provision of a live sheep for ritual slaughter and consumption.

In the last days of September 1915, the launch, now without its horseboats, was ordered on ahead up the sharp bends of the river with the twenty-year-old Gunn effectively in command responsible for finding a channel between the sandbanks for the closely following assorted vessels. The senior naval officer, Lieutenant Edgar Cookson, had chosen to leave the launch for the considerably larger *Comet*, and from this armed tug he conducted a night attack on a boom which barred further progress. That night, as they felt their way up towards the boom, the boats came under fire. Suddenly, Gunn spotted the barrier of chained barges and a dhow from the launch. *Comet* then seemed to surge past into the lead, attempting to fracture the obstruction at its presumed weakest point, the dhow wired to two iron barges. The impact failed to dislodge the dhow and the sailing vessel also withstood gunfire. *Comet* then came right up against the dhow, all the while under heavy fire from the shore. Gunn saw a white uniformed figure, recognisable as Cookson, leap from *Comet* to the dhow, and swiftly wield an axe against the binding hawser. Cookson fell mortally wounded. His courageous attempt had failed. The following morning disclosed that the Turks had retired and the boom was easily dismantled. Cookson, for long Gunn's hero, was to earn a posthumous VC but his death sorely affected the young able seaman in whom

he had placed such trust.

The campaign itself overtaxed the resources for its fulfilment. Townshend's force was unable to defeat strengthened opposition at Ctesiphon, fell back on Kut and there was besieged. In the ensuing tragic drama, the navy was to play a rôle, supporting the efforts of the relief force in January and March to break through the ring of Turkish positions. Kut nestled into its bend of the Tigris where its junction with the Shatt el Hai to the West, made conditions with the river in flood a particular problem for the defenders. In April, after the failure of all else, a desperate attempt to bring relief supplies to Kut was made by the river steamer *Julnar*. Three officers and twelve ratings, all of whom had volunteered and then from a large number had been selected, were embarked aboard *Julnar* on this unpromising mission. At night on 24 April, the attempt was made. Her approach was anticipated and she was fired on by small arms and artillery. A shell hit the bridge killing the Commander but the officer who was second in command, Lt Edward Cowley, though wounded, maintained briefly the progress of the steamer till she hit a deliberately placed obstructing cable. *Julnar* drifted to the shore against a Turkish military position and Lt Edward Cowley surrendered. The survivors were taken off to captivity though Cowley was murdered by his vengeful captors. A few days later the garrison of Kut surrendered. Just over nine months later when Lieutenant General Sir Stanley Maude's counter offensive retook Kut and opened the way for a soundly based advance upon Baghdad, a naval flotilla under Captain Nunn RN exercised a notable role in turning an orderly Turkish retreat into a headlong rout. *Julnar* and her complement had thus, in at least one sense, been handsomely avenged.

9

Blockade

The extent to which the British distant blockade of German trade contributed to final victory has been variously estimated. Even in an awareness that the German military forces in France and Belgium had to be defeated in the field and that many factors interrelatedly contributed to allied victory, most authorities still see the naval achievement as the decisive one. In essence, it meant the gradual economic strangulation of the Teutonic war effort. Protection of British trade and reduction of the enemy's were two sides of the same coin. To these ends, mines had to be laid and cruisers and smaller vessels patrolled, while submarines attempted to fulfil diverse rôles. Nets, searchlights, new weapons and various protection or destructive devices were developed; airships and seaplanes would also play a vital part in due course.

The capture of German merchant traffic at large was seen to remarkably quickly. The 1914 and 1915 midshipmen's journals are studded with references to this effect. Sailing ships were of course particularly vulnerable and it was not always German sail at risk. The three-masted steel-hulled barque, *Kildalton* (1700 gross tons) left Liverpool in September 1914 and, having rounded Cape Horn, was sailing north up the West coast of South America. On 12 December, *Kildalton* fell in with a two-funnelled ship towing a sailing ship without sail. As the vessels drew nearer, the steamship hoisted the flag of the Imperial German Navy and ordered *Kildalton* to stop. It was, in fact, the German raider *Prinz Eitel Friedrich*. A boarding party came aboard and the crew was ordered to muster and then to take to the boats to row to the steamship where they were battened down. The crew had no opportunity to see *Kildalton* sunk by explosive charges placed in her pump wells.

It had been a fine start to his apprenticeship

for one of the youngest of *Kildalton*'s crew, a boy named Phillips.[1] However, good food and treatment were provided by the Germans. At Easter Island the raider coaled from the French sailing ship's cargo and sent the crew of the *Kildalton*, with the French crew, ashore with canvas and timber to construct shelter while they awaited rescue. Basic stores, sugar, flour, yeast, coffee and tea, were provided by the Germans. The whole of the French ship's galley and the master's saloon were removed and re-erected. The island was owned by Chile but leased to a British-owned sheep ranching company under a man called Edmonds who lived there. There was also a Mrs Scorsby Rutledge working on the celebrated monoliths for the British Museum.

Some of the British crew lived in a woolshed but the French preferred the native village. The apprentices and the officers made and erected a tent in a good lookout position. The Germans left them on the last day of the year. The volcanic island was no tropical paradise but a sheep a day was cooked alternately by the French and then by the British. The only drinking water was collected rain. There were fig trees and sweet potatoes. One man died and several were very ill eating the small variety of pineapples which were thus proved unsuitable as food. In February, the marooned mariners were picked up by a Swedish ship, except for five Frenchmen who chose to remain behind. Liverpool and home for the British seamen was reached in early April, after a voyage through the Panama canal, then to the West Indies and across the North Atlantic.

It must be said of this ordeal that the hardships for *Kildalton*'s crew were considerably less gruelling than those suffered by British seamen caught at Hamburg and in the Elbe at the outbreak of war. They were held in prison hulks on the river before being transferred for internment until the end of the war. Their camp was a trotting course at Ruhleben on the outskirts of Berlin and for a few days the camp was to hold Captain Fryatt of the Merchant Navy, a skipper whom the Germans, having captured, chose to execute for his exploit of ramming a U-boat.

For Phillips, the drama of his first service at sea was to have a strange sequel: he was to continue in sail to the end of the war, seeing no sign whatsoever of an enemy vessel.

In far greater numbers German sailing and steamships suffered a fate akin to that of *Kildalton*. However, the securing of control of neutral shipping was to be the key in winning the commerce war. We are not here concerned with the attendant diplomatic problems, though the British boarding parties were to have difficulty in the classification of goods in the three categories of absolute contraband, conditional contraband or goods free from restriction. Politically, there was one neutral of supreme importance. In contriving to offend the United States less than Germany did, Britain did much to bring about final victory. The critical factor governing the issue of boarding and search was whether the real destination from a Dutch or Scandinavian port were thence to be a German port. To prevent goods reaching Germany, mines were laid to narrow the English channel seaway to a passage more easily supervised for inspection. The northern route to Germany from the Americas was round Scotland. The breadth of the seaway here was too great for effective mine laying and it had to be patrolled.

For some six weeks in 1914, Third Fleet battleships formed part of an Anglo-French patrol line across the Channel to intercept ships carrying contraband. The ships were visibility distance apart. They steamed at slow speed west in the day against incoming traffic and east at night, stopping for an hour at daylight and at dusk. The patrol line boarded all incoming ships and it was exceptionally fortunate that

under these operational conditions none of the patrol line was torpedoed.[2]

Weather conditions and U-boat dangers made patrol work in the Northern waters grim. The cruiser *Hawke* had been lost and unsurprisingly a diarist from the cruiser squadron given responsibility for this patrolling referred to their being the 'live bait squadron'. In fact, from December 1914, the 10th Cruiser Squadron was to have more modern, faster ships. These would be better able to cope with the gales and high seas which this officer of HMS *Edgar*, R.A.C. Michell had been recording, with the attendant miseries of hail and snow in November.

'November 11: I was woken by a tremendous crash which sounded like a very loud explosion and then the seas broke over us and we shivered from stem to stern . . . the ammunition for the 6″ guns had taken charge and was rolling all over the upper deck – the main deck was soon flooded and the lower deck as well.' Michell just escaped a torrent of sea water roaring through the after hatch onto the main deck. 'At 6 p.m. when we dived into a head sea and before we had time to recover, another sea struck us just abaft the forebridge on the Port side and completely submerged the upper deck – the water found its way everywhere below. In the engine room where I was at the time we got it "green" for two solid minutes, the water rose in the bilges to above the main bearings. The engine room (top portion) was filled with steam and sea water striking the hot cylinders and steam pipes.' The accommodation was awash: 'The wardroom was a mass of upturned tables, chairs, piano and book cases on the deck, cups, plates, saucers, bottles, tins and the remnants of several suppers charging wildly about in several inches of water.' Michell later found that a large steam pinnace had been lifted bodily out of its crutches and carried across the ship and impaled on an iron stanchion.[3]

The class of vessels patrolling might improve but the weather did not. The misery of ceaselessly vigilant service in these waters, less and less frequently relieved by the stimulus of a steamer to board and search and always at U-boat hazard, can only have been exceeded in its harrowing nature by the North Russian convoys just a generation later. There is a further parallel: the frustration felt by men of those convoys at their graceless Russian reception in the 1940s was matched by the frustration of the 1914–18 Northern Patrol at their own Government's failure to hold so many of the ships perilously brought in for investigation at Kirkwall. Diplomatic niceties markedly constricted the vital weapon of 'board and search' in the waging of war.

Contraband control in the English Channel and Irish Sea was obviously an easier proposition than in Northern waters. The scanty

defence that a drifter could have put up against a U-boat meant that there were still dangers, as a coal trimmer recorded in his recollections that his ship, the *St Combes Haven*, had only staff bombs or small explosive charges on the end of a pole to be flung out at any surfaced submarine adversary. Sometimes a pole was laid across the steam capstan and covered by canvas to simulate a gun. *St Combes Haven* worked out of Poole and once stopped a schooner from which the skipper roared that if the drifter were to come any closer it would be blown out of the water. All was explained in due course by invitation to the drifter's skipper to board the schooner to inspect what was in fact a Q ship, a decoy vessel to draw a surfaced submarine close to her and then blast at it from a concealed gun.

More attention will be paid to Q ships in due course but an idea of the boarding work done by the 10th Cruiser Squadron is given by a Surgeon Probationer, James Shaw, who kept a

Contraband inspection. The Distant Blockade. A contemporary painting by a Surgeon Probationer James Shaw, HMS *Changuinola*. (Dr J. Shaw)

diary of details supporting his statistic that in 1915, parties from his Armed Merchant Cruiser, *Changuinola*, had boarded 159 vessels and had sent fifty into port from this patrolling work in Northern waters.

> *16 May* 'In evening after 9 got a boat flying Swedish flag. Examining party sent over. She had no flags painted on her hull . . . When party returned they told us she was full of munitions of war, 4 aeroplanes, 2 hydroplanes, 2 seaplanes. The ship was French but a British R.N.R. Commander had been picked up in Liverpool . . . yet we were flying the Swedish flag. Playing the German's game.'
>
> *22 May* 'Stopped Swedish steamer but it had green clearance ticket. Two submarines reported the last few days in our vicinity.'
>
> *14 June* 'My nerves are somewhat tense with excitement. Going on deck I observed that the Jack Tars were wearing the life saving apparatus. They were all looking past the Port side of the stern.'

A torpedo track had been observed and the Surgeon Probationer wasted no time in donning his life-saving belt. Later in the day, when doing duty decoding he picked up a signal which confirmed the presence of a U-boat, but they 'had physical drill by Lt. Clarke on the boat deck – a race round the deck afterwards followed by a short game of football in the music room.'

> *15 June* 'After the novelty of it has worn off one realises how monstrous this patrolling in these vessels is. We see nothing but sea and sky.'
>
> *17 June* 'Picked up eleven prize crews from Caesarea. We quickly got rid of them however to other vessels of the patrolling squadron.'

Shaw writes that such visitors were surprised at the social life aboard the *Changuinola* and he himself comments of three P & O officers that 'I never saw such a glum lot. They would have no part in our sports and I hear that one of them, a two striper, remarked to one of our officers that we should have been looking after our guns instead of fooling about.' With no trace of embarrassment, Shaw records for that same day: 'Managed to turn a somersault on the parallel bars.'

> *18 June* '10.15. At the moment at which I write we have almost cut off a small steamer which we are going to board. Our boarding boat is painted white to be easily distinguished at night time . . .'

The steamer proved to be nothing more than a Grimsby trawler. Cod and halibut were the goodwill gift of the trawler, tobacco and meat the naval response.

> *21 June* 'Ships sports were held today . . . Tug of war, obstacle race for men, officers' obstacle race, potato race, bun race, bolster fight, sack race, blindfold boxing etc.'

In the tug of war, the Marines beat the Petty Officers but were beaten by the officers who were themselves beaten by the firemen. Prizes were distributed to the men from an officers' subscription fund. The officer victors earned 'tin Iron Crosses'.

A sailor, who had entered for almost all events and lost in every one, got a special consolation award, a large brass Iron Cross. This much amused the men as 'he is a volunteer and seems to be well brought up and to speak more fluently than the ordinary tar, consequently he is an anathema or at any rate a joke to the latter . . . it does not seem to bother him in the least.'

A Russian and then an American steamer were boarded, abandon ship exercises were practised, and shore leave in Glasgow was enjoyed through June and July. In August, it is clear that precautionary procedures were becoming standardised. 'We steer a circle round the ships we board now when the boarding is taking place so as to give submarines as little chance as possible. Sometimes we go to "general quarters" in fact and train all the guns on the ship which we are boarding in case she is a German in disguise supplied with torpedo tubes.'

The diary quotations are from the good weather of the summer months, it will be noted, and from a happy ship too, but it is clear that the reflective Shaw resented the public attitude he encountered in Glasgow, whose citizens were mindless of the danger and discomfort of their service. 'In tramcars and other places one hears talk "What is the navy doing?" and it is sickening.' Goodness knows what Shaw would have written a year later if he were to have been at Jutland and to have experienced the first public reaction to that battle.[4]

It is a matter of some significance that naval authorities did not relish the idea of a long drawn out struggle which was the natural implication of distant blockade and winning the war by gradually shutting off the life-support system of the German economy. Instead, there was the hope that blockade would force the German High Seas Fleet into risking battle fleet action. Ironically, when this circumstance did arrive at Jutland, its effect was to force the German command into a far greater reliance upon her own blockade. Thus, the British Government and, perhaps less willingly, its naval chiefs were directed into an acceptance of the reality of twentieth century sea warfare, where to hazard battle was needlessly to risk all but to protect one's sinews of war and deny sustenance to the enemy were a sure course for victory.

BRITISH SUBMARINE WORK IN THE BALTIC AND THE NORTH SEA

The record of British submarines in the North Sea and Baltic may be less celebrated than that of British submarines in the Dardanelles but the success of the latter should not obscure the achievement of the former. From the first days of the war, boats from Harwich were on patrol in the Heligoland Bight, the Kattegat, and off the Belgian coast. On 12 October, three E class submarines entered the Baltic by submerged passage through the Kattegat. When shallow water was encountered, as shallow as 21 feet, it was exceptionally difficult to evade the German patrolling vessels. R.W. Blacklock, second in command of *E1* has written: 'Being unable to dive, there was only one action to take if we were caught by enemy destroyers, which was to blow ourselves up. Explosives were therefore fitted to the warheads of our spare torpedoes, and a lead brought up through the conning tower with a switch on the end attached to me. Should we be caught, Laurence (the Commander) intended to have the fore and aft hatches flung open so that all below could have a chance of getting out and swimming for it while he and I blew the ship up (and no doubt ourselves too).'

Two German destroyers, then a Danish and a Swedish lighthouse beam might have discovered them but they revealed their presence by an unsuccessful torpedo attack on a German cruiser. The rendezvous for the three submarines was Libau but only two reached it. The two boats, *E1* and *E9*, then responded to a Russian Naval High Command instruction to report to a naval base in Finland.[5]

The base for the two British submarines attached to the Russian navy was Reval. 'The standard of living on the lower deck of the Russian ships was very low, and the question of food for our sailors was a difficult one which took a lot of working out.' There was no rum, vodka being the substituted daily ration for the men. The men themselves were befriended by the small British community in the town, the officers being welcomed to the British Consul's home to which everyone was invited on Christmas Day.

Patrol work in November was not undertaken by the Russian submarines and the problem of icing is made clear by the fact that when on the surface one man was constantly responsible for chipping ice from the conning tower hatch so that emergency diving was possible. The doors of the torpedo tubes froze up, the periscope could not be raised and under these conditions it was fortunate that no offensive action was called for.

The relationship between the two submarine commanders was sadly not good and as the Russian officers had been admonished by their superiors for being less enterprising than the British, there developed a lack of accord with the Russians too. When local pro-German gossip spread unjustified rumour of loose behaviour at a party given by the Consul, the diplomatic repercussions became so serious as to require *E1*'s commander to give an account of the affair to the British Ambassador. This cleared the air and Russian apologies came forth with a clear exoneration of the British from any scandal.

In January, a Russian ice-breaker saved *E1* from the grim fate of being caught and crushed by newly formed ice in the Gulf of Finland. During the two days of waiting uncertain rescue: 'The sailors were wonderful – I never saw a sign of distress in one of them.' Blacklock saw something of far greater privation when in accompanying Laurence on a visit to Grand Duke Nicholas's army headquarters he saw the 'appalling conditions under which the Army were fighting.' He saw cartloads of wounded men stuck in the roadside mud, having to remain for several days without medical attention. Blacklock was even taken to observe a night trench raid and the subsequent rough interrogation of the prisoners.

Late in April, a German fleet auxiliary was torpedoed by *E1* but *E9* was having more success until *E1*'s great opportunity arrived off the Gulf of Riga. German battle cruisers were in sight and an attack on *Moltke* seriously damaged her, putting her out of action for over a month. This led to a congratulatory visit from the Tsar himself. Blacklock's reward was the order of St Vladimir 4th Class with swords. Among the privileges conferred by the award was one that he could: 'Visit any state school for girls, taste the food and remark on the quality.' No opportunity occurred to allow him to exercise this privilege!

In the autumn of 1915, the British force of two submarines was doubled by the addition of *E8* and *E18* and they brought relief officers thus allowing Blacklock and another officer, posing as civilians, to make their way home via Sweden

Submarine Service: *E34's* Ratings' Mess. (Rear Admiral A. Poland)

Right
Submarine Service: *E34's* officers' accommodation. (Rear Admiral A. Poland)

and Norway, a journey which was itself full of incident in passage through pro-German Sweden.

With the Baltic experience behind him, Blacklock's next duty was North Sea work in a C class submarine being towed at a depth of 60 feet by a trawler with which there was telephone communication. This was an attempt to forestall German depredations on Britain's North Sea fishing fleets. Successes were achieved by this method but not by Blacklock's boat. He was later appointed to one of the Harwich submarines and had a terrifying ordeal in the Heligoland Bight. Stalking a patrol vessel and during a spell on the surface he was alone on the bridge when his submarine commenced diving.

'I only just managed to get into the conning tower without being swept overboard. The hatch beneath me had of course been closed and the pressure of water on my hands and face made it extremely difficult for me to close and clip down the hatch overhead. By some superhuman effort I succeeded in getting the clips on before I was drowned like a rat in a trap, and then fell unconscious to the bottom of the conning tower. The noise of my fall made the First Lieutenant realise that I was still on board, and he quickly dragged me into the control room.'

What had happened was that one of the crew, hurrying down from the bridge, had pressed the switch of the Klaxon horn, the alarm signal for diving, and so the First Lieutenant, following the emergency orders, immediately dived, assuming that the Commander had been killed or washed overboard.[6]

A rare sighting was offered to one submarine officer. While on patrol off Terschelling on one occasion, Allan Poland in *E4* saw six Zeppelins flying in formation for a raid on Britain. Poland did his utmost with an indifferent wireless set to report the sighting but failed to get through.

Submarine work of any nature has special dangers and this was certainly the case in submarine mine laying. A fate for some British mine laying submarines was to be blown up by the very seeds they were sowing and Poland's vessel was near enough in October 1916 to hear in full the monumental explosion which destroyed *E47* when she was engaged in this work.[7]

One of the surface vessels engaged in mine laying in Northern Waters was the very fast *Abdiel*. She carried a hundred mines of two different types and one of her Petty Officers, J.G. Cox, remembers their operations from Scapa. 'We had to get into our area for work under cover of darkness, lay our mines and be away before daylight. We did about three trips a fortnight laying 80 mines each time.'[8] The work was as essential as the patrolling of the cruisers and one presumes that the familiarity of a routine and the security of working from a fast armed vessel minimised the strain on the nerves of those thus engaged.

It might well be asked how submariners coped with the foetid air, lack of reasonable sleeping accommodation, monotonous food, lack of drinking water, cramped conditions and particular danger to life in their service. The answer may lie in the special brotherhood of being in 'the trade', as submarine work was called. That enlistment for the work was voluntary seems to have made acceptable what to others would have been insupportable. The special closeness in every sense of officer and rating, the awareness of being in an irreducibly small working team without a 'passenger', the shared discomforts (though for the ratings in the early submarines living accommodation was virtually merged into the working areas), were all factors which helped to explain the absence from contemporary and recollected personal documentation of any undue concentration upon nervous strain.

Above all, as a healthy influence upon team work, loyalty and mutual relief, there was the clearly apparent responsibility of the submarine commander for the effective work of the submarine and for the security of the crew. To balance this there was his need to be able to rely totally on each member of the crew. Some evidence of the submarine officer-rating relationship forged by such service is contained in the unselfconscious memoirs of a submarine rating. He makes these judgements:

The Captain: 'The crew were fond of him. He was a happy go lucky sort, calm in all he undertook to do, no panic at any time, but at times I thought a little too venturesome, but most of this was to relieve the crew of boredom.'

The Second in Command: 'Very nice in all he did but quiet.' The third officer (Navigator): 'A very nice man. When on the conning tower with me he would be chatting the whole time, sometimes teaching me the names of the stars at others hints on navigation.'

When on passage and the Captain or Navigator were with him in the conning tower: 'They would both talk to me on numerous subjects which I found very interesting and educational.' Once when in the Heligoland Bight the Captain actually asked him: 'Do you realise the trust that I and the crew have in you. They are all shut in down below and you are their eyes.'[9]

THE FIRST U-BOAT SCOURGE, 1915

In February, the German Admiralty announced a new step in its conduct of the naval war. It was a response to the increasing paralysis of German trade by the dominance of the Royal Navy in capturing German trading vessels and deterring neutrals by distant blockade and search for contraband. All the waters surrounding Great Britain were declared a war zone in which enemy vessels would be destroyed by German action. It would not always be possible in such action, the declaration stated, to safeguard the crews and passengers of the ships in question. Quite specifically in the terms of the announcement, neutral ships would be at hazard. A memorandum justified the declaration on the grounds of Britain's unlawful blockade and its flagrant distortion on the whole matter of contraband.

Leaving aside the questions of international law, of high level diplomacy and of propaganda, the actual countermeasures undertaken by the British Admiralty included the strengthening of certain units for patrol areas, the laying of new minefields, placement of indicator nets in the Channel and the addition of some defensive armament and naval gun crews for more merchant vessels engaged in Home Waters. Naturally, armament for merchant ships gave more reasonable justification for German sinking without warning. A redistribution of destroyers for escort support of vital vessels like troop or munition ships was organised but starkly revealed the shortage of destroyers. Decoy ships, the famous Q ships, accounted for only eleven U-boats in all. Success based on surprise by disguise was clearly one of diminishing returns but no one could minimise the human strain of such operations.[10]

The Germans had insufficient U-boats available for a wholesale onslaught on British trade. The initial impact of the U-boat campaign was less than their adversaries had feared; indeed, indicator nets had disclosed two U-boats which were destroyed. HMS *Dreadnought*, skilfully handled, had run down *U29* off Cromarty Firth, and Midshipman P.E. Maitland's journal records the details of the first dreadnought battleship exercising retribution upon the U-boat which had sunk *Hogue*, *Cressy* and *Aboukir*.

'At about 12.30 the officer of the watch, Lieutenant Commander Piercy, sighted a periscope on the port bow about 1200 yards away. We altered course towards her and closed water tight doors. She zigzagged ahead from one bow to the other. At about 600 yards the periscope could be seen through the sights and one twelve pounder was fired at it which missed by about 50 yards. The gun then stuck, run in, and no further rounds could be fired as she was obscured by our bows. The periscope had been about 1 ft. out of the water . . . Finally after a 7 minutes chase while she was crossing from Port to Starboard, while we were turning to the starboard we hit her just abaft the periscope. About 20 feet of her foc'sle showed with her fore foot well clear of the water. She passed aft slowly becoming more vertical until just clear of our stern she disappeared. No survivors could be seen but as we were steaming at full speed this is not surprising. On her bow was a small plate on which the letters U.29 were visible.'[11]

Britain's countermeasures included a retaliatory blockade by 'Order in Council' which attempted still further to restrict trade with Germany and by consequence trod firmly on the toes of neutrals. British anti-U-Boat measures however were only deceptively coping with the German imposition of a war zone. There had been no dramatic increase of sinking in the first months of the campaign despite the major political significance of *U-20*'s destruction of the Cunard liner *Lusitania* on 7 May

BRITISH.

ALIENS RESTRICTION ORDER. 1914.

LANDING CARD.

SECOND CABIN. No. on Schedule 144

Cunard R.M.S. " LUSITANIA. "

Name of Passenger Ekrhardt, Herbert

nd members of family.

N.B.—This card must be stamped by the Aliens Officer at the port of arrival, and will be collected at the gangway before the passenger may land.

The waterstained landing card of a *Lusitania* survivor. (H. Hereward)

1915 off the Old Head of Kinsale. Neither her speed nor her 1250 passengers had rendered her free from an attack which had been openly threatened in New York on the eve of her departure.

Two torpedoes struck her without warning. One passenger, travelling second class, had just finished lunch and saw everyone seem to rush for the stairs as water surged in through open portholes. 'I started to close those nearest to me and was working on the second one when the list of the ship got so pronounced for all the crockery on the tables to slip off onto the floors with a frightening crash.' He was told by a steward to get onto the boat deck having collected his life jacket but it had been taken. He

obtained another one and returned a lost boy to his family: but the list got so bad that people were sliding down the deck and hitting the guard rail. 'When I began to slide the sea met me halfway down the deck. I was sucked down but by keeping my eyes open and swimming towards the light, however much I was turned over in the turmoil I got to the surface.'[12] The great ship had entirely disappeared in twenty minutes from the striking of the first torpedo.

The sinking of a passenger liner and the loss of 1198 lives, 119 of them American, including some celebrities too, amounted to a spectacular gift to British propaganda though it must be remembered that *Lusitania* was carrying munitions, the morality of which was questionable to say the least. When one adds up the 'baby killers raid' on Hartlepool, the *Lusitania*, Edith Cavell's execution and the German encouragement of Mexican designs on United States territory we may admire the successful British presentation to the world of German inhumanity but we still cannot withhold astonishment at such spellbinding German stupidity.

Long before convoy was introduced for merchant shipping as well as for the escorting of troop transports, an impressive degree of regimentation for the security of cross-Channel traffic was in operation. A Great Central Railway mailboat, *Stockport*, was used as HM Transport G.802 by the Admiralty from the RN Victualling Yard at Deptford to ferry military stores and food across to Boulogne and Calais. At the Nore, she was checked by Naval Guard ships.

'From the Nore our route took the inside passage to the Downs, past the Goodwins and the Channel Barrage net supported by flare ships. A further check by Naval Guard ships at the Folkestone Gate gave permission to proceed or anchor. All arrivals after sunset were required to anchor in the Downs and it was not unusual to find in the early morning, a crowded anchorage, where previously there had been a single ship. We always sailed on our own there being ample protection from the continuous movement of naval vessels convoying the cross-

channel troopers and hospital ships on their almost hourly trips. Throughout the war this stretch of water was the busiest in the world and besides being patrolled by naval craft, a watchful eye was kept on the scene from the air by the R.N.A.S. blimps and French flying boats based at Boulogne. Our greatest danger was from floating mines, following stormy weather and during daylight hours extra look-outs were on watch. (A sister ship *Leicester* had struck a mine and only the three on the Bridge had been saved.)'[13]

Before the outbreak of war, despite Admiral Fisher's dire warnings of the likely development of submarine warfare, it had been hoped that speed and zigzagging would provide an answer to the enemy submarine for naval and merchant ships alike. An indication that such answers bore an insufficient relationship to the problem set is conveyed by the anti-submarine picket boat patrol off Portland harbour early in the war which was equipped with a black bag for placing over a periscope to blind the Comman-

U-8 in her last moments off Folkestone on 3 March 1915. The destroyer *Gurkha*, seen on the horizon behind the U-boat, has successfully used an explosive sweep to bring *U-8* to the surface. With his boat in a seriously damaged condition, the German commander has surrendered. The crew awaits rescue by the destroyer *Maori*. (Dr W.W. King-Brown)

der and a hammer to smash it! It was anticipated that the strangely careless prowler, now a hapless victim, would surface to be destroyed by gunfire. It can be recorded without further comment that no such encounter occurred. More promisingly, submarine detection by hydrophone was gradually developed to be effective from fixed positions on the sea bottom connected with shore stations and then, by early 1917, for use at sea by U-boat hunting vessels.

Depth charges, invented early in the war, were developed for specialist use by different types of vessels but it was not until 22 March 1916 that the first depth charge success was achieved.[14]

Wire sweeps with an explosive charge or

several charges came to be used too but with only a single successful return. This was on 3 March 1915 when the Dover Patrol destroyers *Maori* and *Gurkha* cooperated in damaging and then sinking *U-8* off Folkestone. (For Surgeon Probationer W.W. King Brown [*Maori*] it had been a dramatic experience which his camera recorded. However, just over three years later, *Maori* struck a mine off Zeebrugge and the entire ship's company was taken into captivity.[15]) The explosive sweep was replaced by the explosive paravane which could be towed well out, one to either quarter of a destroyer and used in high speed sweeping to a depth of 200 feet.[16] Drifter-towed or held indicator nets also had some success. When the nets were fouled by a submarine, the resultant impact released a carbide flare which drew in anti-submarine vessels. When electro-contact mines were hung on the nets they were still more effective even if only as a deterrent against U-boats which had the new net-cutting capacity. It proved impossible to construct a boom of heavy netting right across the Channel leaving two patrolled gates at either side but it was the nets of the Dover barrage which, until 1917, forced the German Navy Command to order their ocean-going U-boats to proceed to Western waters via the North of Scotland. Unfortunately, the patrol by sixty-two net drifters of the Otranto Straits in the Adriatic was not a success and enemy submarine operations were little hampered by nets which were easily evaded despite the destruction of one U-boat.[17]

Far too much faith was put in patrolling. There was added irony in the reluctance to adopt the necessity of escorting merchant vessels rather than patrolling commercial seaways. A major argument advanced, in a certain sense quite reasonably, against convoying was that there was a shortage of destroyers because so many were needed to cover the Grand Fleet's capital ships. The navy was, however, using these vessels, in their short supply, to patrol empty sea lanes and it was small wonder that the U-boats found easy prey in the vastness of the oceans as isolated merchantmen ploughed their

lonely way so perilously. The very notion of hunting U-boats rather than protecting their vulnerable victims was a fundamental error reinforced by selective considerations which seemed to undermine the practicality of an alternative approach to the problem.

Records at every level from official diplomatic to first hand personal experience, make it clear that submarine warfare had introduced an element of savagery into the war paralleled solely by some German actions in occupied territories.[18] In a period of forty-eight hours around 19 August 1915 there occurred four such incidents starkly illustrating a lack of humanity and a disregard for the conventions of warfare however open to different interpretations such conventions might be. The requirement of historical balance in retrospect makes it necessary to state the obvious in that submarine warfare was new and that taking prisoners or providing for the security of the crews of ships to be sunk while not endangering the submarine were difficult problems.

On the morning of 19 August, two instances, at that moment unrelated, took place. In St George's Channel, the White Star liner *Arabic* was torpedoed and sunk without warning by *U-24*. (Despite the speed with which she sank, only thirty-nine lives were lost out of 429 passengers and crew.) Especially after the *Lusitania* sinking, it seemed a totally callous outrage. That morning, too, the shelling by a German destroyer of a British submarine aground in Danish waters and of their crew attempting to swim to shore or to Danish boats seemed to be similarly beyond reason. The Danes had been guarding the submarine which, for a twenty-four hour period, had been legally entitled to attempt to get free from her stranded position. Two days later a German U-boat fired on the boats of a sinking collier, the *Ruel*, as they were rowed away from the doomed ship, but the incident which had the greatest diplomatic and propaganda repercussions was the fate of *U-24* on the very day she sank the liner *Arabic*.

Eight miles off the Scilly Isles, *U-24* came upon the mule-carrying boat *Nicosian* whose wireless signals were picked up by *Baralong*, one of the mystery Q ships designed to lure U-boats to destruction. *Baralong* had three concealed 12-pounder guns, rifle-armed Marines, a similar number of naval reservists and a well-paid volunteer merchant marine crew, all under the command of Lieutenant Commander Godfrey Herbert whose first officer was Sub-Lt G.C. Steele RNR.

Baralong, with an added mast, was elaborately disguised as a cargo ship but the piled wooden cases were largely empty for floatation ballast apart from those at the top, which held potatoes.

When *Baralong* arrived on the scene, *U-24* was shelling *Nicosian* whose crew had taken to the boats. *U-24* now turned her attention to *Baralong*. The submarine's gun crew was sent below, she trimmed down her profile and approached *Baralong* at high speed. Herbert altered course for *Nicosian*'s boats as if to disclaim aggressive intent. *U-24*'s incautious response was to surface fully and man her gun for further action against *Nicosian*. Herbert skilfully allowed *Nicosian*'s superstructure to come between him and *U-24*, then hoisted the White Ensign and prepared two guns to fire on a target which would soon emerge from behind *Nicosian*'s bows. The 12-pounders (supported by the rifles of the Marines) swiftly destroyed the submarine as well as her gun crew, but while Herbert now sought to shepherd *Nicosian*'s boats together, swimming Germans had reached or were reaching the abandoned mule ship. Their intent might have been sabotage, the sinking of a valuable ship with its cargo. Herbert ordered the Marines to fire and a party was dispatched to *Nicosian* where by now the Germans had vanished from sight, showing no open desire to surrender. They were traced to the engine room and here shot by the Marines.

Commander Steele has left a tape-recorded account of this incident and in certain details it is not in accord with the account given as above from the Official History.[19] Steele does not make much of a point mentioned in the Official History of the fury over *Lusitania* and then *Arabic* that very morning but it is not unlikely that revenge was a strongly motivating factor for the men of *Baralong*.[20]

A propaganda weapon had been given to the Germans who were able to use the untested accounts of American crew members or muleteers once, via Bristol, they had safely recrossed the Atlantic. This British 'atrocity' was used to counter the continuing influence of the British propaganda over *Lusitania*. German

The after part of the famous Q Ship, *Baralong*. (Vice Admiral E. Longley-Cook)

blockheadedness over Edith Cavell in October 1915 and Captain Fryatt in the following month, helped to swing the pendulum decisively in Britain's favour. The second German unrestricted campaign in 1917 left the need for only a final German folly over Mexico to bring America into the war.

A legitimate target for U-boat action and one whose losses in human terms were calamitous was that of the troopship *Royal Edward*, sunk in the Aegean on 13 August with the loss of 850 lives.[21] In the following month, the troopship *Southland* was also struck by torpedo in the Aegean but was skilfully brought to safety in Mudros by a skeleton crew while supporting ships took up all those who had been successful in taking to the boats.

August 1915 was the worst month for British losses to U-boats before the 1917 campaign.

Forty-two ships had been sunk but American protests after the sinking of the liner *Arabic* resulted in the abandonment on 30 August of the German policy of unrestricted submarine warfare.[22]

It was not easy now for the German U-boat commander to operate successfully under the restrictions imposed on him by his Government. The arming of their merchantmen prey was the critical factor. How could such ships be considered 'peaceful merchantmen'? When German policy restrictions were modified, they still, however, specifically exempted enemy passenger steamers from attack. The attack on the French steamer *Sussex* on 24 March 1916 openly flouted this exemption and caused a further diplomatic furore, the end result of which was German discontinuance of any U-boat campaign at all in the war zone.

It had not been submarines alone which had restricted Grand Fleet movements and made so considerable an impact on British trade and hence naval action to protect that trade.

Survivors of HMS *Russell* in the funeral procession of shipmates on Malta in 1916. (F. Jaques)

A long way from Russia! HMS *Hampshire* mined and sunk off Marwick Head, Mainland, the Orkneys on 5 June 1916. Kitchener was lost. (Commander G.C. Harris)

German mines too had struck notable victims which had included two pre dreadnought battleships, *King Edward VII* in January 1916 off the Pentland Firth and *Russell* in April 1916 off Malta.

Fire had swept through *Russell* following upon the explosion and the screeching rush of steam blown from the safety valves. Fumes drove on deck all who had survived the initial explosion. It was just after 5.30 a.m. on 27 April. Most of the sleeping midshipmen had been killed but one who survived because his duties stationed him on the forebridge paid striking tribute to the composure of the crew, unhurried, cheerful amidst the evidence of casualties, pressing danger from fire and the likelihood of overwhelming explosion from the magazines. He remembered one man in particular who had tied a large number of tobacco tins on a string about him for added buoyancy in the water. For those unscathed immediate rescue was at hand, trawlers quickly busying themselves in this work, reducing from disastrous proportions what had already been severe loss of life.[23]

It was a mine to which the cruiser *Hampshire* fell victim off the Orkneys on 5 June but there was still more significance in this loss. Lord Kitchener, the very embodiment of the spirit of the nation, however much he was seen differently in top Government circles, had been the illustrious passenger aboard *Hampshire*, bound for North Russia and a secret Government mission. His body was never recovered. To the gloom of national despondency over published statistics of the battle of Jutland, was added a further sense of national loss.

Again, however unfairly, the fulfilment of naval responsibilities seemed inadequately carried out. As a tragic tailpiece to the sorry affair, numbers of bodies washed ashore after a stormy night of high seas, had broken necks. It may be that in jumping from the stricken *Hampshire* and hitting the water, the life support belt had actually snapped up under the chin of the wearer and thus men were killed outright, losing their small chance in such seas of struggling for the base of the precipitous cliffs of Marwick Head.

A principal mine layer had been the surface raider *Moewe*. Early in 1916, *Moewe* and *Greif* had briefly raised the spectre of being a scourge equal to that of the surface raiders of the first months of the war. *Greif* was hunted down swiftly but *Moewe*, with guns, torpedoes and a high potential harvest from her seed of 500 mines, was to have a remarkably sustained record of success.

On 15 January the Elder Dempster steamship *Appam* was intercepted by *Moewe* north of Madiera. German prisoners from their captured West African Colonies were aboard *Appam*: freedom for them meant captivity for British sailors or soldiers. 'Our quarters were 'tween decks and the place packed with seamen, officers and men of all varieties as we were the 7th boat captured.' Food and medical attention were given and the diarist, an army doctor, N.S. Deane, allowed back to *Appam*, watched *Moewe*'s destruction of a further victim. Strangely, *Appam* was allowed to set course for the United States.

Much less fortunate was a cattle boat, *Georgic*. *Georgic*'s pantry boy, A.G. Newman, who signed on with a false age, was only fourteen when his moment of trial came on 10 December 1916. It had been his third trip to Philadelphia and on their return when nearing Brest, *Georgic* stopped in response to a vessel's signal that she was short of fresh water. Immediately they were shelled, the wireless being destroyed and some ship's boats too. Newman maintained that the bottom of the ship's boat to which he and another took, fell out absolutely rotten, weakened by the axe-blows to free it from the layer of paint which had fixed it to *Georgic*'s deck. The boat had been swung out by davits and hence Newman found himself in the water from which he saw a further shell land among American cattlemen on the deck who had been shouting their nationality and an appeal to cease fire. The *Moewe* put out boats to pick up those in the water but Newman had read in a Liverpool paper of seamen being shot by the Germans and he attempted to elude the boat-hook used to fish him out. The sodden survivors were taken aboard *Moewe* where they joined other captives. A German demolition party failed in its efforts aboard *Georgic* to sink her, so a torpedo had to be used. Bales of cotton were blown as high as the mast and there was a distressing small drama played out before Newman's eyes when a horse, having swum free from the sinking ship, was shot as the swiftest fate possible.

Captivity conditions were crowded and insanitary aboard *Moewe*. In order that she could continue her operations a dangerous sea transfer of the British seamen was undertaken to one of *Moewe*'s captured ships, *Yarrowdale*. Of the alarming prospect of leaping aboard as the vessels came close, Newman vividly remembers the accent of the German's instructions: 'Ven I say yump, yump!'[24] The journey to internment was continued in the still worse conditions of the foetid overcrowding of *Yarrowdale*'s hold.

Moewe went on to further successes, but the new surface raiders in no way paralleled the material threat that the submarine had made in 1915 and was to pose even more seriously in 1917 when a policy of unrestricted U-boat warfare was ruthlessly applied.

10

The Battle of Jutland

In attempting to illustrate how British sailors acted in and reacted to the extended drama of the one major confrontation of the battle fleets at sea, it is useful to note that both the tradition of victory and the public expectation of victory had made a collective impact on the personnel of the Grand Fleet, an impact tangibly felt by individuals. Whether the keenness for a battle to demonstrate the Royal Navy's command of the sea were to have been blunted by what Professor Marder calls the 'mood of frustration and exasperation and uncertainty about the enemy's plans and movements'[1] is difficult to assess. Certainly, the months of watchful sweeping of the North Sea in the vain hope of catching units of the High Seas Fleet away from their bases bent on mischief must have been a considerable psychological strain but so too was there strain for the Germans. Their vaunted fleet had been conspicuously cautious, a caution viewed impatiently by a civilian public suffering from both the impact of the colossal military effort on at least two fronts and the growing influence of the British blockade.

Each side had knowledge of British preponderance in numbers of capital ships and light craft and in gun power. Without regard to vessels not engaged in the battle, Britain had twenty-eight dreadnought battleships opposing sixteen German at Jutland and the German overall speed was to be affected by their being accompanied by slower pre dreadnought battleships. The battle cruiser ratio was nine to five in favour of the British who had also 113 lighter craft to the Germans seventy-two. In weight of broadside from the capital ships, the number and the calibre of the British battleship guns gave them a 2.5 to 1 ratio of superiority. In only two known areas was the Royal Navy at a

disadvantage and that was, first, in the incomplete fitting of director firing gear for the secondary armament of the capital ships and, secondly, in the acknowledged reduction of armour in favour of the accumulation of heavier armament.

It was not to be expected that junior officers, let alone ratings, could have an informed opinion on the quality of the leadership exercised over them and the vessels they served. Sir John Jellicoe's responsibility as Commander in Chief was awesome. Neither the nature of that responsibility nor the effectiveness with which it was fulfilled are to be discussed here. What can be stressed is that there was a wholesome confidence throughout the Grand Fleet in Jellicoe. Of course, there may have been reservations about this or that senior officer and there was before Jutland both a negative as well as a positive side to the intense competitive pride Beatty had inspired in the battle cruiser fleet but, above all, the Grand Fleet awaited the trial of battle in unity and confidence of spirit.

There had been a number of occasions in 1916 when accident or design could have brought about a major action in the North Sea. An attempted carrier-borne seaplane attack by the Harwich Force on the Zeppelin base believed to be at Hoyer was one such occasion; Beatty's battle cruisers, covering the Force, might well have met the German battle cruisers had the latter maintained their search for the intruders.

A month later, the High Seas Fleet came out and Lowestoft was shelled but the Harwich Force put up tough diversionary resistance thus reducing the time available to the Germans for concentrated bombardment to half an hour.[2] When a British seaplane raid at the beginning of

May on the now located Zeppelin sheds at Tondern was essayed, though without success, there was a further chance of action but the High Seas Fleet was not ordered out.

Despite anxieties about the location of his bases so far North from the likely areas of the High Seas Fleet aggression and the unreadiness in terms of security of alternative bases further South, Jellicoe planned in May to lure out German capital units onto his well stationed superior force. Vice Admiral Scheer was to seize the initiative with a not dissimilar plan though changing circumstances brought modification in it. Originally a raid was to be launched on Sunderland but poor visibility reduced to negligible proportions the vital role Zeppelin reconnaisance was to play in this raid. It was intended that a screen of U-boats would weaken Beatty's force critically as it left the Firth of Forth to deal with the flaunted bait of the ships bombarding Sunderland. Adapting from the bad weather, the Admiral still ordered out the lure of his battle cruisers under Vice Admiral Hipper while his own battleships followed as the trap.

British Admiralty Intelligence accurately gleaned from German signals the movement of their units but there was a regrettable delay in informing Jellicoe that Scheer was out too with his battleships. German intentions were not known; they could only be deduced. There was at least the possibility of a realisation of the British plan to bring their superiority to bear. From Scapa and Cromarty the movement to Jellicoe's designated rendezvous off the Skaggerak began, with Beatty to be still nearer the German bases. There was an alerted readiness too for the light cruisers, destroyers and submarines at Harwich and the 3rd Battle Squadron at Sheerness. Beatty's force from Rosyth was led by his light cruisers eight miles ahead of the battlecruisers which had their destroyer

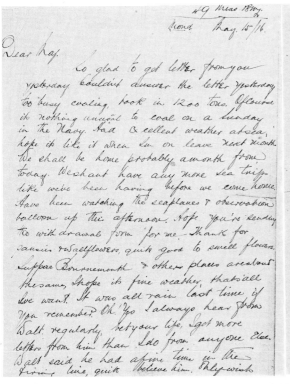

'Roll on next month': a Royal Marine of HMS *Defence* writes what was probably his last letter before Jutland when his ship was lost with all hands. (R. Lugg)

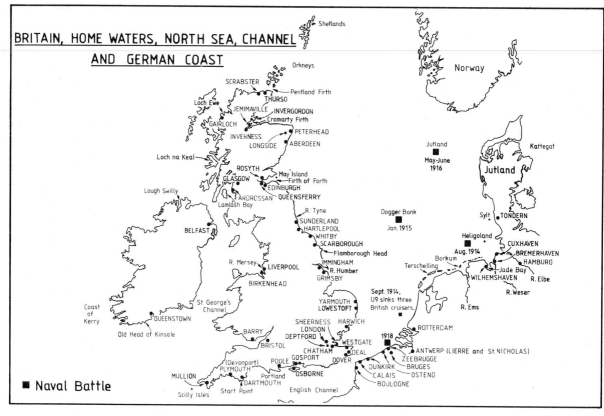

BRITAIN, HOME WATERS, NORTH SEA, CHANNEL AND GERMAN COAST

■ Naval Battle

protection on each beam. Five miles in the rear came the four battleships and destroyers of the 5th Battle Squadron. The U-boat screen was breached without misadventure.

It is not easy to estimate the degree of personal anticipation of battle which permeated the ships as both contemporary accounts and those written later are likely to have been influenced by the events which ensued. Although the view of Midshipman Crawford (*Valiant*) is not supported by general agreement, he had a better overall view than most. 'Returning on my bike from an unlawful visit to Edinburgh I saw from the top of Hawes Brae the unmistakable signs of a fleet getting ready in a hurry. The urgent flag signals, the black smoke beginning to come from the battle cruisers and the destroyers in Port Edgar just beyond Queensferry made it clear to me before I even reached our picket boat at Hawes Pier that this was no exercise but the real thing.'[3] On the other hand, Midshipman Walters, also in *Valiant*, thought as they went out of the Firth of Forth that 'it would not be more than one of our usual periodical sweeps south.'[4] According to a surviving letter from a rating in Beatty's flagship, the battle cruiser *Lion*: 'We were thinking that we would still be able to get back again in time for our coming leave this week and the sole topic of conversation was of that and what we were going to do on our holiday.'[5] A Royal Marine Officer in HMS *Warspite* wrote to his parents on 9 June: 'When we went out we hadn't any idea that there was anything on. We thought we might be trying another air raid but didn't take it seriously as we have been trailing the tail of our coat up and down the Danish Coast pretty consistently lately without anyone treading on anything more than a destroyer or two.'[6]

Contact with the enemy was brought about by the almost simultaneous sighting and investigation by a German light cruiser and the British light cruiser *Galatea* of a neutral steamer. The cruisers in consequence came within sight of each other just after 2.15 in the afternoon of 31 May. Beatty acted on *Galatea*'s information by altering course in an attempt to

106

cut off the German force from its base. He did not however ensure that the really powerful element of his fighting strength, the 5th Battle Squadron, then trailing him, was signalled to follow him closely. When the British battle cruisers were in sight of the German vessels of the same category, the German commander, Vice Admiral Hipper, altered course to starboard to draw Beatty towards Admiral Scheer's stalking battleships. Beatty had delayed firing, strangely in view of the outranging capacity he held over Hipper. Just after 15.45, at about 16,000 yards, the battle cruiser duel began with yet another British error leaving one German ship, *Derfflinger*, without British attention for ten minutes of the action. The range was opened up by deployment from both the opposing forces and the intensity of the shelling was stepped up too. It was at this stage that *Lion* was almost destroyed as a result of a hit on Q turret, the resultant fire being narrowly prevented from reaching the magazine by the action of a mortally wounded Royal Marine, Major F.J.W. Harvey. Harvey, with both his legs shot off, had somehow managed to order the closing of the magazine doors and the flooding of the magazine. This action earned a posthumous VC.

Just after 4 p.m., the battle cruiser *Indefatigable* blew up under salvoes from *Von der Tann*. Fifty-seven officers and 960 men were lost. Two men survived to be taken prisoners of war. The guns of the 5th Battle Squadron now came within range of the German ships. Despite the haze and smoke into which they were firing, their shelling was accurate. Its effect however, was diminished by the shells exploding on impact. At approximately 4.15, the second British battle cruiser loss occurred. *Queen Mary* took a plunging salvo on her upper deck, the impact explosion and fire being almost immediately followed by the huge explosion of one of her magazines going up. As *Tiger* and *New Zealand* went past her, her stern was high in the air before she sank leaving a towering pillar of smoke as an eloquent witness of the disaster.

In compulsion to watch at close hand such a devastating sight as the end of a huge ship, its midships obliterated, William Cave of *Dublin* saw the forepart of *Queen Mary* largely intact. 'In every detail we could see officers and signalmen with others as the ship, already doing twenty knots with the fore section blown forward, causing a higher bow wave than before only listing slightly to Port, then skidding round to starboard towards *Dublin*. We actually ported our helm to avoid her hitting us but it proved unnecessary; with increasing list she dived, her fore turret guns at full elevation hot with firing, giving off a loud hissing as they met the water. It was terrible to see those poor souls so near yet so far and being unable to help.'[7]

Destroyers of the 13th flotilla now attacked Hipper's force driving off the German destroyers attempting to get in an effective torpedo attack on the 5th Battle Squadron. In this action two destroyers, *Nomad* and *Nestor*, failed to return on being recalled. They had been reduced to a sinking condition.

Beatty, on being informed by the cruiser *Southampton* of the approach of German battleships, altered course towards them and, making visual contact, turned north to draw them onto Jellicoe. Yet again he failed to make clear his intentions to the 5th Battle Squadron. When the Squadron approached *Lion* on an opposite course, matters became clear for their Commander, Rear Admiral Evan Thomas and he now manoeuvred to follow his chief.

At this juncture, the cruiser *Southampton* made what seemed a suicidally close approach to the German battleships. She turned and made her escape but concentrated German guns destroyed the crippled *Nomad* and *Nestor* wallowing in the path of the Germans though still getting in torpedo firings. From these attempts and those of another two British destroyers, one torpedo seriously damaged the battle cruiser *Seydlitz*.

Scheer's approach brought the 5th Battle Squadron into action against capital ships of both Hipper's and Scheer's forces with the British at a disadvantage, silhouetted against the lighter western skies. In this action, *Barham* and *Malaya* were heavily hit and there was the added drama of a daring destroyer attack on the German battleships by *Onslow* and *Moresby*. The capital ships' range was now opening beyond effective fire and the first stages of the action were over as Beatty's ships led Scheer on to Jellicoe.

Apart from their fascination, personal accounts of the action are illuminating in three particular ways. The emotional reaction to the experience is often convincingly portrayed; secondly, under some circumstances, the precisely recorded sequence of events for a particular ship or sections of its complement is vividly laid out; and thirdly, the station and responsibility of a young officer in action are described in such detail as to leave the reader with an almost tangible understanding of his work. On rare occasions all three of these elements are present.

On 9 June, writing to his brother (a submarine commander), Captain Poland (Royal Marines: *Warspite*) gave his impression of the action as: 'Confused with one or two momentary exceptions, of haze, paralysing terror, own gunfire and enemy's flashes and a hail of splinters.' He described in graphic detail the severe punishment *Warspite* took and concluded: 'I was in the most dreadful state of terror the whole time. Big gunfire is a beastly thing if you're the target. I don't want to go through anything like our bad quarter of an hour again.'[8]

Concerning emotional response, there is a nice illustration of the release of fear by a sense of the ridiculous in the recall of a Surgeon Probationer in *Onslow* during the gallant torpedo attack on a German capital ship. 'I was sick with fear but I well remember bursting out with laughter at the sight of a huge Channel Islander, Journeaux, bending double, presenting a colossal posterior inside the guard rails each time a salvo came over, shouting: "That was a near one." '[9] A more unaffected illustration of exhilaration is a diary entry of Naval Instructor Frank Bowman (*Colossus*) that: 'Fletcher called through Fore Transmitting Station that he had achieved the ambition of a lifetime by firing

shrapnel at the Hun.'[10]

Action station responsibility is well described by Captain E.S. Brand, a Sub-Lieutenant in *Valiant*: 'My action station was "Rate Officer" in the 15″ Gun Control Tower, a cylindrical armoured tower set more or less in the centre of the Conning Tower which surrounded it. My instrument was what was known as a "Dumaresq". After I had made an estimate of the "inclination of our target" i.e. the angle which the target's course made with my line of sight, and estimated the target's speed, I set these on the "Dumaresq" and was rewarded by being told the "Rate" and the Deflection (left or right), to be set on the gun sights.' Down below in the Transmitting Station, a much larger 'Dumaresq' plotted its own rate of change by means of a mechanically controlled pencilled line on a Dreyer table designed for this recording purpose. Brand was in telephone communication with a midshipman at the Dreyer table so the checking could be done constantly by personal link and he also sat next to the 15-inch Gunnery Control Officer who was able to observe the fall of shot and judge whether he was being advised correctly. Brand's account is far more detailed than can be included here but in considering whether he were frightened he wrote: 'By every instinct of my character I should certainly have been but I do not remember having time to indulge in it which proves the value of "drill" so that one becomes so absorbed in doing what you have been drilled to do that there is no time to wonder if you may be hit yourself.'[11] A contemporary account by a sub-lieutenant in *Barham* affirms and reaffirms that 'the roar and shake of our guns coupled with one's own work left little opportunity to think about outside matters.'[12]

An officer in an exceptional position of observation and with a duty of making notes throughout the action was Assistant Paymaster K.M. Lawder in *Malaya*'s spotting top. Perhaps the feeling of being in so exposed a position was reduced in an emotional sense by the mental concentration required for his duty to observe and record constantly the detail of

S.—1320c. (Established—May, 1900.)
(Revised—February, 1914.)

NAVAL SIGNAL.

P.O. of Watch		
Read By		
Reported By		
Passed By		
Logged By		
System		
Date		
Time		

From   To

5.3 - 6" Splinters of wood flew all over top. There seems to be a fire in the casemate. Another got us shortly after in about the same place

5.35 Another hit all way along starbᵈ battery on ship's side.

.37 Large shell fell just abreast of top, between five & ten yards from ship's side. I was looking at the exact spot where it fell & saw the actual projectile quite clearly. It did not burst on water and at the angle it fell ought to have reached ship's side, but no explosion took place.

.45 We are now on parallel course with other 3 ships of squadron but about ½ a mile on disengaged side. We are being fired at from beam now, firing from astern has nearly stopped. Engaged + small cruiser on starbᵈ beam, range 15000.

.47 Battle cruisers opened fire again. S.1 - 6" fired one round.

.55 We have not been fired at for last 10 minutes, though Destroyers astern are being engaged. There seem to be enemy all along our starbᵈ beam, though they are

M. 1704/1900. Sta. 6/14.
(3312) 16600/D520 200m pads 7/15sv G & S 109 157

Jutland: Captain's Secretary, K.M. Lawder, has copied out the pencilled notes he made while in the foretop of the battleship *Malaya*. (Rear Admiral K.M. Lawder)

the ship's action. A brief extract from his notes typed out after the action will suffice to appreciate the detachment with which immediate danger at its most extreme degree is recorded.[13]

'5.05 Enemy has our range exactly, so hauled out a little to port.

5.12 to 5.30 Enemy's salvoes straddled *Valiant* and *Malaya*. At this time we were outlined against a bright yellow horizon but enemy were nearly obscured by mist and we were under a very heavy constant fire from at least four ships of the High Seas Fleet. Only flashes were visible and six salvoes were falling round the ship per minute and at one time counting some which were probably meant for *Warspite* nine salvoes fell in rapid succession.

Shifted target to what appeared to be the leading enemy battleship, and as soon as a short salvo was obtained broke into rapid Director as it was realised that *Malaya* was presenting a good target. It had been decided to fire the 6″ guns short to make a screen but before this was done the whole starboard battery was put out of action by shells bursting there.

5.14 Enemy's salvo fell close over our port bow, sending spray well over the spotting top and black water into the Conning Tower.

5.17 Altered course two points to port together.

5.20 Shell struck ship on starboard side forward about water line, shaking the ship very heavily indeed.

5.25 Splinter cut steampipe to starboard syren, escape of steam rendering communication with top impossible for a few minutes till shut off.

5.27 Shell struck ship aft (roof X turret).

5.30 Shell struck starboard side of upper deck just above S.3.6″ [gun], followed by another in the same place wrecking the 6″ battery and causing a fire for a short time.'

Near miss shells were actually being seen in their flight from the spotting top. *Malaya* had developed a list and was leaking oil but three factors were now bringing assistance, the arrival of Jellicoe's battleships, *Malaya* being past the setting sun and not such a good target and the German concentration upon the cruisers *Defence* and *Warrior* and the battleship *Warspite*.

An account of the tragic drama played out by *Nomad* in the destroyer action has survived under unusual circumstances. Sub-Lieutenant David Wainwright was reported killed in an Admiralty telegram to his parents at 9.10 a.m. 3 June. News from a private source came to the family on 8 June that four officers had been saved, this information being followed two days later by an Admiralty telegram that Wainwright was safe, uninjured and a prisoner at Mainz. The officer prepared the following account from captivity. 'Think of the worst peal of thunder that you have ever heard, try to imagine it going on continuously and imagine that at the same time you are standing in the corridor of the *Royal Scot* with all the windows open, passing at full speed another express going in the opposite direction on the next set of rails. You

will then have a faint conception of what it felt like on the bridge of a destroyer in the van of the battle cruisers – the state of tension while waiting for the meeting of the destroyers in shell and torpedo battle was the worst period that I passed through because it gave imagination a chance to work. What happened when the shells struck a ship and that dull red glow appeared? Was everyone immediately asphyxiated, burnt or mangled? – I felt very empty inside as though I hadn't had a meal for ages though I didn't feel hungry. My tongue was dry and I smoked a cigarette hard, hoping that with its aid an illusion of sang froid and devil may carishness was accepted by my neighbours at its spurious value. – I busied myself with testing voice pipes and other accessories to my official function, that of fire control.

'Our signal to attack came at last and we increased to full speed to draw ahead, gradually close the enemy, and then swoop down to fire our torpedoes. We were going thirty-five knots, and the whole ship vibrated with the strain. Simultaneously the German destroyers moved out towards us and we opened fire on each other. The din was ghastly. We were going all out, the ship shivering with speed; our three four inch, one on the foc'sle, one aft and one amidships were all firing; the German destroyers' shells were exploding round us, the projectiles from the big ships whistling overhead and the perpetual thunder of their guns rolling eternally. Control of our three guns from the bridge became a farce, what with the din and the fact that our ever-changing course and the movement of the German destroyers meant that each gun's target was continually shifting. The order for "Local Control" was given and I went down to the foc'sle gun. I remember ceasing fire on a destroyer in the belief that she was a friend, then the smoke cleared and we saw her colours plainly and got at her again until she started sinking – I noticed we seemed to be listing to port. The German destroyers had retired and both fleets had turned about to the N.N.W. We seemed to be moving very slowly and gradually we stopped and the list to port increased.

Looking aft I saw clouds of steam amidships and going there found the deck a shambles. A shell had struck the starboard side, entered the engine room and severed the main steam pipe, effectively stopping our motive power. We had fired two of our torpedoes, one was left in a third tube with a merry little fire on deck underneath it which we soon put out and the fourth tube was out of action. A shell had struck just by it and blown the man whose job it was to sit astride it clean over the side. The bilge pumps were out of action, we were leaking badly and two men only were alive in the engine room.

'Out of the haze on the starboard quarter an interminable line of battleships was approaching. *Nomad* was lying crippled in the path of the battle squadron of the High Seas Fleet. Among the best disciplined crew in the world a panic might have arisen but our captain was more than equal to the occasion. Orders were passed to prepare to be taken in tow. This involved getting most of the hands on the foc'sle and ranging the cables along the deck together with various wire hawsers. It kept our minds on a

Jutland: a light cruiser under fire, seen from HMS *Falmouth*. (Rear Admiral S.A. Pears)

definite job of work and it kept us to the opposite end of the ship to the High Seas Fleet. There was however no hope of anyone towing us. A few minutes before, *Nicator* had lain off us and offered to do so but the skipper waved her away. Why risk a second ship? I spent a merry five minutes in the chart room routing out signal books, cyphers and charts and dumping them over the side. Meanwhile all boats were lowered to the deck level and rafts were cast loose.

'We still had our torpedo left, but in order to train the tube on the leading enemy ship it would have been necessary to turn the ship. As we couldn't do this we had perforce to wait until the target ship came into the line of sight instead. Just then the three leading battleships opened fire on us. – We waited. No. 1 and I stood on the foc'sle. Between us and the enemy was a piece of painted canvas and its moral support was enormous. The first salvoes passed over us. The next were short – the next salvo was wrong for direction. We went aft and watched the last torpedo fired but alas it missed. At this moment they got our range and things began to happen. As we sank lower the order "Abandon Ship" was given. The whaler and

motor boat were miraculously unhurt and drew ahead of the sinking ship. The dinghy was splintered but looked as if it would float. I was sent forward and the skipper went aft to see that no-one wounded was left on deck. The stern was now under water and the whole hull was an inferno of smoke, steam, explosions and hailstorms of splintered metal. The skipper returned staggering and badly wounded but we got into the dinghy and pulled clear. She had lain alongside with nine men in her waiting uncomplainingly for the captain to return. Suddenly we saw two wild figures on deck. We went back and took them into the dinghy, two stokers both scalded and half raving in their agony. They must have been knocked out, and missed the order to abandon ship. Only the fore half of *Nomad* was afloat now but the ensign still flew at the masthead.

'All this time the dinghy had been making water steadily and now she gracefully sank under and we swam away. One by one we were picked up by the motor boat and as I was hauled over the side I turned and saw *Nomad* take her final dive. The Germans put a few parting salvoes into the middle of the survivors in the water and then disappeared into the N.W. leaving two torpedo boats to collect us as prisoners.'[14]

For all the difficulties involved, it still seems reprehensible that Jellicoe was not kept fully informed of the progress of the battle cruiser action and of the relative position of the engaged and then disengaged units as Beatty set course north for contact with the main force of British battleships steaming south from their bases. Only *Southampton* seems to have fulfilled her function properly in this respect. Compounding these omissions of accurate signals there was an excess of Admiralty caution in holding back the Harwich Force from its Commander's eagerness for effective deployment.

The 1st Cruiser Squadron on the starboard wing of the Battle Fleet making headway south was the first to make contact with the advance units of Beatty's force but it was on the port wing where the next phase of the action commenced with the 3rd Battle Cruiser Squadron and supporting units becoming engaged. The light cruiser *Chester* was: 'Smothered in bursting shell,'[15] the mortally wounded young Cornwell staying at his gun amidst a scene of grim shambles.[16] The German light cruisers which had wrought this damage then suffered heavily themselves from the battle cruiser *Invincible* but the latter had to turn away to avoid torpedo attack. The British destroyers of the 3rd Battle Cruiser Squadron were now unprotected by *Invincible*'s guns but, led by Commander Loftus Jones in *Shark*, the destroyers *Acasta*, *Ophelia* and *Christopher* launched a daring attack on the German light cruisers and attendant destroyers. The attack protected the British battle cruisers but *Shark* was reduced to a wreck. A tow by *Acasta* was gallantly offered and with equal gallantry refused. Though *Shark* was given a momentary respite by a British light cruiser diversion, she took further concentrated punishment and sank. Loftus Jones's heroism is well described in the Official History[17] and the action is remembered by Cdr C.G. Vyner, then a sublieutenant in *Acasta*. Vyner was on the bridge with the Commander. His main responsibility was with the foremost 4 inch gun. 'The enemy against which we were directed seemed almost innumerable. We were steaming almost directly at the enemy and they were steaming across us South to North. We soon took a hole in the foc'sle big enough to drive a motor car through. The shelling was so intense and the splashes all round so much a screen that I could see nothing much of what happened to my own shells. Furthermore it seemed that our little gun was only a pea shooter and perfectly useless. This was extremely depressing. I don't think I was really frightened just frustrated. *Shark* was in trouble and we went to her. She was a complete shambles, totally destroyed. We went round her to see if we could take her in tow though we were in fact unready to do this. *Shark*'s Commander told us to clear out and we proceeded to do this but immediately took two shells in our engine room and this more or less finished us as a

Jutland: HMS *Defence* five minutes before she was destroyed with all hands at 18.20 hours on 31 May 1916. It is likely that the pall of smoke above the ship to the right of the photograph is that from *Wiesbaden* the German light cruiser, which was soon to sink. (Rear Admiral D.J. Hoare)

fighting unit. We lay stopped, the Grand Fleet passing us firing over our head at the enemy beyond.'[18]

During the night, *Acasta*'s fires were brought under control. Her wireless was still operating and the surviving leading signalman picked up a signal from *Iron Duke* to a destroyer to search north for *Acasta* and tow her home. In the morning, a destroyer in fact appeared, took *Acasta* in tow and brought her successfully to a jetty in Aberdeen. Here, as if in final exhaustion, she sank though she does not appear as a battle loss.

Returning to the development of action between the battle fleets as Jellicoe's and Scheer's forces converged – Jelllicoe still with no clear understanding of what was happening south of him and Scheer with no intention whatsoever of confrontation with the full Grand Fleet – it was the Grand Fleet's 1st Cruiser Squadron which now came into action. A suicidally bold attack on German battle cruisers led to an inferno of shells upon *Defence* and *Warrior*, the tragedy clearly visible from *Warspite*, herself in serious trouble, her involuntary manoeuvre out of line protecting *Warrior* from *Defence*'s terrible fate. Captain Poland of *Warspite* wrote: 'I saw the *Defence* coming down our starboard bow (engaged side) heading straight at the enemy, with a cloud of white smoke amidships and aft. She was banging away and going full speed, masthead colours and all the rest of it and made a very gallant show. I saw three salvoes fall across her in quick succession, beauties. A flicker of flame ran aft along her forecastle head and up her fore turret, which seemed to melt. Then – whoof, up she went, a single huge sheet of flame, 500 feet high, mixed up with smoke and frag-

Jutland: HMS *Engadine* alongside the stricken *Warrior*, taking aboard her crew.

ments. As it died down I saw her crumpled bow, red hot, at an angle of sixty degrees, and then she sank. I nearly vomited – God it was an awful sight. I couldn't get to sleep that night for thinking of it.'[19]

Warrior's plight, momentarily near disaster, was more prolonged. A Royal Marine, J.C. Jones, whose action station was manning a telephone in a 9.2 inch gun turret, wrote a contemporary account for his family which is an unselfconscious tribute to the conduct of all during a harrowing experience. In all the bustle of action stations 'our Captain of the gun was ever cool and all the gun crew, as if from his inspiration, the same.' Again, as news of the annihilation of their sister cruiser was given, it was in the Marine Captain's 'very quiet voice'. Their turret filled with smoke and fumes as their gun continued in action. Then that voice again: 'Put your gas masks on men.' The turret was struck a glancing blow as it traversed. Once outside they saw the turret had been opened as if by a 'tin opener'. The order 'fire stations' was

given, dead and dying had to be ignored to secure the ship against a magazine explosion or uncontrollable fire. Like a great wounded elephant leaving its herd, *Warspite* then made a circle round them which shielded them from likely destruction. *Warrior* herself now strangely seemed to have been left alone on the scene of her torment. Wreckage and human bodies were 'continually floating past us'. As darkness closed in, the sea became rougher and *Warrior* was taking in far too much water. 'We went down below to bring up our dead and wounded, to strengthen our bulkhead doors, to plug the holes in our ship's side with blankets and hammocks.' But it was of little avail for she seemed doomed and was listing over. 'Some of us were ordered to our anti-submarine guns. We carried on bringing our mates up from down below and laid them out on the deck, the dead to be buried overboard.'

The ship's boats had been destroyed and there was an anxious expectancy of the order to abandon ship. 'Captain and Officers moved amongst us helping and cheering us. We managed to eat some sandwiches and drink a little cocoa – it passed a little time away. We had a bad list, the water was washing our upper deck and the wounded continued to moan.' Jones, went to his mess down below to search for his money and treasured photos. 'I made my way over wreckage of all description, slipping on blood covered decks but gradually worked my way down below.' He found his small box but it was jammed, perhaps by blast. The water was swirling round him and he slipped actually to immersion beneath its surface. He abandoned the box.[20] There were further tense minutes as a ship approached the weakened *Warrior*. The ship proved to be the seaplane carrier *Engadine*. *Warrior* was far beyond aid. Daylight revealed the extent of her unseaworthiness. The fit men abandoned ship, swimming to jettisoned floating material. They were picked up by boats from *Engadine*. Somehow the wounded were transferred too, the doomed cruiser being left low in the water not to be sighted again.

Returning to *Warspite*'s problems, Captain

Poland's letter outlines them clearly. 'Just then our troubles started. The hit aft appears to have upset our steering gear and we careered off out of line, heading towards the enemy and made two 32 point turns. The others of course went on and we had to take all that at least a couple of divisions of the H.S.F. [High Seas Fleet] could give us. I gave up hope of seeing Rosyth again then. They hit us and hit us damned hard. Beautiful salvoes, fired as ripples, and three out of five guns hitting. No spread for direction and very little for elevation (the latter of course rather a defect until you hit).' *Warspite*'s guns were put into divided control as the battleship's gyrations made detector firing from all four turrets useless. Poland's position was particularly trying. 'I couldn't get any-thing from X turret so went into local control. Then I couldn't find the enemy – I could see his splashes and feel them all over us but I couldn't see him. I started training around but apparently the ship was turning the other way. My 2nd officer was howling for permission to fire at something, but I refused to do so until there was something visible to fire at especially as just about this time I was under the impression I only had a round or two left as I thought my magazine was flooded – I got a report that my magazine was shot through, so I ordered the crew out and told them if there was any danger of fire – to flood. Then I went down and found that it was only the compartment above that was full of water, so we got the crew down and went on, keeping the cordite dry with tarpaulins over the hopper. The N.C.O.'s were V.G.I. [Very Good Indeed] They stood fast with one or two men until I came down although they had a lot of smoke down from above as the repair party opened the hatch for a moment.

'We had about a $\frac{1}{4}$ hour of this hammering and then the G.F. [Grand Fleet] arrived. I've never been so thankful for anything in my life.'[21]

The Grand Fleet's arrival could scarcely have been more opportune. The timeliness of *Warspite*'s rescue is indicated by the fact that she was not now making way. It was an hour before repairs were carried out and the dangerous journey to Rosyth essayed. With rafts constructed and placed on her upper deck against the anticipated swift effectiveness of even one torpedo, the great ship set course for the Firth of Forth. Cautiously, she worked up from 15 knots to high speed. She was met by torpedo boat destroyers off May Island and safely escorted to Rosyth. The Forth Bridge was passed at about 5 p.m. on 1 June. 'Damn thankful to be afloat' Poland added in his letter. His description of *Warspite*'s damage and the necessary shoring up which had to be done by 'Chippies [who] worked like Trojans' makes it clear that *Warspite*, at what became known as 'Windy Corner' or on her way home, might very easily have been the single post dreadnought battleship sunk at Jutland. Her losses in killed or died of wounds were only fourteen from a complement of over a thousand. She was hit by thirteen large calibre shells and such statistics set against the material and human losses of three British battle cruisers make one pause soberly at the incalculable judgement of fate.

One man soon to drink a variety of celebratory libations on behalf of his shipmates was Assistant Clerk Bickmore who was dispatched at Rosyth with a letter to deliver to the Captain of HMS *Elizabeth*, the battleship of Dardanelles fame which had however missed Jutland through being in dock. After champagne with the Captain, whisky in the Wardroom and beer in the gunroom, it may well be that the clerk's account of *Warspite*'s exploits lost little in the retelling.[22]

Jellicoe's deployment as the enemy was encountered unexpectedly on his starboard side has received deserved praise. At the moment of execution, it must have been an unforgettable image of immense power in changing symmetry. 'The ships seemed to be in a great arc, stretching as far as one could see, indeed a most imposing spectacle. All the guns trained on the beam, smoke poured from the ships' funnels, and numberless ensigns fluttered from every ship. The fighting was drawing nearer, and everyone knew we would soon be in action. One

Jutland: the deployment of the battleships of the Grand Fleet, photographed from HMS *Orion*. (Commander J.B. Mitford)

Jutland: the terrible fate of HMS *Invincible* and her crew. (Commander C.F. Laborde)

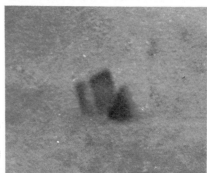

Jutland: the tomb of a thousand men, the bow and stern of HMS *Invincible*. (Commander C.F. Laborde)

wondered what would be the result, who would be sunk and who would live through it.'[23] Deployment was ordered to port. Defensively this did something to protect the more vulnerable, older and less powerful squadron of his fleet and offensively attained in time the line ahead station with which he had real prospect of crossing the enemy line's 'T'. This was the classic tactical position from which maximum punishment for least return could be wrought upon the enemy. The full effectiveness of Jellicoe's deployment was diminished by his having to reduce speed sufficiently to allow Beatty's battle cruisers to cross his own battle front. For Beatty's part, it must be stated that by Grand Fleet Battle Orders his station was at the head of the line and with little time to reach that position he made full speed in the attempt to achieve it.

Nothing heightens nervous tension more than having to await passively for a moment of supreme testing in the performance of duty. In the gun turrets of Jellicoe's battleships the minutes must have passed like the slow filling of

sand in the lower half of an hour glass. 'The worst part of the whole thing was waiting for that 1st round to go off. The gun was at 'Ready' for about half an hour. However as soon as the first round went off they were all as happy as sand boys.'[24]

In the van of Jellicoe's line was his 3rd Battle Cruiser Squadron. *Invincible*, the flagship, was hotly engaged until her magazine exploded rending the ship in two, stem and stern starkly angled in the air appropriately like displaced tombstones for over a thousand men. Of the few who survived the explosion, some were swept under to drowning by the passage of British ships across the tragic spot. The destroyer *Badger* plucked to safety the tragically small number of six in all.

Despite the grim loss of a further battle cruiser, the British battleships were now to exercise their material advantages over Hipper's and Scheer's ships. Their guns fired

Jutland: HMS *Orion*'s 13.5 inch guns firing over British destroyers. (Commander J.B. Mitford)

salvoes into *Lützow* and *Derfflinger*. Scheer ordered the disengaging manoeuvre for the escape of his force. It was in translation known as 'Battle Turn Away' and was to be covered by a destroyer attack and laying of a smokescreen. The smokescreen, aided by the fear of mines laid by the retreating Germans and of course an understandably exaggerated fear of submarines, prevented or deterred close pursuit. Instead, Jellicoe set course to cut off the High Seas Fleet from its home bases.

The German cruiser *Wiesbaden*, wallowing in her disabled condition awaiting final dispatch, got off one final defiant blow in damaging by torpedo the battleship *Marlborough* but this did not affect the tactical situation. The Grand Fleet was in position athwart the return path of the German capital ships, some of which had been seriously damaged. When Scheer attempted to break through, his ships took another pounding, *Marlborough* playing her part in this. Thus baulked, Scheer ordered a further destroyer attack and smoke screen so that he could disengage. On realising the unlikelihood of success in this, Scheer now ordered the move to be covered by the battle cruisers attempting to break through the British line. The German battleships, thus protected by the attack of their battle cruisers, destroyer action and smoke screen, completed their disengaging turn in the gathering gloom. The battle cruiser charge ordered could now be modified to one of manoeuvring off the British van. Before recall, the German destroyers had been in unsuccessful action against British battleships and light cruisers. Of this action a Cruiser Squadron Commander, Commodore C.E. le Mesurier, wrote to his son from *Calliope*: 'My little unit has been credited with two German destroyers and we claim a fat big battleship as well – tho' I hear other people are on to the same lay – Great pity the failing light and thick haze saved 'em.' The Commodore's cabin had been used for a number of the *Calliope*'s badly wounded and of the casualties he wrote: 'We lost a lot of men, I'm afraid. Poor fellows, close on a dozen – and still a good many more crumpled up rather badly.

Wonderfully cheery over it all.'[25]

British communication during this next stage of the battle was again woefully inadequate. An absence of signals, incorrect positions given, apparently incomplete instructions, each played a part with the darkening night in reducing the extremity of danger of the High Seas Fleet's position. It was now well to the west of the German bases, altering course south in a desperate attempt to evade pursuit so that it could work back east. The German battle cruisers were in a seriously damaged condition, *Seydlitz* down by the bows and without wireless communication, *Derfflinger* and *Lützow* even more severely affected.

Soon after 20.00 hours there was a further cruiser action in which *Calliope* received hits, vividly recalled by Cdr W.J.A. Willis, then a Gunnery Petty Officer, Captain of a 4 inch gun. In the gunlayer's seat and with vision through his telescopic sight, Willis would be aware of the shells coming up the hoist from the magazine, of each being taken from the hoist by one of the gun's crew, passed to a loader who placed it on a tray. The tray would be rammed up against the breech thus inserting the shell with its cordite charge, the breech would be closed by the breech loader who would shout 'ready'. All the guns were under the direction of the Gunnery Officer in the foretop but Willis's trainer would have a pointer to guide him in the training of the gun in its horizontal plane as would the sight setter responsible for elevation. On orders from the foretop it would be Willis's finger which would act on the firing trigger. When *Calliope* was hit, it was as the cruiser rolled. A shell had hit the rear of the gun and its explosion burst out the back of the gun. The whole team was wounded but 'Wiggy Bennett, my sight setter, was decapitated, his head falling in my lap. I was wounded in the left side. I can remember moving Wiggy Bennett's head, turning round to the crew and ordering the continuance of action procedure.'[26]

Cruisers *Caroline* and *Royalist* from the 4th Light Cruiser Squadron had got their turn to play a part through the Senior Officer, Captain

A sketch by one of *Caroline*'s telegraphists, William Crick. (W.R. Crick)

H.R. Crooke (*Caroline*) taking responsibility to ignore the cancellation of his attack by the Admiral, Sir Thomas Jerram (2nd Battle Squadron). Jerram was searching for Beatty's battle cruisers and judged that they might have been mistakenly identified as German. Though the cruiser attack, in which *Caroline* fired two torpedos and *Royalist* one, achieved no material damage it had at least revealed the hitherto unknown position of some of the German units.

Jellicoe faced the choice of the hazards of night action for which his fleet was little trained or holding his position to the east of the escaping Germans. By steering south he could keep the stable door locked – the decisive engagement would follow in the morning. It was this alternative he chose.

What happened in the night, as probing efforts by the Germans were made to break through the moving screen athwart their route home, was a number of destroyer and cruiser engagements. In one, the German cruiser *Frauenlob* was sunk but heavy damage was suffered by *Southampton* and *Dublin*. This was between 22 and 23.00 hours. Immediately after this, scouting vessels again encountered each other at close range and a hurricane of shells rained down on opposing ships. A deliberate ramming took place jointly by the destroyer *Spitfire* and a German battleship, the dreadnought firing her forward guns as their bows crashed into each other. The blast effect de-molished the destroyer's bridge though the guns could not be sufficiently depressed for the shells to hit. Miraculously, *Spitfire* survived, but involuntary collisions and enemy shelling dramatically reduced the effective strength of one destroyer flotilla, the 4th.

Two more British disasters remained, the cruiser *Black Prince*, caught by German searchlights, was destroyed by an inferno of shelling and the destroyer *Ardent* suffered a similar fate. From *Black Prince*, none was saved of her complement of 903, of *Ardent*, two were saved of eighty.

With all this action, the British battleships remained but sketchily in touch. When the darkness was riven for *Malaya* by a British destroyer's torpedo explosion on what was revealed as a German capital ship, even this information was not passed on to the Commander in Chief. Jellicoe was in fact now getting information from a number of sources, including both Admiralty and scouting vessels, which was confusingly contradictory in its reporting of and prediction of Scheer's course. As Jellicoe continued south, Scheer boldly in the darkness altered course to head for home, astern of the Grand Fleet. The tail end of the Harwich flotilla of destroyers was blundered into by the Germans and a further British destroyer was sunk with all hands as a result of a high speed collision with a German battleship. The suddenness, the confusion, the noise and the blinding flashes led the commander of the flotilla to write afterwards that 'it was literally awful – far worse and utterly different to anything I've been through in daylight.'[27]

One more slight possibility remained to redeem the ineffectiveness of the British destroyers' attacking endeavours, a further flotilla, the 12th, well to the NNE, was in a position for attack. This time the sky was perceptibly lighter with the first hint of dawn though the time was only in the region of 02.00 hours. The powerful German searchlights which had been the herald of destruction for several destroyers were now less dazzling and there was mist from which destroyers emerged and re-entered with some security. The pre-dreadnought battleship *Pommern* was struck by a torpedo and exploded into smithereens to leave no survivors. The flotilla commander's wireless signal of the renewed fighting failed to be picked up by *Iron Duke*. The fierce engagement did attract more destroyers but no larger ships. As the sky lightened, Jellicoe, without his far flung destroyers, reluctantly had to accept that pursuit of the elusive quarry, now reported east of him, was too dangerous in enemy waters sown with mines and harbouring submarines. Setting course north to resume contact with his cruisers and destroyers there was but one false hope when firing was heard but proved to be nothing but the efforts of naval units to drive off a scouting Zeppelin.

As the High Seas Fleet neared its bases, it was to lose Hipper's flagship, the battle cruiser *Lützow*, from which the crew was first evacuated. In her totally disabled, wrecked condition she was sent to the bottom by German torpedo. The other three battle cruisers, in a seriously damaged condition, avoided the mines sown across their path by the minelayer *Abdiel* but a battleship, *Ostfriedland*, was damaged in striking a mine.

The limping home of some of the British vessels has been described. The scene in Scapa and at Rosyth was sobering as scarred, holed, blackened ships with smashed superstructures moored beside others showing less clearly the evidence of battle. At their berths there was still movement, that of sad necessity as viewed from *Caroline*. 'June 2nd Scapa 2.30 Hospital ship comes alongside *Barham* to take off injured. *Malaya*'s quarterdeck with dead covered by Union Jack. 7.15 Funeral ship took away dead from *Barham* and *Malaya*. Crews lined up on quarterdeck and last post sounded. Ship passed us close. We stood at attention. Very sad sight.'[28] Not all the ships returned to their home bases, the Tyne and Aberdeen receiving some in their damaged condition.

Despite the perkiness pluckily scrawled in one letter to a distinguished sailor father: 'I am very much alive and kicking after a most enjoyable little scrap',[29] officers and men were ready for leave. As the gunnery officer of *Southampton* wrote home: 'We are all very glad to get a spell of leave as we had a trying time and I don't think the ship's company escaped a considerable shock to the nervous system.'[30] A further shock to jangled nerves would be administered by the public's reception of the men. The unwise release by the Admiralty of the extent of British losses before those of the enemy was known, was one of the few propaganda battles lost by British authorities in the war. Drawing upon the Communique, banner headlines in, for example, *The Daily Express* of 3 June 1916 were the result, bringing dark depression, disappointment, even anger: **'HEAVY UNACCOUNTABLE BRITISH LOSSES – THREE BATTLECRUISERS SUNK. GERMAN BATTLESHIP DESTROYED. MANY SMALLER CRAFT LOST.'** As Commodore le Mesurier wrote to his son on 10 June: 'A thousand pities the Admiralty ever made such asses of themselves as to sing 'Miserere' that Friday night or evening.'[31]

Controversy developed over the early release of such bleak news. The authorities knew, even at that stage, that there were clearly balancing factors: the Germans had chosen to break off the engagement, statistically Britain could take the losses without her superiority in naval power being really affected and, of clinching significance, the Grand Fleet would be ready for action immediately on refuelling and re-stocking with ammunition. Such was certainly not the case for the High Seas Fleet. It would be weeks before the German battle cruisers would be fit for action again.

Countless letters home protest at the public reaction. 'I don't think it was nearly such a bad show for us as the losses show', wrote T.S. Fox Pitt to his mother on 2 June. The following day, he wrote to his brother in the army: 'Don't be down-hearted about the navy until you hear the worst or the best.' Then, two days later, he wrote again to his brother: 'I know we were fearfully surprised when we came in to hear that all the people thought it was disgraceful, but I

S.—1320c. (Established—May, 1900.)
(Revised—February, 1914.)

NAVAL SIGNAL.

		P.O. or Watch	
		Read By	
From	To	Reported By	
		Passed By	
		Logged By	
		System	W/T.
Pr. Alla News		Date	3·6·1916
		Time	3·00 m

London June 2nd Secretary Admiralty makes following announcement. Afternoon Wednesday May 31st. Naval engagement took place off JUTLAND. British ships on which brunt of fighting fell were Battle Cruisers Fleet some cruisers and light cruisers supported by four fast Battleships. Amongst these, losses very heavy. German Battle Fleet aided by low visibility avoided prolonged action with our main forces and soon after these appeared on scene, enemy returned port, though not before receiving severe damage from our Battleships. Battle Cruisers :— "QUEEN MARY", "INDEFATIGABLE", "INVINCIBLE", and Cruisers :— "DEFENCE", "BLACK PRINCE" SUNK. Cruiser "WARRIOR" disabled and after being towed some time abandoned by crew. Also known destroyers :— "TIPPERARY", "TURBULENT", "FORTUNE",

M. 1704/1900. Sta. 6/14.

S.—1320c. (Established—May, 1900.)
(Revised—February, 1914.)

NAVAL SIGNAL.

		P.O. or Watch	
		Read By	
From	To	Reported By	
		Passed By	
II. Continued.		Logged By	
		System	
		Date	
		Time	

"SPARROW HAWK", "ARDENT" lost and six others not yet accounted for. No British Battleships or light Cruisers sunk. Enemy's losses serious. At least one Battle Cruiser destroyed, one severely damaged. One Battleship reported sunk by destroyers during night attack. Two light Cruisers disabled probably sunk. Exact number enemy destroyers disposed of during action cannot be ascertained with certainty, but must have been large.
Latest Campaign Intelligence Western Front British Official. Yesterday our aeroplanes on reconnaissance had long running fight with three hostile machines, one enemy machine driven down, one our machines missing. During night hostile aircraft dropped eight bombs on POPERINGHE doing no damage.

M. 1704/1900. Sta. 6/14.

Wireless Telegraphy relays text of Admiralty's Communique on Jutland. (Commander A.G. Bagot)

---

don't think anybody minded as we were all rather pleased with ourselves. *The Daily Mail* says it is a drawn battle so I suppose its a pretty complete victory for us.'[32]

The British losses of three battle cruisers, three cruisers and eight destroyers compares unfavourably with the German loss of a pre dreadnought battleship, one battle cruiser, four light cruisers and five destroyers. The imbalance in the loss of personnel seems still worse, 6097 against 2545. In terms of materiél and technology, there was a need for action to be taken immediately on some lessons which could have been learned earlier and others which were from newly demonstrated experience. British shells were indifferent, too many failing to explode or exploding on impact without pierc-ing the German armour. A Naval Instructor diarist wrote that they did not explode because the fuses were defective. He reported that the Magazine *Bystander* had dubbed such shells 'Yankees' because they were 'too proud to fight.'[33]

The most disastrous defect was in the failure to prevent the flash of an explosion in a gun turret from travelling down the trunk of the ammunition hoist to the magazine. It was lamentable too that we had carried out no real exercises in training for night fighting. There were also secondary areas of inferiority to the Germans, for example, with regard to searchlights. Concerning the arrangements for interpretation and transmission of intelligence of German activities to the Commander in Chief, matters had gone woefully adrift. Matching this critical area of disappointment was British ships' signalling intercommunication during the battle, though in making so sweeping an indictment, balanced judgement would require an appreciation of the technical difficulties involved. As to the quality of high command leadership, this is something which is as arguable as is the broader side issue of the wisdom of the tactical caution exercised first by Jellicoe and then by Beatty himself when the mantle of Supreme Command fell upon him, the supreme advocate and proponent of vigorously harrying the enemy.[34] It should be stressed that the conditions of naval warfare had so changed since Trafalgar and, in terms of quality, since Tsushima too, that to look for Nelsonian or Tojo-like victory in the North Sea in 1916 requires a genie-like lamp. The real consequence of the German failure to crack the Royal Navy's supremacy on the sea effectively was their decision to search for victory under the sea. Though this would be fearfully damaging to Britain, unrestricted U-boat warfare was a weapon of suicidal potential politically. In short, the writer believes that logic is not being stretched in claiming the April 1917 American declaration of war quite considerably as a fruit of Jutland. All the more then is it clear that while there is agreement over the navy having been a fundamental factor in securing victory over Germany it should also be stressed that the victory was assured by Jutland.

AFTER JUTLAND

Only chance prevented an early repeat trial by battle for the opposing Commanders in Chief. On 19 August 1916, the High Seas Fleet was approaching Sunderland to bombard the town when Admiral Scheer redirected it to a wrongly identified weaker British force to the south. From being in a position to catch the raiders well in Home Waters, Admiral Jellicoe was once again to be in forlorn chase. At an early stage in the operation he lost the light cruiser *Nottingham* to U-boat torpedoes and, later, another light cruiser, *Falmouth*, foundered after two separate U-boat attacks.[35]

Falmouth was rejoining the fleet after an excursion to drive off a Zeppelin. The light cruiser's speed was about 26 knots when two torpedo tracks were observed. One torpedo was avoided but the other struck *Falmouth* in the ram. The Gunnery Lieutenant S.A. Pears was on the forecastle anticipating the explosion. 'I turned aft and gripped the foremost boiler casing. There was a great "WUMP" which shook the ship, and then a rather surprisingly quiet roar which lifted the whole forward part about four feet up and the ship hove herself up and down as if trying to shake something off. This was followed by great solid seas which swept all loose gear, including many men before it. I saw men being whirled past and some were hurled down into the waist, but none were killed. The sea struck me with great violence in the back, but I was able to hold on, and as soon as the great 300 foot column of water had descended I began blowing my waistcoat up which, by the way, I was wearing for the first time. I did not feel very excited or in any panic but I was just quietly afraid of what was coming.' A second torpedo struck, Pears went aft to see to the readiness for lowering the two big port boats. 'There was no panic. No one jumped overboard and no raft or boats were set adrift.' Pears did not like his next job – to go into the inky blackness below to attend to a water tight door not properly closed but 'one has to obey an order.' A trawler appeared next and it took off the wounded and 'our boys and our old reserve men.' Pears, hearing that he was to be sent with those men to be evacuated actually hid in order that someone else was sent in the consequent need to avoid delay. *Falmouth* had first been struck at 16.50 hours. At 18.30 hours, a further torpedo track was observed. It was watched with fixed fascination approaching the ship below the forebridge, but there was no explosion and the track continued on the far side of *Falmouth*. Pears's letter describes the watching of destroyer endeavour to sink the stalking U-boat and he claims it was successfully accomplished. Despite the fact that 'for the last 30 or 40 feet of the ship there was only the upper deck projecting out over the sea, carrying, like cur-

Now aboard the destroyer
Porpoise, officers of the
cruiser HMS *Falmouth*
watch their ship sinking.
(Dr H.V. Edwards)

HMS *Falmouth* torpedoed
and sinking. (Dr H.V.
Edwards)

tains, the frayed sides of the ship' and only the outer propellers remained, some progress was made at a knot and a half but the distortion of shattered plating tended to turn the ship constantly to starboard. A burial of two stokers was conducted. 'They were wrapped in white sheets and weighted with fire bars. When all was ready the Commander came and said "Off caps; God rest their souls: they died doing their duty" and over they went. The dusk, the white figures which shot so phosphorescent downwards, the men, dirty, queerly dressed, cap in hand but solemn and stern, and the Commander's quiet simple words, form a memory I shall not lose.' When the men were mustered later, the Commander's demeanour impressed Pears. There were no prayers for men to fidget through but simply: 'I am not a religious man from what I know of you neither are you; but Off caps! Thank God. On caps! And if you are always as lucky as you have been today you will do well.' For food, the breaking into and looting of the ship's canteen were sanctioned. The men even put on an impromptu concert during the night. *Falmouth* was not to survive; towing by a tug brought her near Flamborough Head at noon on 20 August, but in sight of the Yorkshire coast the light cruiser took two more torpedoes and that was that, though she floated till 20.00 hours. Touchingly, Pears writes of a ship which had been to him 'a symbol of my home, my work, my play, my life, my companion in danger.' *Falmouth*'s reluctance to die had moved him deeply and the whole experience was one he was never to forget.[36]

According to the recollections of *Falmouth*'s newly appointed clerk, G.H. Bickmore, one man whose imperturbability impressed him was the Captain's steward who, soon after the torpedo struck *Falmouth*, presented her captain with a whisky and soda on a silver salver and then not long afterwards informed each officer in turn that he had prepared a cold collation in the Captain's cabin.[37]

As a result of the loss of *Nottingham* and *Falmouth*, it was decided to reduce the operational zone of the Grand Fleet considerably. In consequence of this wise British caution, matching that of the Germans as far as their capital ships were concerned, the chance of another general fleet action was made markedly less likely. The North Sea and, of course, the Channel were still to hear the earsplitting crack of the guns of destroyers but the deeper thunder of big guns in action was now a much more remote possibility.

The official deliberations over every area of proven naval inadequacy led to wide ranging, swiftly instituted reform, the impact of which was felt in a diminishing ratio down to the lower deck; nevertheless, from the post Jutland records and recollections left by officers and ratings in the more cautiously deployed capital ships – in fact, spending extended periods at base – it seems that the individual sailor reacted to the diminution of the dangers of his service with a greater awareness of self than hitherto.

Anticipation of the British equivalent of 'Der Tag' seems not to overlay thoughts on service conditions, food, recreation and keeping boredom at bay while still being involved in the proper maintenance of a well-run ship. Such an alteration of outlook was by slow process. It is undeniable that morale within the Grand Fleet remained at a high level while that of the personnel of the High Seas Fleet was broken by the various factors associated with inaction but a change of outlook there was. Letters from Scapa Flow written in the period from Jutland to the end of the war tell a tale of a reduction of the tension of high expectation of action and its replacement by something quite different.

11

Life on the Mess-Deck and in the Gunroom

THE MESS DECK

From HMS *Iron Duke*, the flagship of the Grand Fleet, a senior rating, Harry Miller, wrote on 2 December 1916: 'We are always cheerful, the papers say so so it must be right.' Six months later: 'the regatta is coming along again in a couple of months so we are all mad on boat racing just now. There are crews away practising and racing all evening'. In July: 'We had some sports ashore. It was a great success too, everybody seemed to enjoy themselves, it was such a change – I wish we could have a day like it more often.' When the time for training for the 1918 regatta came round, Miller anticipated being away on a course and considered at first that there was no point in training 'but I suppose I had better make up my mind that I shall, and do my best for the old ship once more . . . There are not many of us left in the ship now who first commissioned her, the old faces keep going on, new ones coming gradually.'[1]

From the Commander in Chief's office down through individual ships, their distinctive Wardrooms, Gunrooms and Messes, war was waged against boredom in Scapa. It was waged with the weapons of training, ships exercising at sea, organised entertainment and competitive physical activities. There was sub-calibre firing practice in the Flow, full calibre in the Pentland Firth, cinema shows, whist drives and concert parties aboard ship and then in rotation the opportunity of attending the more professional entertainment provided from a stage erected within *Gourko*, a ship specially adapted for entertainment or in *Borodino*, primarily a canteen ship. In a programme for HMS *Valiant*, no

Sketch by Surgeon Probationer James Shaw. (Dr J. Shaw)

rank is given for any of the actors, entertainers, writers or producers but F. Pickles played the actress Flossie Fluff, J. Newton played the Labour Parliamentary candidate Joe Jenkins, A.W. Mallinder and E. Sidebotham the boy and girl lovers, all in a revue entitled *Who's your man?* The chorus was drawn from the 'Leading Opera Houses on Flotta'.[2]

Housey Housey legally, but Crown and Anchor illegally, provided gambling opportunities on the mess decks. As C.C. Twiss (*Victorious*) recalls, a scout had to be stationed in the latter case to give warning of the approach of the Master at Arms.[3] Boxing displays or competitions were a regular source of entertainment, frequently taking place in a ship secured alongside *Gourko* from which parties of men from a whole squadron might watch. A.W.

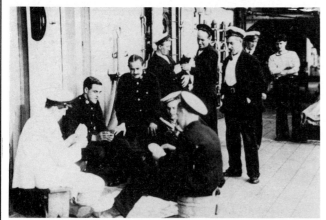

Top left
Gunlayers Trials, HMS *Malaya*. (Dr D. Lorimer)

Above
HMS *Valiant* uses the stage of Gourko to present a musical. (Dr A.B. Emden)

Above
When not at sea, an afternoon off could mean 'make and mend' for the repair of socks or other personal articles, but Marines and sailors are relaxing here over cards. (F.A. Foxon)

Battle Cruiser Squadron Boxing Competition on board HMS *Tiger* at Rosyth, with the Forth Bridge in background. (Commander P. Haig-Ferguson)

Royal Marine Band playing during Dog Watches (late afternoon and early
evening) aboard HMS *Colossus*. (F. Bowman)

Thomas had written in January 1917 that 'one week passes very much the same as another' but in May he was pleased to note: 'We have the piano on deck now after supper and a dancing class has been started so things are a little pleasanter now that the evenings are longer.' The tribute he was to pay to a newly appointed Commander in *Malaya* is eloquent testimony to the officer's successful leadership in maintaining a happy ship. In October 1917, Thomas wrote that two concerts were to be held every week, that toy making for children at Christmas had been started and a Squadron football league inaugurated. The cinema programmes had been improved and there were drum and fife band entertainments. 'The Commander is the prime mover in all the new ideas and he is a great sport and takes a great interest in the ship's company and seems to be doing all he can to make the ship comfortable and contented . . . he has stopped all overtime work and won't have it done.'[4] Perhaps innocent of the significance of his observations, Thomas was drawing attention to that most important welding factor in the securing of good morale, a concern by the officers for the welfare of the ratings. Just as in the army the 'separated closeness' of officers and men enabled so much that was grim to be endured, so too in the navy the uncongenial was made acceptable by the accompaniment in a ship's routine of much that was thoroughly good fun. Officers' gifts of cigarettes at Christmas were welcome and so was the officers' concert party staged for the men but in the long run they were perhaps of less influence than the officer who played regularly in a ship's football team.

FOOD, RUM AND PAY

Every man was entitled to a standard ration, part in kind and part in money value. Each mess detailed one or two hands as 'cooks of the mess'. The 'cooks' drew the rations for the men in bulk, spending the money element on what the men fancied from a narrow range of choice. They then made up the food into what had been chosen or, more usually, what the leading hand of the mess wanted and in the galley the qualified cooks saw to the final preparations of the meal.

Concerning the destroyer *Hind*, serving in the Adriatic in 1918, A.L. Jones wrote of the store run by the 'pusser' issuing 'meat, flour, tea, tinned milk, rabbit, salmon, potatoes, corned beef, jam etc., all paid for at the end of the month out of rating messing allowance.'[5] Other goods were obtained in a canteen run by civil contractors who were usually Maltese.

Mealtimes when at sea were never at precisely fixed times but a breakfast of tea, bread and butter would be at about 07.00, dinner, a cooked meal, at around noon, tea at 16.00 and the evening cooked meal, supper, at approximately 19.00. Meals, presided over by a leading hand, would be taken seated on stools at long tables for twelve or sixteen men. The mess was not only where the men ate but where they relaxed and slept too, their hammocks slung above the tables at night, lashed and stowed during the day with the sailor's ditty box and kit bag on racks in the bulkhead.

As an almost constantly available beverage, thick navy cocoa, 'kye', warmed everyone without the timed formality of the rum issue which was an important daily ritual. Not all ratings took up their allowance of rum and they could opt out receiving an allowance in lieu. The rum itself in its small cask was treacly and was watered to weaken it and diminish its keeping qualities so that it could not satisfactorily be 'bottled-off'. In smaller ships the rum issue was seen to by the Coxswain in the presence of the officer of the day. Highly polished copper jugs were used as measures, the mixing being done in a large wooden tub bound with copper bands. The measures were usually two of water to one of rum but Petty Officers enjoyed the privilege of having theirs undiluted – 'neaters'. When the time for the issue arrived, the Boatswain's Mate would be sent forward and would pipe 'Hand from a Mess for Rum'. One member from each mess would assemble on the Quarter Deck and receive the proper allowance from a dixie. The

The strict rules of membership in HMS *Bacchante*'s Dance Club. (S.J. Allen)

HMS *Inflexible*: dancing in dinner hour relaxation to the Royal Marine Band. (Commander C.F. Laborde)

Roller skating exercise aboard HMS *Queen Elizabeth* at Scapa: top left, Leading Seaman Fowler; centre left, Able Seaman Evans; bottom left, Petty Officer Treib and Armourer Crew Flemington. (Captain L.A.K. Boswell)

Signalmen and Telegraphists of HMS *Caroline*'s 'Racing Whaler', the Regatta winners in June 1917. (W.R. Crick)

4th LIGHT CRUISER SQUADRON PULLING REGATTA, 1917.

No. of Race.	Time.	Crew.	Boat.	Course (miles).	First.	Second.	Third.
	FORENOON.						
1	9.30 a.m.	Daymen and Excused Daymen	Whalers	1	Constance	Cambria	Caroline
2	9.50	Stokers	Cutters	2	Comus	Cambria	?
3	10.10	Marines	Whalers	1	Constance	Caroline	Comus disqualified
4	10.10	Seamen	Galleys	2	Comus	Calliope	? (Caroline will)
5	10.35	Signalmen and Telegraphists	Whalers	1	Caroline	—	Comus	?
6	10.50	Commissioned Officers	Galleys	1	Comus	Cambria	
7	11.20	Boys	Whalers	1	Comus	— Calliope	? (Caroline will)
8	11.20	Seamen	Cutters	2	Comus	Constance	? (" ")
		INTERVAL FOR DINNER.					
	AFTERNOON.						
9	1.30 p.m.	Stokers	Whalers	1	Comus	Comus	Caroline
10	1.45	Marines	Cutters	1	Comus	Caroline	×
11	2.10	Seamen R.N.V.R. & R.N.D. and [Ord. Smn. (H.O.)	Whalers	1	Comus	Constance	Caroline
12	2.10	Petty Officers (of all branches)	Galleys	2	Constance	Comus	Cambria
13	2.45	E.R.A.'s.	Whalers	1	Constance	Comus	Calliope
14	3.0	Racing	Skiffs	1	Constance	Comus	Caroline
15	3.20	C.P.O.'s. (other than E.R.A.'s.)	Whalers	1			
16	3.35	Ord. Smn. & Boys (act. service)	Cutters	1			
17	3.50	Warrant Officers	Skiffs	½			
18	4.45	All Comers	—	3			

Above
Relaxation of a sort! Note the victory of HMS *Caroline*'s Signalmen and Telegraphists, of whose crew William Crick was a member. (W.R. Crick)

Right
Wireless Telegraphy Staff HMS *Caroline* 1915–16: top row left to right, Lock, Lockyer, Crick, Owen; bottom row left to right, Moore, Poore, Saunders and A.N. Other. (W.R. Crick)

Master at Arms distributes mail on
HMS *Caroline*. (F.A. Foxon)

Right
Cooks of Messes lined up with mess tubs
containing vegetables supplied by well-wishers
ashore. The issue, Harry Freemans or Harry
Frees in naval parlance, is being supervised by an
Instructor Lieutenant (the 'Schoolie'). William
Crick is about to receive his allotment. (W.R.
Crick)

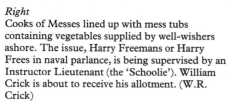

Seaman's mess at night. (F.W.H. Miller)

Slinging hammocks. (F.W.H. Miller)

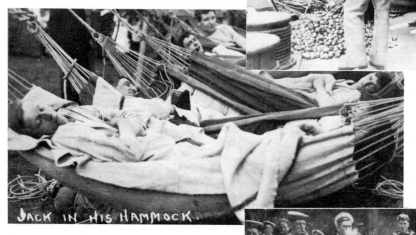

rum would be drunk from a crock basin, cups not being issued to lower deck ratings. To 'Splice the Main Brace' meant a double issue of rum on perhaps the King's birthday or some other special celebratory occasion.

In 1917, an ordinary seaman's rate of pay was 1/3d a day, that of an able seaman 1/8d and that of a Seaman Chief Petty Officer 4/-.[6] A boy 1st class got 7d, a boy 2nd class 6d. Some idea of the sailor's cost of living to set against his pay is given by the price of beer in the Rosyth Naval Canteen at 2d a pint and of ship's tobacco on board at 1/- a pound in weight. There were extra allowances for the years of service and for the holding of proficiency badges, a torpedo-man getting 3d extra a day but there were also pay stoppages for cutlery losses and breakages.

CRIME AND PUNISHMENT

Churchill's jibe of rum, sodomy and the lash being the components of naval tradition seems singularly inappropriate in any consideration of crime in the navy during the Great War. That there would be some drunkenness, the occasional fight going beyond an acceptable scrap in off duty hours, the discovered fiddle over rum, food or stores, the gambling school, the unfortunate man subject to bullying or the rare incident when a homosexual relationship was officially notified, is scarcely to be wondered at in a confined all male community. If service in the navy were to have reflected the poor elements of society at large as well as the better, that is surely to be expected but there was strong naval discipline to root out anything deemed disruptive of the well being of the crew and the smooth running of the ship.

For minor offences, boys might be awarded six or ten cuts with a cane administered by the Master at Arms, extra drill in the dog watches or have their leave stopped. The officer of the watch or day could deal with minor offences by boys and seamen, such offences merely requiring a reprimand or a couple of hours of extra duties. Anything requiring more severe treatment was passed on to the Commander or 1st

Lieutenant who usually held a 'defaulters' session every morning. For anything judged beyond the Commander's power, the Captain held a 'defaulters' session once or twice a week, a Post Captain having the power of sentence of

Men on 10A Punishment, holystoning decks, HMS *Colossus*. Note the smiles for the photographer. (F. Bowman)

confinement in cells on board his ship. The next step, when there was a question of detention ashore, required a warrant approved by a flag officer and then finally there was the rare, ponderous and lengthy matter of a Court Martial which required a court of some five captains.

Aboard ship, ratings were liable to 'No. 10 punishment' which involved extra work and intensive physical drill. Stoppage of leave was of course also available as a punishment. For the very serious crime the ultimate penalty was 'dismissal with disgrace' by Court Martial which meant being put ashore with no collar silk or lanyard and given a railway pass to one's home. With no civilian clothes held aboard, the sailor's incomplete service dress would denote clearly his ignominious discharge.[7]

Leave breaking by missing the 'liberty' or leave boat's return was perhaps the most usual crime as such. There is a philosophical note in the March 1917 diary of an officer whose boat, *P14*, was in the last day of her refit: 'Some of the liberty men returned but the majority had broken leave. Personally I can understand it as

HMS *Caroline*'s string band: rear left, W.R. Crick, centre rear, F.A. Foxon. (F.A. Foxon)

Burial at sea of HMS *Triumph*'s Chief Ship's Steward. *Triumph* was en route to the Dardanelles from China where, off Tsing Tao, she had been in successful co-operation with Japanese naval and army units against the German shore-based force. (P. May)

practically all the men are West Country and Irish.'[8] Leave breaking would mean at least the loss of a day's pay and probably some stoppage of leave. Longer periods of absence without leave could lead to the loss of a proficiency badge if one were held and a reduction in rating as well as in pay and leave.

It was good for no ship to have its detention cells or accommodation regularly occupied. Skulking to avoid duties, slowness to obey orders there will always have been and always will be. When it affected more than the occasional individual and so permeated the atmosphere in a whole ship, then in those infrequent cases there was something wrong with the senior end of a normally successful working relationship between officer and rating.

RELIGION

It would seem that, as with the soldier's spiritual identification with his regiment, so was the sailor's spirit more exercised by the personification of his ship rather than by religious inspiration. Sunday church parades were compulsory; they were a part of a ship's routine in an age which quite naturally saw the navy reflecting the formalised practices of society at large. There were variations from ship to ship and a pious officer would influence the way of worship under his command. Sailors sang their traditional hymns lustily whether or not they were accompanied instrumentally. The light cruiser *Caroline*'s Sunday services were led by an harmonium supported by signalman Crick's violin but, as this rating observed, 'religion was apparently accepted and rarely discussed. It was known that certain people held strong beliefs – one Petty Officer sometimes read scripture to anyone who cared to listen on the upper deck, this being by permission of the Commander.' Just as the dispenser of religious tracts would be known as a 'Holy Joe', it was likely that a man who so openly displayed his convictions as to read to others from the scriptures would be known as a 'God botherer', though Crick makes no reference to this in the case he described.[9]

Certainly, the presence of a good Naval Chaplain would have an impact on a ship's company. The Chaplain, though a commissioned officer, customarily wore civilian clerical dress as if to eschew rank and thus make himself more readily accessible to all. Pastoral guidance on worldly perhaps more than in spiritual matters was easier to seek from a figure whose apparel set him apart from those in everyday authority. The Chaplaincy was as effective as the man who administered its functions: accordingly, respect for the office and for religion itself was earned or diminished by individual chaplains appointed to particular ships. It is noteworthy that eight sea chaplains died in the battle of Jutland. A Catholic Chaplain of *Warspite*, A.C.H. Pollen bravely rescued two seamen from a cordite fire during that battleship's time of trial at Jutland and C.J.E. Peshall made repeated journeys on to the Zeebrugge Mole on 23 April 1918 to carry wounded men out of the field of fire to some shelter in *Vindictive*.[10]

LEAVE

To move from the question of religious observance to that of naval leave is not to move deliberately from matters of the spirit to those of the flesh but rather to move from one matter of mixed constraint and opportunity to another. The amount of leave it was possible to give was naturally dependent on the location of the ship. 'Short leave' implied being allowed ashore for the afternoon and evening and occasionally for the night. For those in capital ships at Scapa, Invergordon and Rosyth, 'long leave' was given when one's ship was refitting. With the ship's Company divided into parties of 'Port' and 'Starboard' watches, alternate watches would have from ten to fourteen days of 'long leave'.

Destroyer boiler-cleaning took such ships out of action for only three or four days and so only one watch would have an opportunity for leave. Such a short period would not be taken from Scapa because of the time used in the necessary travelling and the lack of worthwhile facilities for spending such leave in the Orkneys at Kirkwall or Stromness. There was at Longhope a YMCA hall and canteen but the only form of short leave at Scapa was more a recreational break in routine in that football parties would be landed and for the officers there was the newly constructed golf course for the 'Grand Fleet Golf Club'.[11] A canteen and a cinema and better football pitches at Invergordon began a southward trend in improving Scottish leave resources, completed further south still at Rosyth where the proximity of Edinburgh provided a full range of leave opportunities from the castle and concert hall to bawdy house and bar.

Each officer and man was entitled to a very small number, usually two, railway warrants a

Seamen of HMS *Swiftsure* falling in to go ashore in the 'Liberty Boat' for the first time since the ship was commissioned some eight months previously. This photograph was probably taken at Chatham in 1916. (F. Jaques)

The spick and span YMCA Canteen at Stornoway on the Isle of Lewis, awaiting its seafaring clientele. (Miss D.M. Abbott)

Seamen in the YMCA Canteen at Stornoway, Isle of Lewis. (Miss D.M. Abbott)

year for the nearest station to his home. This invited much abuse at the Railway Company's expense but there was heavy punishment for those caught in trafficking with the warrants.

London and the bright lights of other cities were magnets for many on long leave. The lines of a revue produced on board HMS *Monarch* expressed a general intent even without much lyrical flair:

> 'Goodbye I've got to go
> From dear old Scapa Flow
> I'm heading for Soho.'

Nothing less than a great deal of drinking and a compelling desire for female company could be expected after being cooped up in a totally male society for months on end, to say nothing of the stimulus of being free from naval discipline.

Welfare organisations, of which Miss Agnes Weston's Royal Sailors' Rests were the most well known, offered a very cheap bed and food but were strictly teetotal. In London, the Union Jack Club near Victoria Station was dominated by its soldier clients but was patronised by sailors too. For those with strong family ties there was no substitute for a truly home-orientated leave, the excitements and contentment of which were only likely to be matched by the heartache for all concerned as the remaining hours of the leave dwindled and departure time approached. The keenness of the senses in anticipating a family reunion after long months of separation is given evidence even sixty-nine years later as William Crick recalled the end of a train journey leaving him well short of his home

An Expeditionary Force leave boat departing from Boulogne, a reminder that no soldier arrived at or left the Western Front except by courtesy of the Royal Navy. (Lord Braybrooke)

in East Molesey. At that hour of the early morning there were no more trains. Even with the long trudge involved, 'I retain most vividly the recollection of the sweet smell of lime and chestnut trees and flowers in the gardens.'

Glasgow offered a warm welcome when the Molesey rating's ship, *Caroline* was in the Clyde. 'Dances, concerts, up to date films, very good food and accommodation in the YMCA, 6d for a bed, one shilling for ham and eggs and a pot of tea . . . We remembered the kindness and friendship of Glasgow.' A thoughtful action also remembered by William Crick was that of the YMCA in getting a photographer to call on his family and send to HMS *Caroline* the resultant print of: 'Father, mother, two sisters and the baby, the grey parrot and the cat.'[12] By such gestures, home must certainly have been brought closer when leave seemed far distant.

THE GUNROOM AND ITS MIDSHIPMEN, 1917–18

In a battleship's Gunroom, the junior officer's accommodation, there might be sixteen midshipmen, two sub-lieutenants and an assistant clerk or paymaster midshipman. The essential individuality of each Gunroom was a simple matter of fact though in few ships did this go to the extreme of the battleship *Ramillies* where the most senior sub-lieutenant, the 'President' of the Gunroom, decreed that 'olde worlde' charm was to be the character of their abode. Wooden beams were found to box in steel girders, an open fire was built in and material-covered cane chairs as 'arm chairs' set the scene. On 5/- a day, life in this realm could raise expenditure above income but there were other matters of practical concern too. At sea the 'chimney' had to be dismantled; the hole in the roof as a flue stopped up. When the guns fired all the cement around the fire cracked.

Resolution's Gunroom, lit by several scuttles[13] looking out to Port, had a sort of ante room at one end sacredly reserved for the more senior occupants. A long dining table lay fore and aft, an L-shaped settee offered seating or daytime sleeping space round portions of two sides of the room. Mess chairs on the other sides or at the table completed the furniture except for the arm chairs in the ante room. There was a coal stove at one end and a trap hatch down the inboard side of the room, from which food was brought to the table by the stewards. Guest nights were Thursdays when a midshipman from another ship or an officer from the Wardroom might be invited and the meal taken more formally.

The Gunroom bathroom was a fair sized white-tiled compartment holding a full-sized bath (sub-lieutenants only!) and several sparrow dishes 2 feet 6 inches in diameter and less than 6 inches in depth. The floor was usually awash despite the economy on the fresh water, all of which had to be distilled. A junior midshipman of *Ramillies*, H. Dalrymple Smith, has written that he and his fellows had to keep the Gunroom clean but there were stewards to set and serve meals and to wash up. In the main, meals were taken without undue formality because such formality would have been destroyed by the necessary comings and goings of officers on duty.[14]

The officers got the same rations as did the ratings. It was drawn in bulk by a Messman. In the case of *Ramillies*, the Messman served both the Gunroom and the Wardroom. He was allowed to charge the officers of the former 1/- a day and the latter 2/- a day to supplement the ration but items additional to this supplement, perhaps fruit or cake would be charged as 'extras' to the mess bill of the officers ordering them. Drinks, of course, were 'extras'. Midshipmen were allowed a 10/- a month wine bill (duty free!) but there were restrictions by age on the drinking of spirits. Each week, the Captain would inspect the wine books, stopping an officer's bill if he were to judge his consumption to be excessive.[15]

In the case of *Resolution*, Bandsmen servants slung the Gunroom officers' hammocks in a cabin flat two decks below the Quarter Deck. The servants lashed and stowed them in the morning. They also saw to the officers' washing

After end of HMS *Malaya*'s Gunroom, 1918. (Vice Admiral Sir Charles Norris)

HMS *Collingwood*'s Gunroom, 1917. (C. Foster Hall)

Below left
'The best, fastest, cleanest, most economical and generally the most select picket boat in H.M. Fleet. Also containing the best crew and only run by the very best Snottie.' The battleship *Valiant*'s second Picket Boat as described in his photograph album by the self-same Snottie. (Captain J. Crawford)

Below right
HMS *Indomitable*'s Gunroom: left to right, Troubridge (feet only), J.G. Sutton and J.C.Y. Loveband. (Air Marshal Sir Thomas Elmhirst)

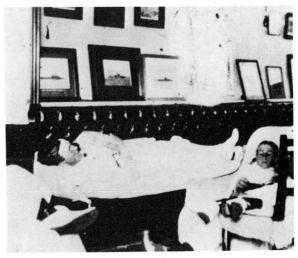

and a certain amount of mending. In the cabin flat was stowed the midshipman's sea chests holding their uniforms, equipment and personal treasures.

In harbour, there would be two or three midshipmen on watch from 06.00 till 22.00 hours except for offical instruction hours. At all functions and ship's evolutions, the Captain and the Commander had a midshipman in attendance (a 'doggie') and the Navigator had a midshipman at his beck and call too (a 'tanky').[16] Each midshipman had a station for evolutions, an action station and a defence station. Dalrymple Smith was given a succession of stations by his turret officer so that he had experience of the shell room, then the magazine, the handling room, the working space, the gun house and finally the local control position at the back of the gun house where the huge range finder was mounted. For these young men there was far too much to do and to learn without being bored by service in a Grand Fleet which did not seem likely to be in action against the High Seas Fleet.

Appointed to the battle cruiser *New Zealand*, C.A.G. Nichols was to learn that *New Zealand*, with its thirty-three huge boilers, used what seemed to him a phenomenal amount of coal. 'Something over 1,000 tons was an average intake. I always shovelled coal into 2 cwt. sacks at the bottom of one of the coal lighter's four holds – you had to keep your wits about you as the "hoist" of about a dozen sacks was no respecter of persons on its way up to the deck of *New Zealand* and the empty hook lowered for the next hoist could knock your brains in from above as you concentrated on the coal below you.'[17]

RECORD OF EFFICIENCY.

TORPEDO.

Ship	Period of Service in Ship	Number of days in the Department during the period	Marks	Signature of Lieutenant (T)	Captain's Initials
Temeraire	March 5th 1917 to June 30th	15	75	John Wilkins	JH
Temeraire	June 30th to Dec. 31st /17	21	75	S.G. Spickernell	JH
Temeraire	Dec. 31st to June 30th /18	40	80	S.G. Spickernell	JH
Temeraire	June 30th/18 to Aug 30th/18	Under 3 months		S.G. Spickernell	JH

Wartime does not interrupt the formal practical education of a midshipman at sea as this page from the Record of Special Entry Cadet Guy C. Harris illustrates. (Commander G.C. Harris)

Fishing on Kirbister, Orkneys: left to right, Royal Marine officer, Lt Reginald Portal, Lt Hill, a Rating and Commander Paine. (Admiral Sir Reginald Portal)

Right
Membership card of the Grand Fleet Golf Club. (Vice Admiral J.S.C. Salter)

Admiral Sir William Davis, a midshipman appointed to *Neptune* in September 1917, has written of a full daily routine of physical training on the quarter deck at 6 a.m. in a freezing Atlantic gale, Divisions, instruction in navigation, gunnery, torpedo and engineering and practical training in seamanship. There were sub-calibre firing practices in Scapa Flow and full calibre firing against practice targets in Pentland Firth. 'The firing of our 12″ guns, sometimes all together in broadsides made a tremendous and quite frightening noise. I thought the end of the world had come and from then onwards always wore ear drum protection with scrupulous care.' About every six weeks, full tactical exercises known as PZ exercises were undertaken at sea but now the Grand Fleet was not undertaking regular sweeping of the North Sea, as it had before Jutland, some variation in routine was provided when units were sent to cover Scandinavian Convoys after the *Mary Rose* and *Strongbow* convoy disaster. In a heavy sea, and battleships tend to go through seas rather than over them, a tremendous amount of water is shipped. 'Climbing up the struts of the foremast in such a sea was a rather hazardous job, for if one fell off or was blown off one would probably fall into the sea where the chances of

rescue were negligible.'[18] In such duties the Grand Fleet midshipman educated his way towards the Armistice and anticipated advancement in his chosen profession.

The need to expand the supply of junior officers to the navy had led in 1913 to a new category of special entry, direct from school after application, successful Admiralty interview, medical and entrance examination. The first cadets were appointed to the cruiser *High-*

GRAND FLEET GOLF CLUB.

Name .... Date 191

Marker's Signature ....
Before starting insert H'cp. (thus 1) in Bogey Col.

Length in yds.	No.	Bogey.	Strokes.	Won + Lost — Halv'd 0	Length in yds.	No.	Bogey.	Strokes.	Won + Lost — Halved 0
221	1	4			164	10	3		
400	2	5			260	11	4		
299	3	4			134	12	3		
433	4	5			164	13	4		
257	5	4			122	14	3		
245	6	4			240	15	4		
130	7	3			326	16	5		
252	8	4			277	17	4		
200	9	4			291	18	4		
							IN		

BOGEY RESULT.   OUT

Holes Up ....
or
Holes Down ....

TOTAL...........
H'CAP...........

....

Officers from battleship *Hercules* working on an allotment on the Island of Flotta, Scapa Flow. (F. Bowman)

Below
Officers of HMS *Tiger* picnic in the grounds of Dalmeny House: front, left to right, Gilmour, Ouvry, Campbell; back, left to right, Rawe, Sweetman, Moore, Mr Poore, and (seated) Mr Mackay. (Commander P. Haig-Ferguson)

Above
A full-sized cricket net used at sea aboard the battle cruiser *Indomitable*. (Air Marshal Sir Thomas Elmhirst)

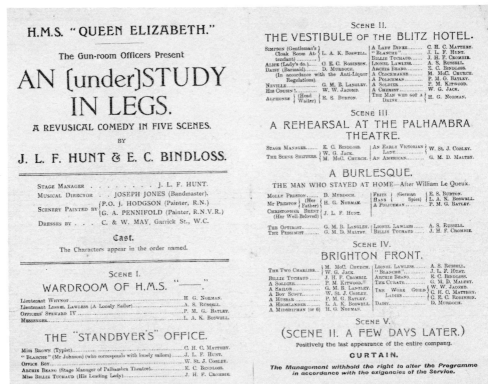

H.M.S. "QUEEN ELIZABETH."

The Gun-room Officers Present

AN [under]STUDY IN LEGS.

A REVUSICAL COMEDY IN FIVE SCENES.

BY

J. L. F. HUNT & E. C. BINDLOSS.

STAGE MANAGER . . . . J. L. F. HUNT.
MUSICAL DIRECTOR . . JOSEPH JONES (Bandmaster).
SCENERY PAINTED BY {P.O. J. HODGSON (Painter, R.N.) / G. A. PENNIFOLD (Painter, R.N.V.R.)
DRESSES BY . . . C. & W. MAY, Garrick St., W.C.

Cast.

The Characters appear in the order named.

SCENE I.
WARDROOM OF H.M.S. "——."

Lieutenant WHYNOT .... H. G. NORMAN.
Lieutenant LIONEL LAWLESS (A Lonely Sailor) .... A. S. RUSSELL.
OFFICERS' STEWARD IV .... P. M. G. BATLEY.
MESSENGER .... L. A. K. BOSWELL.

THE "STANDBYER'S" OFFICE.

MISS BROWN (Typist) .... C. H. C. MATTHEY.
"BLANCHE" (Mr Johnson) (who corresponds with lonely sailors) .... J. L. F. HUNT.
OFFICE BOY .... W. ST. J. CORLEY.
ARCHIE BRANO (Stage Manager of Palhambra Theatres) .... E. C. BINDLOSS.
MISS BILLIE TUCHAUD (His Leading Lady) .... J. H. F. CROMBIE.

SCENE II.
THE VESTIBULE OF THE BLITZ HOTEL.

SIMPSON (Gentleman's Cloak Room Attendant) .... L. A. K. BOSWELL.
ALICE (Lady's do.) .... O. E. C. ROBINSON.
DAISY (Barmaid) (In accordance with the Anti-Liquor Regulations) .... D. MURDOCH.
NEVILLE .... G. M. B. LANGLEY.
HIS COUSIN .... W. W. JACOMB.
ALFONSE (Head Waiter) .... E. S. BURTON.
A LADY DINER .... C. H. C. MATTHEY.
"BLANCHE" .... J. L. F. HUNT.
BILLIE TUCHAUD .... J. H. F. CROMBIE.
LIONEL LAWLESS .... A. S. RUSSELL.
ARCHIE BRANO .... E. C. BINDLOSS.
A CLOCKMAKER .... M. McC. CHURCH.
A POLICEMAN .... P. M. G. BATLEY.
A SOLDIER .... P. M. KITWOOD.
A CHEMIST .... W. G. JACK.
THE MAN WHO GOT A DRINK .... H. G. NORMAN.

SCENE III.
A REHEARSAL AT THE PALHAMBRA THEATRE.

STAGE MANAGER .... E. C. BINDLOSS.
THE SCENE SHIFTERS {W. G. JACK. / M. McC. CHURCH.
AN EARLY VICTORIAN LADY .... W. ST. J. CORLEY.
AN AMERICAN .... G. M. D. MALTBY.

A BURLESQUE.
THE MAN WHO STAYED AT HOME—After William Le Queux.

MOLLY PRESTON .... D. MURDOCH.
Mr PRESTON (Her Father) .... H. G. NORMAN.
CHRISTOPHER BRENT (Her Well-Beloved) .... J. L. F. HUNT.
FRITZ (German Spies) .... E. S. BURTON.
HASS .... L. A. K. BOSWELL.
A POLICEMAN .... P. M. G. BATLEY.

THE OPTIMIST .... G. M. B. LANGLEY.
THE PESSIMIST .... G. M. D. MALTBY.
LIONEL LAWLESS .... A. S. RUSSELL.
BILLIE TUCHAUD .... J. H. F. CROMBIE.

SCENE IV.
BRIGHTON FRONT.

THE TWO CHARLIES {M. McC. CHURCH. / W. G. JACK.
BILLIE TUCHAUD .... J. H. F. CROMBIE.
A SOLDIER .... P. M. KITWOOD.
A SAILOR .... W. ST. J. CORLEY.
A BOY SCOUT .... P. M. G. BATLEY.
A HUSSAR .... P. M. G. BATLEY.
A HIGHLANDER .... L. A. K. BOSWELL.
A MIDSHIPMAN (or 6) .... H. G. NORMAN.
LIONEL LAWLESS .... A. S. RUSSELL.
"BLANCHE" .... J. L. F. HUNT.
ARCHIE BRANO .... E. C. BINDLOSS.
THE CURATE .... G. M. D. MALTBY.
THE WORK GUILD LADIES {W. W. JACOMB. / C. E. C. MATTHEY. / C. E. C. ROBINSON.
DAISY .... D. MURDOCH.

SCENE V.
(SCENE II. A FEW DAYS LATER.)
Positively the last appearance of the entire company.

CURTAIN.

The Management withhold the right to alter the Programme in accordance with the exigencies of the Service.

A dramatic offering by *Queen Elizabeth*'s Junior Officers. (Group Captain T.G.G. Hutchinson)

---

flyer for eighteen months training in 1913. The outbreak of war interfered with these plans and for further Special Entry terms, the Royal Naval College at Keyham was to provide a much shorter period of training, at first for three months intensive training before service appointment. This system was maintained until the end of the war. The cadets were overwhelmingly but not invariably from Public Schools. Between 1913 and 1919, Bedford and Charterhouse sent twenty-two boys each, St Paul's twenty-three and Haileybury twenty-five but Bristol Grammar School sent two as did Ilkley and Watford Grammar Schools, with the number from Portsmouth Grammar School actually reaching five.

These cadets answered the need for an expanded navy and they were a distinctly new element in the Gunroom. At first, they were a source of considerable discord until service life blurred the contrasts of age and differing background for junior officers living and working closely together. The new entry men, some almost nineteen years of age, were much older than their counterparts in service seniority. They did not take kindly to the traditional treadmill towards seniority in the Gunroom. Initiation rites were less willingly accepted by or exerted upon young men who had long since passed through the miseries of fagging and prefect punishments at the public schools. The Dartmouth midshipmen saw their promotion prospects being 'unfairly' crowded by less well-trained 'New entries'. The 'New Entries' saw those already established in the Gunroom as mere boys. 'For them to order us about in the Gunroom was gall and wormwood. However, by the time we became Senior Midshipmen, we got on well together.'[19] Clearly the most awkward stage was that of sharing that lowest of landings on the stairway to promotion, the status of a 'snottie'.[20]

Above
Destroyers at sea. (Dr H.V. Edwards)

Above right
Improved 'Leader' class destroyer HMS *Parker*, looking aft. Torpedo tubes and searchlight platform are distinctively apparent. (Dr A.B. Emden)

Right
Ratings of HMS *Parker* embarking and assembling depth charges. Note the Range Clock to indicate to the next astern the range of the target being fired at. (Dr A.B. Emden)

Below
HMS *Parker* in the Medway, with the Duty Signal Rating on the signal platform Portside looking aft. (Dr A.B. Emden)

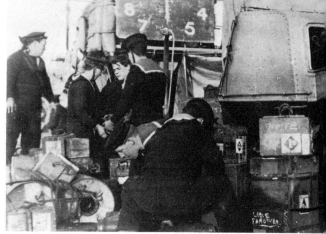

12

Destroyer Service and the Witness of Disaster

The cramped accommodation for men serving in destroyers might be expected necessarily to produce a special rapport if the ship were to be an efficient fighting unit. Destroyer service was certainly a special school of experience. At the end of October 1916, Cdr Goldsmith described a typical day of service from Harwich: 'I was on the bridge practically all the time from 2 a.m. till 10 p.m. being blown, rained and sprayed upon by one of those almost perpetual hurricanes, arrived in stiff and aching and utterly worn out.' He aired an opinion generally shared by men in his class of vessel when he wrote a year later: 'The destroyers still doing all the work of the navy as usual – you shore goers never realise the blessing of going to bed.'[1]

The miseries and the compensation of Scapa Flow based destroyer work are brought out well in the memoirs of Surgeon Probationer R.H.J.M. Corbet aboard HMS *Raider*. *Raider* was so crowded that he and another officer had no regular sleeping accommodation. Corbet's hammock was slung in the cabin flat and the steering engine was bolted on the other side of the bulkhead. The swing of the hammock was arrested at one side by a rack of rifles, at the other by the chimney of a stove, and underneath it was one of the main oil tanks, sounded at least once a watch. 'I used to think the Chief Stoker used to derive pleasure from pushing the end of the sounding rod into the middle of my back.' Corbet does not describe the sleeping area for the hundred ratings; it may have been more suitable but was probably as cramped as his.

Seasickness was this medical man's particular curse. It plunged him into the depths of personal misery. In his first trip he was washed against the lowest of the three strands of guard wires threaded through the stanchions. He clung on desperately. 'A violent roll to Starboard enabled me to pull myself back, push off the wire and slide back down the quarter deck until I found something to which I could cling. I scrambled to my feet, shot down below and was very sick. Next morning I got up, it was bright and clear but blowing very hard. I put my head up the companion way to see on our Port quarter an enormous wave over the top of which was the stern of a large oiler with her rudder and propellers in the air as she slid down the opposite side of the mountain of water. That was enough, I had a great wish to be home or elsewhere on dry land. I retreated to my hammock, remaining there, alternating between bouts of seasickness and coma until we returned to Scapa some four days later . . . That was the pattern of my life that winter.'

Though *Raider*'s flotilla base moved south to the Forth, memories of Scapa and, in particular, the dismally bleak outlook of Gutter Sound between Hoy and Flotta remained vivid to Corbet – the football fields laid out on Flotta, the heather, the stone walls, walking or climbing on the bigger island of Hoy – here there was the joy of reaching Risa Lodge, providing tea, boiled eggs and home baked bread after which by lantern light the satisfied adventurers went down to a small stone jetty to their boat. Small compensation it might seem for the purgatorial tribulations of mal de mer but significant for all that.

Corbet's memoir has amusing recall of the restricted area regulations which obtained for Inverness and the continuation of the much-

Officers relaxing: the destroyer HMS *Kempenfelt*. Note the gramophone and splinter protection mattress round the bridge. (Dr H.L.G. Foxell)

Above
Wardroom 'Picture Gallery', HMS *Kempenfelt*. (Dr H.L.G. Foxell)

Left
From one naval base to another: a ticket for the railway part of the journey from Scapa Flow to Immingham. (Commander T.G. Michelmore)

144

travelled sailor's 'Scapa Express' rail route to Thurso and its little port of Scrabster for the Orkneys. At Inverness, 'I had not got the proper stamps on my papers so would not be allowed off the station platforms. I could see the office where I could get my papers stamped but could not get to it. I wandered around the station wondering what to do when I saw a door labelled "Hotel". No one stopped my going through that so I went out of the front door of the hotel, got my papers stamped and all was well.'[2]

Whether implemented with such laughable looseness or with ruthless restriction, security regulations for base areas were designed to make espionage or sabotage impossible; they could not, however, prevent disaster striking from within the bowels of a ship. Three tragedies in separate locations exemplify the fact that it was not necessarily by enemy action alone that fearful calamity occurred.

HMS *Natal*, which was destroyed by internal explosion and fire in December 1915. (Commander G.C. Harris)

NATAL, VANGUARD AND *GLATTON*

On 31 December 1915 in Cromarty Firth, fire aboard the cruiser *Natal* led to her after-magazines exploding. A senior rating of *Natal*, Edward Meyers,[3] was at a mess table when the bows of the ship went down and he seemed to be in space. There was a terrific trembling. He went on deck and as he passed the hatch leading to the decks below, he saw the ladder had gone. Flames were roaring up the main mast. He helped up some who had succeeded in scrambling from below. They were dreadfully burned. Then there was a terrific explosion. The main mast toppled over and the ship turned over to Port enabling the rating standing on the Port side of a 9.2 inch turret simply to step into the water, using the foremast as a sort of lifebelt by pulling on trailing ropes and actually standing on the bridge as it went under. He remembered what seemed to be lots of footballs which were the heads of the men in the water suddenly disappearing and he presumed that they had

Wreckage from the *Vanguard* explosion which fell upon HMS *Neptune*. (F.W.H. Miller)

been sucked under as the funnels came level with the water and drew them in.

Severe as had been the loss of life from *Natal*, that of the dreadnought battleship *Vanguard*, blown up by internal explosion at Scapa on Monday, 9 July 1917, was much worse, though some by kinder fate escaped through being in attendance at a Concert Party. One of the fortunate midshipmen, R.F. Nichols, remembers that on the fateful morning the Captain had addressed the ship's company on the importance of proper procedure if disaster were to strike the ship. He judged that the ship might survive even three torpedoes but that every emergency must be prepared for and each man must know his 'abandon ship' stations. Accordingly, this exercise was thereupon practised.

Each evening of that week, the Concert Party

of the new battleship *Royal Oak* was to entertain the personnel of the fleet in the theatre ship *Gourko*, lying alongside *Royal Oak*. That Monday night was officers' night but as Nichols had the Tuesday morning watch, turning out at 05.45 hours, he chose at first not to go. Not long before the boat was to leave *Vanguard* for *Royal Oak*, a signal came for Nichols from a Dartmouth term mate aboard *Royal Oak*. The signal, personally inviting Nichols to the concert, led to a change of mind and, putting aside concern about the morning watch, Nichols left for the evening's entertainment.

Just as the 'Goodnight Song' was being sung 'we were heavily shaken by two terrific explosions at no great distance from us. All the same, the "Goodnight Song" was finished and the National Anthem sung, then we streamed on deck to find out what had happened. In spite of the darkness of the night, a heavy cloud of smoke could be seen against the starlit sky, and amidst the tense atmosphere that prevailed no one could say just where the explosion occurred. Fully an hour passed before the *Vanguard*'s officers were summoned to the Quarter Deck to be told the fate of our ship – that she had blown up and sunk in a matter of seconds. We were shocked, sickened and horrified . . . Everyone spoke in hushed tones and treated us (miraculously spared from death) almost with reverence.'[4] Nichols observed that a cruel fate waited upon even some men from *Vanguard*'s advance party on leave at the time. This party was to man *Vanguard* during its refit but with no ship to which to return they were ordered to Chatham Barracks at the end of their leave. They were at Chatham on the night of 3 September 1917 when two bombs dropped in a Gotha bombing raid wrought the worst single raid casualties of the war and there were *Vanguard* men among the 130 killed in the naval barracks drill hall.

While dealing with some of the worst tragedies outside of battle action, mention must be made of one grim event, the sombre colours of which are given some relief by the shining courage of men who chose to ignore the imminence of a colossal explosion and embark

HMS *Glatton* burning in Dover Harbour in September 1918. (C. Foster Hall)

upon a ship in Dover harbour, the monitor HMS *Glatton*, where explosion and fire had already produced appalling scenes vividly described in the diary of a principal in the rescue attempts, Sub-Lieutenant D.H. Evans RNVR.

On 16 September 1918, in the early evening a mighty explosion in *Glatton* led to a furious blaze amidships. From the destroyer *Trident*, half a mile away, a motorboat and a whaler were swiftly manned and despatched to the stricken monitor, soon to be surrounded by small boats 'anxious to help but doing nothing'. A few men were lowering themselves into these boats but there was obviously no organised evacuation. 'We managed to push ourselves under the ship's bows, Belben, our 1st Lieutenant scrambled up the cable and lowered two desperate cases into the boat. The doctor dosed these with morphia and "behaved splendidly throughout".... The motorboat went off with the wounded while I and A.B. Clark scrambled up the anchor cable on deck.' Evans was astonished to see that only four rescuers were aboard. 'I found a door behind the foremost turret through which smoke was pouring out in great clouds, I stepped inside and groped along a passage and soon heard groans ahead of me. I piloted myself along the passage by the sound till I came to a spot where, by the light of the flames, I found three ghastly huddled forms in a heap, the clothing of one being still on fire. I smothered the flames and lifted the man up while his burnt flesh came off in flakes in my hands. He drew his ghastly arms across my face as I staggered, choking back along the passage while I prayed aloud that the shell rooms would not send us all to eternity before I could get my burden away.' Evans got lost but he found his way to the deck where he left the man he had been carrying, made his way back for the second who was unconscious, apparently blinded by the fire and burned naked. This man Evans carried out but had not the strength to complete his rescue of the third, finding a member of *Glatton*'s crew to help.

Belben was now below, attaching a bowline to a wounded man and Evans attempted to haul him up through a hatch but had insufficient strength. It was not easy to get volunteers to come aboard from the small craft standing off *Glatton*. Evans secured some help from a man already aboard, perhaps a crew member, and two men were hauled up through the hatch. Belben then came up in a condition of collapse from the heat and flames. Evans went below and spotted a man lying in a deep grating. 'I clambered over the rail and got down to him. A brand fell on my head setting my hair alight, while another bit of wood fell on his lips. This I removed while I smothered my hair with my other hand.' Somehow he hauled the injured man over the rail and prepared a bowline around him so that when help arrived above, he could be hauled up. Another victim was singing tunelessly – Oh don't let me die – me die – me die. Yet another was groaning. Help arrived in time for them to be rescued and Evans assisted in hauling aboard a fire hose from one of two fire tenders now alongside. He and a rating used the hose to put out the fire on the upper deck but it was quite useless to think of tackling the fire below.

By this time, the abandonment of *Glatton* had been ordered. A last look below satisfied Evans that no one still alive had been left and the small party of rescuers was itself evacuated safely.[5]

The bravery of those who came to aid the victims aboard *Glatton* was, of course, outside conditions of enemy action and, with the exception of the celebrated Zeebrugge raid and Ostend operations, which will be dealt with separately, it is to the war's remaining naval engagements in waters close to Britain that attention will now selectively be drawn. In the main they involved units of the Dover Patrol and the Harwich Force.

13

The Dover Patrol
and the Harwich Force

Certainly, the British public, as reflected in as well as informed by the national newspapers, was seriously shocked to learn in October 1916 that German destroyers had crossed the Dover Barrage. The enemy force had penetrated the eastern end of the English Channel and had then sunk several hired drifters and a destroyer and so severely damaged two destroyers, *Zulu* and *Nubian*, that their total loss was only avoided by their less damaged halves being quite remarkably joined so that a new vessel was created from them appropriately named *Zubian*. It was not to be readily acceptable in the eyes of the general public that modern destroyers at speeds in excess of 30 knots could carry out such a raid with a fair chance of evading strong opposition.

This book is not the place to examine the large question of the effectiveness of the Dover Patrol in controlling submarine and surface entry into Channel waters, but it must be summarised. For nearly three years, command of the Patrol was held by Sir Reginald Bacon stationed ashore at Dover. In deep resentment at both neglect of the achievements of his force and at criticism of his method of operation, he listed in his memoirs the operations successfully carried out; conducting the safe passage through the straits of 120,000 merchant vessels, ensuring the security of five and a half million troops in cross-Channel traffic, bombarding the enemy's coastal positions and the laying of mines and net barrages. He had suffered from the overall shortage of destroyers and he had failed to prevent damaging German destroyer raids into the Channel and to have any marked impact on U-boat penetration of the Channel in 1917. It has to be acknowledged that in these

respects his record, even allowing for the demanding circumstances, is not outstanding.

In early 1917, a small action, but one of high drama, did a great deal to restore faith in the Dover Patrol's capacity to punish enemy surface raiders. A German raid took place during the night of 20/21 April 1917. First Calais then Dover was shelled. In the darkness, two patrolling destroyers, *Swift* and *Broke*, came upon a German destroyer force and attempts were made to ram their nearest opponents. Commander E.R.G.R. Evans (*Broke*) was successful in this though his ship came under heavy fire. *Broke* had got her bow in so far that she had actually to repel boarders before she drew clear again. Commander A.M. Peck (*Swift*) missed his intended victim but his ship passed through the German line and rapid shell fire was exchanged. Torpedoes were fired from both British vessels. Damage to *Broke* was so severe that she could not follow *Swift* in pursuit of the German destroyers escaping from the action and instead she made for the two remaining German ships, one sinking, the other disabled and on fire. *Broke*'s shell-fire silenced the guns of her opponents, both of which were attempting to defend themselves despite their desperate condition. Calamity now struck *Broke* as her engines stopped and she drifted right up to her burning quarry, thus risking her own destruction in the pressing likelihood of a magazine explosion. In the event, *Broke* was towed out of danger, first by a destroyer and then by tugs, back to Dover while her enemies were sunk and survivors from their complement rescued. Commander and ship had well earned a linked immortality as 'Evans of the *Broke*'.

The destroyer *Lydiard* took part in the last

Top
HMS *Lydiard* picks up Germans from the *Swift/Broke*
action, depicted in a contemporary painting by a Surgeon
Lieutenant James Shaw, HMS *Lydiard*. (Dr J. Shaw)

Bottom
Destroyer action in the Channel: the *Swift/Broke*
engagement depicted in a contemporary painting by
Surgeon Lieutenant James Shaw, HMS *Lydiard*.
(Dr J. Shaw)

stages of the engagement and in the rescue
work. James Shaw, *Lydiard*'s surgeon, wrote
home on 24 April: 'The night all round us was
rent with the cries of drowning men. The
shrieks of men struggling in the water. It was
agony to hear. We went sailing through them in
pursuit of the enemy. We were somewhat
relieved when we realised they were shouting in
German "Kamerad" and other gutteral sounds.
Still it is awful to see men drowning and you do

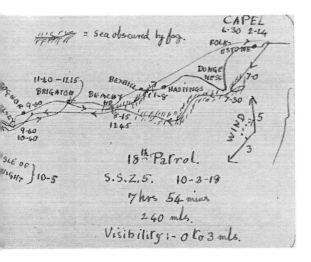

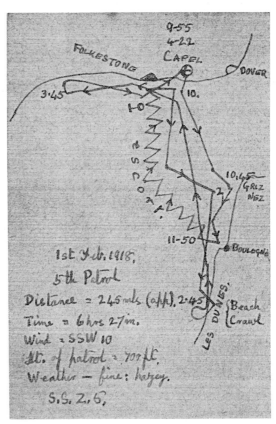

Dover Patrol airship work in 1918. The personal track chart of *SSZ 5*'s commanding officer on cross-Channel escort work on 1 February 1915. He has faithfully reproduced the convoy's track. (H.R.H. Ward)

Above left
A Dover Patrol airship's track chart of 10 March 1918. (H.R.H. Ward)

Left
Uncle Billy and Auntie Bertha sighted from an airship. Note written on the reverse of the track chart of 10 March 1918, on a coastal patrol of seven hours 54 minutes during which the sea from Folkestone to Beachy Head was obscured by fog. (H.R.H. Ward)

nothing for them. We had just got a line round one of them to haul him on board when we had to leave him to go ahead.' Coming upon the two German hulks, *Lydiard* was not to fire a shot and they were destroyed by torpedoes from other British vessels. After this, rescue work was undertaken, Shaw dressing the lacerations of four German sailors.[1]

An indication of German daring in the Channel was demonstrated when their destroyers brought an end to the cross-Channel steamer service of *The Queen*. By day *The Queen* ferried troops to Boulogne and she usually returned empty to Folkestone at night. On the night of the 26 October 1916, she was intercepted by the raiding destroyers, boarded, her evacuation ordered and explosive charges set to destroy her. In fact *The Queen* had a single passenger, a not undistinguished one, G.R. Roupell, a Staff Officer and Victoria Cross holder who had special permission to cross that night to attend his father's funeral. Hearing the shot across the bows, he had made his sleepy way on deck. Here, the Master agitatedly explained that carrying a combatant rendered all the crew more likely to be taken captive. Almost before he had given thought to the personal implications of his disguise proving ineffective, the Staff Officer had obediently jettisoned overboard his cap, Sam Browne and service jacket and had donned over his riding breeches puttees and army boots, a khaki shirt, a blue mackintosh and a sailor's cap. With the crew lined up for German inspection, Roupell's place, taken in the back row, shielded him somewhat from the searching light of a torch; he then had to busy himself appearing to aid the lowering of a life-boat and inexpertly assist in the rowing of a boat whose damaged rudder led to the making of an erratic course away from the steamer. Even with the ultimate rescue of the crew and the passenger, the loss of The Queen in these narrow, heavily used waters further tarnished the record of the gate keepers of the Channel, the Dover Patrol.[2]

That the work from Sheerness of the small P boats with their complement of about sixty brought almost daily adventure to say the least, is demonstrated by Sub-Lieutenant A.W. Clarke's diary for March 1917. On 18 March: 'Soon after midnight the alarm was sounded and we all prepared to leave harbour. The Aircraft signal was made and P.22 reported from her position on patrol that she had seen illuminated shell fired'. P.14 was not ordered out but in the morning Clarke learned that Zeppelins had been dropping bombs on the shipping in Black Deep, that submarines had torpedoed two British patrolling L boats and that the enemy destroyers had been bombarding Margate. Three days later: 'Having arrived alongside Port Victoria [Sheerness] we accidentally dropped one of our depth charges which, had it gone off, would have smashed the Lightfoot alongside us and ourselves to smithereens.' On 24 March, there is an entry which could not indicate more clearly the concern felt

as the P boats faced an anticipated raid by the new, exceptionally fast and well armed German destroyers. 'We got all our arms up on deck and served them out. There is only one thing to do if we are attacked by the latest Hun destroyers. That is to ram and keep off boarding parties. There is no hope for us with one gun against modern destroyers with three.'

Just a month after P14 had narrowly avoided a collision with P13 which had stopped without warning, a collision occurred which, Clarke wrote, could have destroyed both patrol boats in the resulting explosion of depth charges: 'the awful thing has happened. I have been in collison. Thank heaven I am in the right. But even so it is a rotten thing to happen.' Fortunately, no calamitous explosion occurred but an unusual experience was still awaiting officers and ratings of P14. On June 8: 'Proceeded to meet convoy coming from America but no luck, we missed it owing to lack of information. At 4 a.m. this morning were thoroughly shelled by a U.S. destroyer at a hopeless range of about 12,000 yards. None hit us and we closed and explained we weren't a submarine.'[3]

From Harwich, Commodore Tyrwhitt's force of light cruisers, destroyers and submarines established a deserved reputation for dash and esprit well before Jutland when they were so frustratingly held back from active participation. This reputation had been earned not by striking successes but by a policy of constant offence against the enemy. This was maintained despite the obvious difficulty of effective cooperation with the Grand Fleet and the need to support the over-extended resources of the Dover Patrol.

A member of Commodore Tyrwhitt's staff, H.G. Pertwee, recalled occasions which help to explain why: 'Everyone in the force would have done anything for him. He wasn't a very clever man but he would go hell for leather after the Germans.' In February 1916, Tyrwhitt's flagship, Arethusa, struck a mine and actually broke in two. When an accompanying destroyer came close alongside to render aid, Tyrwhitt shouted

from the bridge 'Go away I'm not sinking'. He wanted and achieved, remembered Pertwee, an orderly, calm, abandoning of the ship. A month later with his Commodore's pennant transferred to *Cleopatra*, this light cruiser deliberately rammed and cut in two a German destroyer encountered with her sister ships at night. Damage to *Cleopatra*'s stern from an accidental collision with a British ship in this incident necessitated a further transfer of the pennant to *Conquest* and again a month later the force

Top
Gun Drill under the watchful eye of the officer, Haig-Ferguson, aboard HMS *Lurcher* of the Harwich Force. (Commander P. Haig-Ferguson)

Above left
Ship's dog and two hands, HMS *Teazer*, Harwich Force. (Commander P. Haig-Ferguson)

Above
Proof that even a 'Gunner T' (Mr Worsh of the destroyer *Swallow*, Harwich Force) could have a sense of humour. Is he displaying knitted 'comforts for the troops'? (Commander P. Haig-Ferguson)

Left
Men from HMS *Lurcher* in a Carley Float Race during the Harwich Force Regatta. (Commander P. Haig-Ferguson)

Below
Motor lighter of 1st Portsmouth Hydrophone Flotilla which was severely damaged in collision with a French destroyer during bombardment of the German occupied coast of Belgium. The lighter caught fire, having been towed to Dunkirk. (G.A. Mooring-Aldridge)

Bottom
Monitor bombardment of Zeebrugge. A contemporary painting by a Surgeon Lieutenant James Shaw, HMS *Lydiard*. (Dr J. Shaw)

Monitors approaching Belgian Coast (Zeebrugge) at Dawn to Bombard Zeebrugge etc. accompanied by Motor Launches and Destroyers.

attempted to interfere with a German battle cruiser raid on Lowestoft. 'We went straight for them and started pooping off at them with our forward 6 inch guns at maximum elevation.'[4] Return shelling from the battle cruisers' far heavier calibre guns caused damage and considerable casualties to *Conquest* and the pennant was thereafter to flutter defiantly from *Carysfort* until a more suitable replacement ship for *Arethusa* was ready.

A major responsibility involving units from Harwich was to watch over commercial traffic with Holland. Such traffic was at risk from German destroyers based at Zeebrugge. The unfortunate Captain Fryatt, in command of the packet *Brussels*, lost his ship and ultimately his life from this threat.

The Government had negotiated with Holland to ensure that food which, under the pre-war conditions, had been sold to Germany was now being allocated to Britain. Protection patrolling of the route of these ships and later convoying of the merchant ships concerned, was known as the 'Beef Trip' and it was undertaken by Harwich destroyers. From Harwich too, help was given to cover the Dover Patrol's bombardment of Zeebrugge and Ostend in May 1917, a bombardment designed to destroy the lock gates at the entrance of the harbour basin. Destruction of these gates would make the artificial canal and harbour for Bruges behind the gates, tidal and hence dramatically lessened in utility if not blocked altogether. In the event, an hour's shelling by monitors was narrowly to fail in its purpose. Two months later, Harwich light cruisers and destroyers stifled a German attempt to resurrect their own traffic between Rotterdam and the Heligoland Bight and Tyrwhitt's Force had, of course, played no negligible part in combatting the U-boat menace.

HELIGOLAND BIGHT: NOVEMBER 1917

As far as action for the Grand Fleet was concerned, there was a real possibility in November 1917 that a major confrontation might develop from British operations designed decisively to frustrate German protection of her mine-sweeping operations in the extensively mined waters of Heligoland Bight. A German force was caught at this work and in its retirement laid effective smoke screens, making British pursuit less swift and sure than was necessary for success. Shelling causing damage to both sides was exchanged and in this inconclusive fashion the last sparring of the opposing battle squadrons and their support ships took place. It was not the last sortie of the war for the High Seas Fleet but it was the last time that any action was joined. On one final occasion, in April 1918, the High Seas Fleet did seek advantage from carefully concealed plans to trap both a convoy off the Norwegian coast and deal with a detached British battle squadron and light cruisers. The presence of fog and lack of precise knowledge of convoy departure dates rendered the operation fruitless but, by ironic coincidence, its timing was also that of the dramatic endeavour planned by the Dover Patrol to block exits at Zeebrugge and Ostend of U-boat bases.

Far From Home Waters

ADRIATIC AND AEGEAN

It must not be forgotten that the Adriatic and the Aegean both provided the navy with surface action. Playing a creditable part in the supplying and then the evacuation of the Serbian Army in its courageously endured retreat before the Austrians in December 1915, British cruisers cooperated with Italian and French ships against an Austrian force but failed to do more than inflict damage on the principal Austrian ship which made good its escape. In May 1917, the drifters of the Otranto Barrage bravely but ineffectually attempting to seal off enemy U-boats based at Cattaro, were them-selves completely outmatched by three Austrian cruisers. Some of the drifters sur-rendered rather than engage in so unequal a battle, but others, *Gowan Lea* and *Floandi* outstandingly, conducted heroic defence. Of forty-seven drifters, fourteen were sunk and three others seriously damaged.[1]

Reference has already been made to the lack of success in allied cooperation in the Mediter-ranean and Adriatic but shelling from British monitors, seaplane carrier support and feint landing operations did assist General Allenby

British drifters assembled for the Otranto Barrage. (Vice Admiral E. Longley-Cook)

in his attack on Beersheba and Gaza at the end of October 1917. French vessels assisted in this naval work but success was at the price of U-boat sinking of several ships which were insufficiently protected in their anchorage off shore.

THE *GOEBEN/BRESLAU* SORTIE: JANUARY 1918

The long awaited Aegean sortie of *Goeben* and *Breslau*, challenging the mine fields and allied naval and air capacity to hold them penned within Turkish controlled waters, took place in January 1918. It was wrongly assumed that the intent behind such a sortie would be to join with Austrian naval forces in the Adriatic; in fact, the British naval bases on the island of Imbros and Lemnos were the intended focus of German aggression. Though *Goeben* was damaged by striking a mine, the two German ships shelled shore installations on Imbros and sank two monitors, *Raglan* and *M28*.

Captain P.W. Dumas was the British Senior Naval Officer at Mudros on the island of Lemnos. His diary records for 19 January that, at a staff conference, consideration of reports of aerial reconnaissance concluded that 'at any rate the *Goeben* wouldn't come out'. The diary indicates in every sense a rude awakening on 20 January: 'Had my tea as usual at 7.15 after which fell asleep again and was called at 7.55 to hear that GB [code abbreviation for *Goeben* and *Breslau* "out" alarm signal] was made from Tenedos and *Goeben* and *Breslau* out and attacking *Raglan* and *M 28* in Kusu Bay.'

The prospect of a major engagement in the Eastern Mediterranean was removed as the German ships, intent now on shelling the naval base at Mudros, instead struck mines. *Breslau* sank but *Goeben*, badly damaged by mines and under bombing attack by RNAS aircraft (even if the missiles as Dumas wrote were 'wretched little bombs . . . nearly worthless'), worthily reached the security of the Dardanelles, there running aground. The force despatched by Captain Dumas was too late to intercept her, bombing was ineffectual though consistently essayed and no submarine was operationally available to attempt the destruction of the German battle cruiser before she had been refloated and towed to safety. A British submarine was destroyed in a tragic attempt to sink a ship no longer in the exposed position in which *Goeben* had lain for a full five days. Honour and blame had been perhaps equally shared; *Goeben*, in fact, was not risked again, quite apart from the serious nature of her damage, but Dumas's concluding point in the report he made to the Rear Admiral Commanding the British Aegean Squadron indicated the insecurity felt by the navy even in the last year of the war: 'I would venture to call to your notice the fact that when I left Mudros yesterday morning the sole remaining defences of this important centre of information and stores was a broken down submarine, the *Heliotrope* [a sloop] and a few sailors and marines. I submit that this is not satisfactory.'[2]

A British officer demonstrates readiness to co-operate with the Italians: Taranto, August 1915. (Vice Admiral E. Longley-Cook)

157

LAKE TANGANYIKA AND THE EAST AFRICAN COAST

Certainly one of the most extraordinary naval operations of the Great War, and a successful one too, was that of Lieutenant Commander G.B. Spicer Simson in transporting two 40-foot long motor boats through hundreds of miles of bush and across mountains in East Africa to reach Lake Tanganyika. In destroying the German armed boats which had hitherto dominated the region, he and his men had made a notable contribution to the difficult work of securing overall control of German East Africa.

In the first week of the war, a tiny British armed steamer had destroyed her sole rival in Lake Nyasa, finding her conveniently on a harbour slipway. In March 1915, British armed steamers secured control of Lake Victoria, trapping a German armed tug which had been a considerable nuisance. Lake Tanganyika, however, lying between Nyasa and Victoria, remained open for undisturbed transport of German troops and thus British east/west and north/south communications were blocked or threatened.

Spicer Simson's force was assembled in Britain and carried by Union Castle liner to Capetown and then by rail reached Elisabethville, the capital of the Belgian Congo's Katanga Province. The railway line ended 140 miles north-west of Elisabethville and from here the motor boats and stores were conveyed by teams of oxen, lorry and traction engines on a path through the bush hacked out by 400 African labourers. There were bridges to construct and then perilously to cross as August and September were spent in slow progress eastwards towards the lake. A 6000-foot mountain range had to be crossed and then a narrow gauge railway assisted the expedition to reach a river made navigable in its shallowness by raising the two motorboats on empty petrol drums and

Sorting the mail on the Quarter Deck of HMS *Talbot*, East Africa, 3 April 1917. (J. Falconer)

HMS *Talbot*'s Concert Party, off East Africa 1917. The King, crowned and standing, is Petty Officer Fear, his daughter, seated centre, Sick Berth Attendant Wilshaw. (J. Falconer)

poling them downstream to deeper water where the drums could be dispensed with. A stern-wheel steamer carried the force to another small gauge railway and at last, in the final week of October, Lake Tanganyika was reached.

A small camouflaged naval base was constructed and the two motor boats, *Mimi* and *Toutou*, were launched in December. Almost immediately, opportunity arose for them to use their forward mounted three-pounder guns against a German tug's six-pounder. The German tug was shelled into surrender but *Mimi* damaged herself in collision coming alongside to board the German vessel. The small victory had the considerable bonus of adding a new ship to the British strength, renamed *Fifi*, upon which a new twelve-pounder was mounted.

On 9 February, a small, armed German steamer, *Hedwig von Wissmann*, was fought and sunk by her one time sister ship *Fifi* supported by *Mimi*. The remaining German armed vessel on the lake, the new steamer *Götzen*, for some time armed with one of the guns from *Königsberg*, was not to fall to Spicer Simson. Before Belgian forces entered Kigoma in July 1916, she had been scuttled in the harbour.

East Africa was not without further varied naval operations because whalers and cutters manned by officers and ratings from cruisers were involved in the capture of coastal and river forts in 1916. Sometimes a river bar had to be crossed by a steam cutter: 'The method was to steam up with all the ship's company forward, then on the bugle sounding, run aft and jump. I forget how many times we had to do this but eventually we got through. The Germans had one or two guns up on top of a cliff well hidden with foliage. So as to get at the guns we had to list the ship and this was done by moving the coal and other things to one side so that the ship

159

was canted with a good list. It worked [and later, on the coast when] Dar es Salaam surrendered in September 1916, I was in the first boat to go in. First we cut the wires of a Merchant Ship that was across the entrance to block the Channel. There was rather heavy rifle and machine gun fire whilst we were doing that and also clearing wire strung across a floating dock but we got through without any casualties . . . We then went on down the coast to another lovely bay, a jetty was built as a depot, troops landed, the jungle cleared and a very good road built.'[3]

By no means was naval work in East Africa limited to the shore, river and lakes, as the diary of a rating from HMS *Talbot* indicates. He was involved in entirely land-based operations. '23.11.16 At Kilwa-Kissiwani. I was told off for field gun's crew. 24.11.16 I landed to join up with Naval 12 pdr. Field Gun Detachment at 10 a.m. with motor convoy to Kilwa Kivenche. Arrived there about 1 p.m. All the gun's crew are complaining of malarial fever. 25.11.16 Proceeded a few miles up country with field gun. Took up a gun position and opened fire about 6 a.m. . . . Trying to get lyddite shell to explode in the air like shrapnel but they failed to explode. Returned to camp and piped down for remainder of the day.' These action exercises continued despite being flooded out of their beds, their huts collapsing in a tropical storm and having to be rebuilt. On 12 December, with porters, army signallers and the necessary mules, the naval detachment moved more deeply inland. The rain was torrential and made progress difficult as well as ruining the supply of food. Pioneers assisted with the hacking out of a road for the gun but Able Seaman Falconer, the diarist, clearly did not enjoy 'crossing very shaky bamboo bridges.' The gun and its toiling mules regularly slid off the road. Sharp bends in the track forced the men into manhandling the gun. '19.12.16 I feel very bad with dysentery. C.O. returned from Kibata and told us we could not hold a position with our gun, as the Germans had got all the most favourable observation posts and their firing is very accurate.

20.12.16 We are still on short rations. Two biscuits a day. British askaris reported 4 white and 20 German askaris making towards this camp. King's African Rifles went out to look for them and we had to take the gun to a position where it could command all the hills around. Had to do sentry duty all night.'

With Indian troops, the detachment made its way to Kibata. Here they were shelled and so built a protective dugout. On Christmas Day 1916: 'The aeroplane flew over Kibata and dropped a note and a box of fags with compliments of the *Daily Sketch* to the troops at Kibata.' By the 28th the gun had been moved into a firing position. 'Fired 14 rounds and one round of shrapnel but it burst short of our own trenches.' The Germans returned the fire but did not hit the British position. Their camp was attacked too and by this time many of the porters had fled. Falconer's health finally succumbed and he was taken to a field hospital, rejoining HMS *Talbot* in March 1917 after a lengthy spell of land service.[4]

THE CASPIAN NAVAL FORCE

Though it was much later in the war, mention might be made here of similarly less well known naval work, this time against a different foe but in another area remote from Home Waters. A full account of service with the Caspian Naval Force falls outside the parameters of this book because the operations continue into 1919. In brief outline, the idea of establishing a naval force on the great landlocked Caspian Sea grew from the threat of Bolshevism to Persia and the strategic railways linking Russia with India through Turkestan. The Persian port of Enzeli provided seaborne access to the oil at Baku. If British forces were able to control Caspian shipping, the continuation of the spread southwards and eastwards of Bolshevik influence

The Caspian Naval Force: the Russian Steamer *Emile Nobel*, fitted with 6 inch guns at Baku. Note that, as in Royal Navy practice, a Range Clock has been fitted. (Captain A.B. Lee)

would be markedly checked. From Tigris gunboats, guns and men were secured and further guns came from the Bombay arsenal. At the end of July 1918, an advance party left Baghdad by lorry with one 4 inch and two twelve-pounder guns.

Three steep mountain passes had to be traversed, one between 7000 and 8000 feet high. To balance the thrilling evidence of historical sites associated with Alexander the Great and Darius was grim contemporary evidence of famine in Persia.

The advance party was reinforced until perhaps a thousand officers and men were gathered at Enzeli. A confused situation reigned in Baku where the anti-Bolshevik forces had overthrown the communists but were being beseiged by Turks and Tartars. The defence of Baku was being assisted by Armenians. British help had been requested but British army forces in the vicinity had been attacked by independent bandits. Within such a scenario there were complex ethnic cross-currents to make the

situation still more difficult to unravel, even in retrospect. Overshadowing all considerations was a further political reality; behind the Turk stood the German as needful of Baku's oil as Bolshevik or Briton.

Russian steamers were acquired, armed and re-named at Enzeli, a seaplane base was organised and, on 16 August 1918, the Caspian Naval Force made for Baku and attempted to establish its base there on the following day.

Baku could not be held and the British returned to Enzeli in mid-September. More systematic arming of steamers was now undertaken and anti-Bolshevik mercantile crews were put under Royal Naval discipline, the guns newly mounted on the ships being manned by Royal Navy and Royal Field Artillery personnel. Each of the five ships so prepared had two naval officers, one, of course, in command. H.G. Pertwee, as Secretary to the Senior Naval Officer of the force, had to take on wide-ranging duties like making sets of flags and ensigns from coloured calico bought in the bazaar, writing

signal books, devising codes and acting as executive officer on one of the steamers. Shells for the guns came by camel (six 4 inch projectiles to a camel) and camel transport superceded lorries as rain and snow made the mountain passes en route from Mesopotamia so difficult in winter.

Baku was re-occupied in November with Turkey now out of the war. A Bolshevik naval attack was beaten off and a Bolshevik naval base destroyed by bombardment but the main actions in a struggle dominated by the iron laws of political and logistical reality were fought in the following year. In fact, victory at sea brought no decisive blow against the Bolsheviks. The converted ships were handed over one by one to the White Russians and the British evacuated their base, the work of the Caspian Naval Force having been concluded as it began, with no ships whatsoever.

Except perhaps at sea the whole affair had been confusing and frustrating for all who served in the force. Seaman Harold Beevers wrote from hospital in Baku: 'Is there any use in clenching teeth in rage at these people when the Government does not allow one to fire on them, although they fire indiscriminately about the streets.'[5] Commodore David Norris, the Senior Naval Officer, wrote of Baku that the 'town was full of dust and matters are one long smell of disturbed fungus-dungus.'[6] In a later communication, he defined the situation in simple terms: 'The Russians have ships and guns but little ammunition, we have guns and ammunition but no ships and it remains to be seen if we can get them to understand that we do not want to stay in their rotten Caspian Sea but we want to beat the Turks and Germans and get the war over.' The problem was never to be satisfactorily resolved.

NORTH RUSSIA

It has been made clear in the outlining of the gallant service of British submarines in the Baltic that the naval links with Russia had by no means been limited to the unusual operations of the Caspian Naval Force. Far to the north at Archangel and then from 1916 at the newly constructed port of Murmansk on the Kola inlet, munitions, coal, food and a range of manufactured goods were landed to sustain the Russian war effort. Ice froze Archangel into inactivity from November to May and U-boats and mines threatened steamer and naval traffic throughout the 630 miles passage from Scottish ports to North Russia. Political events in Russia with mutiny in the Russian navy soon after the February/March revolution in 1917 provided problems of unforseeable dimension as the Royal Navy continued its efforts to maintain supplies for a continued Russian war effort against Germany. The British Government was becoming inexorably embroiled in a social upheaval cleaving the country into civil war to defend or overthrow the successful Bolshevik Revolution of October/November 1917. This revolution attempted to take Russia formally out of the war against Germany by a Bolshevik acceptance of the draconian peace terms demanded by Germany at Brest Litovsk in March 1918. Reducing a problem of glutinous aggregation to its most simple ingredients, the questions were the ultimate destination of hugely expensive vital war supplies brought at such cost to Russian shores and the fear of a tremendous German onslaught in the West if the Germans were freed from their Eastern Front commitment.

The losses suffered in bringing supplies to Russia are reflected in the diary of a seaman recording the torpedoing in October 1917 of SS *Zillah* and SS *Ilderton*.[7] 'Sighted *Zillah* still floating. *Stephen Furness* picked up survivors of SS *Ilderton* torpedoed 7 p.m. yesterday and we found derelict *Ilderton*. We got out straw cable and half towline but decided not to attempt towing for fear of carrying away bits. She was torpedoed in No. 3 hold, had shot holes in forecastle and midship house and was burning in poop and engine room . . . it would have been difficult to board with such a sea running.'

On the following day they 'came across *Zillah* again. She had drifted 60 miles since being torpedoed and will probably not be seen again. She was distinctly lower forward. Our lifeboat, with me at stroke, went alongside and looting party did well with sextants, barometers, telescopes, clocks, binoculars, food, clothing, rifles, furs, wireless and electrical gear.' Gear of that nature may well have been saved but two ships and their cargoes had gone and one of *Zillah*'s lifeboats with sixteen aboard was never sighted again.

In Russia herself competing agencies strove for local or regional ascendency while overall authority seemed insecurely held, whether by the Provisional Government or by its successors, the Bolsheviks. From a point of view of actual collaboration with the Murmansk Soviet in May 1918 against a pro-German faction of Finns eager to take advantage of confused conditions in Russia by seizing a port just

The Navy and the Bolsheviks: A Seaman's diary, North Russia, July 1918. (W. Kennedy)

within Russia, the political kaleidoscope offered the first of its changing pictures – the Royal Navy cooperating with Bolsheviks to secure Russian territory from pro-German Finns. The pictures were to change more bewilderingly then can be related here as, step by step, a small British military force, despatched in May to assist in the training of Russian forces willing to oppose the Germans, became transformed into the North Russian Expeditionary Force committed to the support of the White Russian anti-revolutionary forces in a Civil War of vast scale.

Something of the confused nature of the experience of naval service in North Russia in the last year of the European war is caught in the diary of a rating in the light cruiser *Attentive*.

7 July '[At Saroka on the Murmansk Petrograd railway.] Forced landing with field guns. Bolsheviks retreated setting fire to engine sheds, overturning engines and trains and tearing up the lines and blowing

prisoners fetched aboard, having been concerned in a murder of a Serbian officer ashore. HM Yacht "Kathleen" arrived from Kandalaksha.

5th. Warm & cloudy. Russian steamer left for Saroka with workmen & passengers, the Bolsheviks having blown the railway bridges up. All the railway engines & steamers, burn wood, as coal cannot be got for "love nor money".

6th 2.45 p.m. Captain of Port of Saroka appeals for help, as the Bolsheviks are burning the town & won't allow the passengers to land. 6.0 am proceeded to Saroka, with two more boats full of passengers. 9.0 a.m. Thick fog. Boats get separated. 10.0 am Arrive at Saroka. 10.30 am proceeded to sea to look for passenger boats. 11.45 am sighted them & arrived, with them,

at Saroka at 1.30. Thick fog & rain. Very Cold. Troop ship brought on board.

7th. Very thick. 9.30 a.m. Forced landing, with field guns. etc; Landed passengers. Bolsheviks retreated, setting fire to engine sheds, overturning engines & trains & tearing up the lines, & blowing bridges up. People greet us with great joy. Proclamation read, asking to surrender all fire-arms, and join the army which is being formed to defend Northern Russia. 300 Recruits obtained. (Some thousands of men have joined further up the line). Over 400 rifles, pistols, swords, & 8 machine guns surrender-ed, also over 80,000 rounds of small arm ammunition. Cold & Damp.

8th. More recruits joined. More arms surrendered. Our Captain takes bridges up. People greet us with great joy. Proclamation read asking to surrender all firearms and join the army which is being formed to defend Northern Russia. 300 recruits obtained, over 700 rifles, pistols, swords, and eight machine guns surrendered, also over 80,000 rounds of small ammunition.'

9 July 'Armed guards put aboard surrounding ships. More prisoners fetched aboard.'

10 July 'Several German, Austrian, and Turkish spies fetched aboard.'

13 July 'Ships company give Russian children in Saroka a treat. Tea cakes (baked by ourselves) games etc. Music provided by the ship's band . . . Three prisoners shot for killing a monk. Trotsky[8] handed over to military authorities. Received three roubles and 50 kopecks from him for a packet of cigarettes.'

Naval landing party at Archangel, 1918. (Rear Admiral R.M. Dick)

17 July '400 sailors off Russian cruiser *Askold* arrive here from Murmansk after killing their remaining officers. Refused to allow them to enter town, therefore they start off to walk to Petrograd (157 miles). Nice walk. Hope they enjoy it.'

20 July 'Captain goes up in seaplane to reconnoitre Bolsheviks' positions. Seaplane returns slightly damaged by fire from Bolsheviks.'

27 July 'Ship proceeds to dear knows where –. Very foggy can't see a hand in front of you.'

29 July '50 of ship's company sent to Russian cruiser *Askold* which has been taken over by us.'

1 August 'Captured lightship off Mudyugski Island, island in Bolshevik occupation and guards approach of the Dvina river and Archangel which is some 30 miles up the river. 9 a.m. Anchored off island and asked for their "unconditional surrender". Half an hour given for consideration. They surrender but as we are about to send in the landing party of French marines, they inform us that they will fire on them if they attempt to land . . . 9.35 Fired first salvo. Several salvoes fired before they replied. 10.50 Still banging away. Bang. 6 inch shell hit No. 1 funnel and exploded inside making the funnel like a large sieve. No casualties. 10.53 Bolsheviks ceased firing. 11.10 a.m. We ceased firing. Seaplanes machine gun and bomb retreating enemy. 11.20 Landed landing party without a shot being fired.'

On the following day, *Attentive* made her way up the Dvina past hastily and ineffectively sunk blockships. Archangel was reached, the Bolsheviks having cleared out or been cleared out of the town by their Russian opponents, encouraged by the approach of the British warship.

'As we approach, you can see thousands of people running down to the jetty. By the time we got abreast the jetty about 10,000 people were there. The jetty, roofs of houses, walls and every place were black with people and then a tremendous shout arose and the cheering and blowing of sirens continued for about half an hour or more . . .'

3 August '[off Bakharitsa island up the Dvina.] Arrived just in time to prevent Bolsheviks burning and wrecking the place. Landed troops and commenced bombarding the enemy. Trains, houses used as barracks by the Bolsheviks destroyed and enemy put to flight.'

Attentive returned to Archangel where the ship remained as shops, parks, banks and theatres reopened and an aspect of normality returned, though shelling continued from British monitors up the Dvina. The diarist noted that in September when the 'tramway people [came] out on strike . . . American troops take over and run tramcars, with one armed sentry on each.'[9]

In October, before *Attentive* could be caught by the encroaching ice, she left for Britain, Sub-Lieutenant R.M. Dick, the ship's signal officer, bringing with him copies of messages which reveal more of the confusion than could be expected from the diary of a rating: 'Station train has not yet proved itself definitely hostile. If you stop bombardment, will send patrol to station to investigate. If it advances we hold both sides of a cutting.' Then on another naval signal form: 'From ship to train, Blow whistle when you approach so we know you.' Another: 'I have two prisoner suspects. What shall I do with them?' Reply: 'Turn them over to military if you can, if they won't have them, bring them on board.'[10]

Officers of the cruiser *Cochrane* seemed to find opportunity for a variety of activities during their stay in North Russian coastal waters. Charles Drage described in his diary the complex construction of a punt gun for duck shooting. Quite as much ingenuity seems to have gone into it and its operation as in the Anglo-Russian and French cooperation to build and use an armoured train against the Bolsheviks. Refugees also attracted the concern of *Cochrane*'s officers: 'The Commander, the Fleet Paymaster and I gave a tea fight for the

Left
HMS *Cochrane* icebound, North Russia, 1918.
(Commander C. Drage)

Above
Tobogganing, North Russia, 1918. (Commander C. Drage)

Above
Landing Party from HMS *Attentive* under Lieutenant
Richardson RNR (note the Serbian Officer), North Russia,
Saroka, 1918. (Rear Admiral R.M. Dick)

Below
HMS *Cochrane*'s landing party of sailors and Royal
Marines, sleighs, reindeer and their Lap drivers.
(Commander C. Drage)

elite of the refugees. We had a band and danced on the aft deck. The most interesting of our guests was a little Yankee hospital nurse from Chicago, by name Miss Torrance.' According to Drage, the prospect of action was viewed by his company with 'immense jubilation coupled with a complete indifference as to whether they were going to fight Red Guards, or White Guards, Huns or Finns or Bolsheviks.' In the snowy wastes of the Pechenga inlet, the ratings had opportunity of action but in the safer excitement of tobogganning.

Reindeer-drawn sleighs were used to transfer men and stores when a decision was announced by the Captain on 4 May that the ship's company was to land. 'The seamen in fur caps and duffel coats, with rifles at the slope, the reindeer with their picturesque Lap drivers and

HMS *Sagitta* in one of the Bays of the Kola Inlet, North Russia. (Sir James Corry)

With *Cochrane* in these northern waters was the steam yacht *Sagitta* which was to some extent equipped to repel the pestilential insect boarders, with fine wire grilles to all port-holes. When out on deck or on land, 'veils and gloves were necessities, and it was a sound idea to wear sea boots inside trousers and tie strings tightly round your legs. As to numbers, visibility was impaired as by a mist and a man with moderately big hands could kill twenty or so by clapping his hands once.'[12]

A source of cheer, necessary in the heat and under mosquito attack was HMS *Cochrane*'s concert party. Serbian troops were especially pleased by such entertainment, one Slavic officer shouting 'with joy at a brawny stoker's impersonation of a coy maiden.'[13]

Cochrane, joining *Attentive* at Archangel, had assisted in the establishment of a British military presence in North Russia. When the ship left to escape Winter's clutch, there was no more that could be done, but only the first chapter of an unfortunate story had been written.

the ship herself wedged in the ice, all combined to present a picture which must be unparalleled in the annals of the Service.'[11]

Soon after this *Cochrane*'s Royal Marines and then a detachment of ratings under their officer were in action against Finnish forces. Casualties were suffered in this fighting but something which seriously affected Drage and many others was not wounds in action but snow blindness, an affliction replaced by another unfamiliar misery in July, mosquito bites even on skin surfaces seemingly protected by thick serge.

'An auxiliary small craft', the steam yacht *Sagitta* in the Kola Inlet, North Russia. (Sir James Corry)

15

Nautical Steps
in the Right Direction

Perhaps it is a strange leap from the privations of the Arctic to the relative comfort of the Admiralty and certainly the living conditions of shore-based naval work during the war may well have attracted derogatory observations from both junior officers and ratings at sea, but few can have grasped the full extent of their dependence on one particular section of one department of the Admiralty, the department being that of Naval Intelligence. Room 40, officially designated I.D. 25, was the section of the Intelligence Division of the Navy concerned with the interception and decoding of the wireless traffic of the German navy. The decoding of German diplomatic wireless traffic was also to come within its responsibility with quite astoundingly successful results in the case of the Zimmerman telegram. The decoding and brilliantly judged use of this piece of intelligence in January and February 1917 did much to persuade the President and people of the United States that they could no longer be too proud to fight. Despite limitations being imposed on the effectiveness of its work by the policy of over-centralisation of the Director of the Intelligence Division, Rear Admiral H.F. Oliver, and the failure of the Director of the Operations Division, Captain Thomas Jackson, to make full use of the fruits of Room 40's work, Patrick Beesley in his book makes bold claims on behalf of Room 40, equating its contribution to the 1914–18 War effort to that of Bletchley Park's decoding work in World War Two.[1] Certainly, from late October 1914 until the end of the war,

reliable information was pouring into the Admiralty to be used by the Naval Staff in the conduct of the war at sea and by the Foreign Office for the naval blockade of Germany, for action against German colonies and for the trade war in general.

When W.H. Bruford was appointed to Room 40 in 1917, the group of people working there was quite large and worked in watches all round the clock. Bruford recalls his famous chief, Captain Reginald Hall with his nervous twitch which gave him his nickname of 'Blinker Hall', briskly entering the room exuding authority and self-confidence. Quick judgements were made. He was 'no respecter of persons and his limitless self confidence put many backs up' but, nonetheless, he was admired and trusted by staff who felt themselves engaged in 'highly urgent team work'. Bruford, a Cambridge scholar with First Class Honours in Languages, had been appointed to the political section of Room 40 where there were recruits from the Foreign Office, the RNAS, and the Universities. There were also bankers from the city, an author, a critic, a legal man, a newspaper foreign correspondent, a Dartmouth schoolmaster, an actor and a man who became a dress designer. Immaculate in the uniform of a Lieutenant RNVR, Bruford's special pass admitted him to the Admiralty Building for work in a room very close to Room 40 itself. About six officers in this room were engaged in decoding German and Spanish signals or other wireless messages from German naval and diplomatic sources to the German naval attaché in Madrid and from Spanish officials in Germany to the Spanish Government. Bruford and his colleagues in

251A

their decoding work were using a code book fished up by a trawler but when the system changed it was Bruford who broke the new code.

Room 40 was the main room in an isolated suite of rooms in the Old Admiralty Building in Whitehall. It received its most important traffic from intercepting stations by landline to the basement of the Admiralty and then up to Room 40 by message tube for the signals to be sorted out and distributed. The actual copies of the signals as written down by the wireless operators came later by despatch riders. They were essential to check for 'corruption', letters or figures not distinctly heard and guessed at or omitted and replaced by some description of the noise.[2]

The development of wireless had added a new dimension to the securing of knowledge of the enemy's intention. Neither intelligence gathering nor decoding was in any sense new in 1914 but the established and increasing sophistication of working methods to decode wireless transmitted intelligence, was Room 40's achievement. In this, its naval officers had enormously advanced an essential element in

Women's Royal Naval Service. The training of officers: smartness. Miss E. Gledstanes is second from the left, in the front rank. (Miss E. Gledstanes)

Britain's armament for war or indeed peace in the twentieth century.

THE WOMEN'S ROYAL NAVAL SERVICE

Though women did civilian clerical work in the Admiralty and the Royal Dockyards, it was not until the end of November 1917 that an advertisement in *The Times* asked for 'Women for the Navy. New shore service to be formed'. The first course for officers in this new Women's Royal Naval Service was in fact one for the Women's Auxiliary Army but naval courses were quickly established instructing in squad drill, physical fitness and revolver target shooting and giving lectures in naval history and the naval way of doing things, first aid and self defence. With newly fledged officers enthusiastically if nervously ready to command, the next step was the enlistment of female ratings to the new service. From employment exchanges, women over eighteen years were recruited and

Women's Royal Naval Service. The training of officers: fitness. (Miss E. Gledstanes)

Women's Royal Naval Service. At the wheel, Miss Dorothy B. Greig, Motor Transport Division. (Miss D.B. Greig)

maintenance were opportunities soon added to the range of work and the numbers rose until there were a thousand Wrens at Portsmouth and over seven thousand in all, with Training Schools, hostels for accommodation and a network of organisations all round the British coast. Some Wrens served overseas at naval bases as did Kathleen Ussher whose swift action in mopping up spilled ink at a naval conference in Gibraltar saved blushes as well as white uniforms of superbly smart staff officers.[3]

That the Wrens did invaluable work, whether in driving officers on East Anglian roads or decoding signals in Devonport, is unquestionable. That it was not always appreciated by those entrenched in their ways is also evident. Not representative, but certainly not without parallel, is the diary verdict of a Yarmouth seaplane pilot: 'Wrens only waste time and retard work. Women are no use whatsoever as outside workers and these dear souls are in the Women's Royal Naval Service because of its novelty rather than its utility.' As the pilot expressed concern about the 'enormously greater wages they receive com-

The Chief of Staff being told that his signals have a lower priority for decoding than those of the Flag Commander which are being attended to. Sketch by Miss Gledstanes. (Miss E. Gledstanes)

Innocent and inexperienced Decoder tells the COS to take his ▌▌▌▌ to the ▌▌▌ ▌▌▌▌

(P.S. This is not a true story)

reported to the Crystal Palace in batches of twelve to twenty for a fortnight's basic training in squad drill, physical training and, again, lectures about the navy. They were then appointed to clerical duties or as storekeepers, messengers, cooks, printers, postwomen and waitresses in officers' shore-bound messes. A badge of cross quills denoted a clerk and keys a storekeeper and the rating proudly wore her pudding basin hat with pleated crown and round brim.

More specialist areas like wireless telegraphy, cypher and decoding duties, driving and vehicle

Officers Dinsdale, Moore, Duggan and Fox enjoy the comforts of their accommodation, the 'mortuary', in Grimsby. Sketch by Miss Elsie Gledstanes. (Miss E. Gledstanes)

For their good work, the Wrens are given eggs, welcome in view of their frugal fare. Sketch by WRNS officer Elsie Gledstanes, whose work as an artist was to become well known. (Miss E. Gledstanes)

pared to the paltry pittances doled out to the unconsidered men' it may be assumed that the issue of women's pay caused concern or raised prejudice in more than merely the industrial sphere![4]

Elsie Gledstanes did signalling decoding work at Immingham. Her hostel ('the mortuary') was but a row of empty shops in Grimsby. Night shift work was physically demanding and the food provided was barely adequate. The confidentiality of their work imposed its own strain too, a strain not relieved by a female perception that the shore-based naval officers at Immingham had far too great an addiction to navy issue rum and spirits.[5] Working at the Wren Headquarters, Great Stanhope Street in London, Miss Gaitskell had the opportunity of examining closely the outstanding Katherine Furse, the Commandant, at work. Dorothy Gaitskell had led a sheltered life, had no experience of using a telephone and no typing or shorthand skills but the organisation of Dame Katherine's papers became her responsibility. She was at first alarmed at handling papers marked 'secret and confidential' but she so took to the work in the happy office atmosphere that she burst into tears when influenza forced an abrupt end of her service.[6] Her departure was not long before the demobilisation of the whole force. In late 1919, economy and the seeming absence of a need for Wrens closed a chapter in the history of the navy. Twenty years later that chapter would seem to have been closed prematurely.

On and Above the Sea:
The U-Boat War, 1917–18

THE U-BOAT WAR AND CONVOY 1917–18

The opening of a new campaign of unrestricted U-boat warfare was designed quite specifically to lead to the defeat of the whole allied coalition by draining the capacity of its strongest member, Britain, to sustain its own warfare, let alone render aid to her hard pressed allies. Such a plan, put forward by the Chief of the German Naval Staff in December 1916, received Government authorisation for commencement on 1 February 1917.

In the first three months of the campaign 345 British ships were sunk. The delayed introduction of convoy as the answer to a problem of such catastrophic proportions is not infrequently cited as a perfect illustration of the blockheadedness of the executive level of Britain's Senior Service but there were factors which cast doubt on the capacity to mount convoy and the efficiency of convoy itself. That these factors were outweighed by their counterpoints was only self-evidently true for a small number of men, notably Commander R.G.H. Henderson at the Admiralty. There are others deserving of credit, none claiming it more for himself than Lloyd George. Certainly it has to be accepted that Admiral Sir John Jellicoe who had earned such loyalty as Commander in Chief of the Grand Fleet, was sunk by overwork and indifferent health into a degree of enfeebled pessimism as 1st Lord and seemed reluctant to espouse the one course which, by the reasoned arguments of some, offered hope of reversing the balance of shipping losses and U-boats destroyed.

From May 1917, mercantile convoy pro-

The end of the destroyer *Scott* by U-boat torpedo in the North Sea on 15 August 1918. (Commander P. Haig-Ferguson)

cedures were introduced on an increasing scale. Gradually North Atlantic and other vital routes were made safer by the work of cruisers, destroyers, trawlers (some with hydrophone equipment), airships, kite balloons and seaplanes. On the North Atlantic route in July 1917 only one convoyed ship out of 245 was lost and only two convoys in the war, both on the vulnerable Scandinavian route, were seriously hit and these convoys were attacked by German surface vessels.[1]

The twin enemies of foul weather and potential German interception of the Scandinavian convoys were a considerable strain on all concerned. For some ratings in one destroyer, the strain in the autumn of 1917 whatever its precise source, proved too much though the subsequent court of enquiry spread the blame between an officer and the twelve men concerned. In port at Lerwick, the men 'broke out of the ship at noon and had to be fetched. They were absolutely mutinous when caught and had to be placed aft under arrest. Another had fired the foremost gun. Luckily only a blank charge but it upset the whole town. The ship breakers then broke away from the guard and broke open the Wardroom wine. This made them mad drunk. Eventually a Marine guard had to be sent for and they were handcuffed and put down in the stokers' flat. The Marines standing guard with ball ammunition.' The destroyer was promptly isolated from her sister ships while an enquiry was succeeded by an even more detailed investigation. This latter enquiry was being conducted when news came in of the loss of the destroyers *Mary Rose* and *Strongbow* together with most of the merchantmen they were escorting from Scandinavia. Rather surprisingly, the diary which gives an account of these events provides no information on the formal findings of the enquiry other than: 'Poor No I is leaving the ship. He has been severely criticised over the ship breaking business although it wasn't his fault but the Captain's.'[2]

AIRSHIPS AND AEROPLANES

With the logical extension of convoy to coastal shipping, the significance of the airship's anti-U-boat role was reinforced. The value of airships in convoy duties was not to be measured by successful attacks on U-boats, of which there seem to have been very few, if any, but in terms of the observational capacity which the airships possessed. Sightings were transmitted by wireless or signalling lamp to surface craft, enabling the latter to move in to attack. The observation capacity of airships had proved itself in locating mines during the Dardanelles Gallipoli campaign and off the Macedonian coast, but actually to score a hit or near miss on a U-boat with a bomb was another matter. On one occasion off Cornwall, T.P. Yorke-Moore actually had to climb out of his observer's cockpit and kick

loose a half-released 60 lb bomb which was being used in a practice drop. This may seem dangerous, but worse was to follow: dropping a bomb in Mullion harbour in the summer of 1918 in order to kill fish for an easy haul by a small naval-manned boat, York-Moore saw local fishermen approaching the scene ahead of the naval party. A burst of Lewis gun fire discouraged the enterprise of the local men but severed a petrol pipe, allowing a free flow of petrol to drench the determined aerial desecrators of Isaac Walton's memory. It took just under a worrying quarter of an hour to get back to base, a disastrous fire ignited by the uncovered spark plug narrowly averted. 'What I do not think the crew even knew was that I had had incendiary bullets with the ordinary ones and I can only assume that one did not pass through the pipe.'[3]

On another occasion, airship victims were claimed but by reason of bad weather: loss by

Fishing by bomb. A bomb provides fish collected by RNAS officers Sketchley and Read of the seaplane station at Cattewater. (Wing Commander J. Bentham)

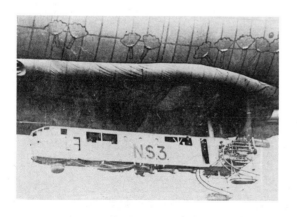

drowning of half of the crew of ten of North Sea Airship Number 3 in the Firth of Forth on 21 June 1918. Gale conditions had forced the airship to abandon convoy duties and it was returning to base at East Fortune when it was thrown out of control by air turbulence and struck the surface of the sea, tearing off the engineer's compartment. The airship then rose a few hundred feet in a vertical position, those crew members in the remaining compartment certain that their death was minutes or even seconds away. P.E. Maitland, 2nd Officer, recalled that the Commander, Flight Commander

Wheelwright, actually bade formal farewell to the Coxswain, a man with whom he had served a number of years. When the airship crashed down again into the sea, five of the crew were fortunate in being able to scramble onto a portion of the envelope which remained afloat. They were rescued by destroyer.[4]

Anti-submarine airship work from Scapa was frequently affected by the high winds. Getting out of the unscreened hangar on the west side of the Flow, despite some shelter from low hills, was difficult, landing and mooring being perhaps still more alarmingly so under

Top right
Squally weather problems as an airship attempts to enter the shed at Longside, near Peterhead, in 1918. (Air Vice Marshal P.E. Maitland)

Right
Non-rigid airships had a panel at the top which could be pulled out by a cord in an emergency, the gas escaping quickly and the airship envelope collapsing. C10A has been deliberately 'ripped' in such an emergency in front of her shed in the autumn of 1918. (Air Vice Marshal P.E. Maitland)

Below
The seaplane carrier HMS *Campania*, losing more than her seaplanes, sinking after collision in the Firth of Forth on 5 November 1918.

Above right
RNAS Flanders aeroplanes and non-rigid airship personnel greet Christmas 1916 with this card. (Squadron Leader C.P.O. Bartlett)

Above left
RNAS officers defending the beach at St Malo in 1917. (Squadron Leader H.A. Buss)

Left
RNAS Station Great Yarmouth Sunday Parade. (J. Sellers)

Below left
Close up of the floats of a Short seaplane, Great Yarmouth, 1918. Flight Sub-Lieutenant Gordon is at the extreme left. Note the interesting diversity of uniform, RNAS flying kit and RAF. (Rev. Dr. T.C. Gordon)

Below right
An early 'Digging for Victory'. RNAS officers starting a garden at Manston. (Squadron Leader H.A. Buss)

A Felixstowe F3 flying boat at Houton Bay, The Orkneys in 1918. (Rev. Dr T.C. Gordon)

The seaplane station at Houton Bay, The Orkneys: hockey team to play against a team from a cruiser 1918. T.C. Gordon is fifth from the right. (Rev. Dr T.C. Gordon)

windy conditions. In one instance, Sir Ralph Cochrane recalled, the rip cord had to be pulled, creating a large slit in the top of the envelope to allow gas to escape. 'Unfortunately as the internal pressures collapsed, the handling party lost control and the ship lifted into the air nose first before settling down. A ship had been hazarded and I therefore faced a Court Martial, which was however turned into a Court of Enquiry with two Post Captains. I found the situation humorous because in the Flow at that time lay H.M.S. *Campania* a seaplane carrier which was losing seaplanes at a steady rate, yet nothing was ever said although each loss represented many times the value of a fill of gas for an airship. But then one was a ship and the other a plane!'[5] Cochrane, however, suffered some embarrassment without official reprimand on another occasion when he followed an oil slick, convinced that it was evidence of the presence of a submarine, only to find that he was following a trail made from the drip tray of the engine of his own airship.

Well over a million miles were patrolled by airships on anti-submarine work in 1918 but seaplanes and land-based aeroplanes played their part too in 1918, providing escort cover on 4869 occasions, with only two ships attacked in those convoys. T.C. Gordon, a seaplane pilot, recorded in his diary that engine unreliability

177

Left
Sopwith Camel gun turret take-off: HMS *Renown*.
(Commander G.F. Evans)

Above
A Sopwith Camel on Q Turret of the battle cruiser HMS
Tiger. (C. de L. Bacon)

Right
A kite balloon aboard the battle cruiser *Renown*.
(Commander G.F. Evans)

could prove disastrous. '21 February 1918 One of our pilots went off in search of F.S.L. Budd, but he had not gone very far when his engine stopped and he had to land on a tremendous high sea, and of course he sent the unfailing pigeons for help. A little later, one of our scouting seaplanes saw the stranded Short, and made quickly for two trawlers beside which I landed and while one proceeded to the help of the Short pilot and his observer the other was compelled to take the Schneider pilot on board and abandon the machine. No result was obtained by five seaplanes and three M.L's searching for the missing officer and in the process two more machines were lost and three pilots almost done in.' In the same month, Gordon lost a Hamble Baby seaplane during take-off: 'rising ten feet from the water, the wind caught one wing tip and turned me over. I went splashing into the water in the centre of a maze of wires and guns and bombs and fabric and the whole wreckage began to sink bodily.'[6]

MERCHANTMEN IN PERIL

From looking at the experience of those engaged in protecting merchant ships, it is appropriate to consider the dangers to which the crews of these ships themselves were exposed. It is a salutary reminder of the range and reality of deep sea merchant service during the war to look at the bare detail enscribed in so many diaries of men whose way of life was the sea. 'Dec. 14 1916. Joined ship in Glasgow. Jan. 14 1917 Sailed from Barry to Dakar, Durban, Delagoa Bay, Beira – Sydney, Brisbane home via Freemantle, Durban. June 24 Torpedoed and sunk by German submarine. June 25 Landed Plymouth by British destroyer. June 27 Arrived home.'[7] Twelve men lost their lives in this sinking of *Clan Davidson*.

In September of that year SS *Carlisle Castle*, leaving the Mersey, was in collison with two ships but nevertheless took her place in a North Atlantic convoy. A U-boat was sighted and chased off by destroyers and New York was

reached safely. After dry dock repairs she took on oil and shells, grain and flour in Philadelphia but: 'Chief Engineer fell into dock. Pulled out by Chief Officer. Pantryman attempted suicide by drowning. Rescued. Taken ashore and detained as a lunatic.' The diary is censored so it is not possible to read where cordite, listed next, was loaded or where a convoy was awaited. Whatever the destination of the convoy, huge seas smashed into *Carlisle Castle*, so damagingly that she had to put in for further repairs in New York. Bad weather again delayed the journey to Boston, USA and from Boston a convoy of seventeen ships departed on 13

On Convoy, Wireless Telegraphist B.C. Bishop decodes messages of U-boat sightings. (B.C. Bishop)

November. The weather deteriorated again and the whole convoy had to hove to. 'Driving rain and spray obliterate surrounding ships. Gale increases. Give up attempting to keep station. Every ship for itself. Huge confused sea running . . . November 20 rejoined escort. Starboard lifeboat stove in and port lifeboat damaged. Carpenter and hands on repairs. Captain in nervous breakdown. November 21. Convoy reformed. Ten ships remaining.' Yet again the weather worsened and the convoy hove to, the gale again snapping the Quadrant which swept clear off the deck everything within its reach. 'Rolling to extreme and shipping thunderous seas over all. Chief Officer Wren again to the fore. Captain remains in cabin.' Men trying to secure the quadrant were badly injured, one side of the bridge being 'smashed to matchwood . . . Iron stanchions flattened. Iron Jacob's ladder twisted into knots.' All the accommodation and the galley were washed out, steam pipes torn up and gun screens demolished. Distress rockets were fired and cargo oil dumped to lighten the ship. When *Carlisle Castle* had to hove to again, off the Irish coast: 'What a chance for a Hun pirate to do the dirty on us.' 'November 29 5 p.m. Sighted light through fog . . . Proceed full speed for Liverpool [crossed out but still legible]. Arrived battered and bent but not broken spirited at 5 p.m. November 30th. Now safe. Thank God.'[8]

Of the torpedoing of *Port Hardy* near Gibraltar, former apprentice officer, now Captain E.T.N. Lawrey, remembered that, having waited for escort from Sierra Leone and none being forthcoming: 'We left on our own, bound for Genoa . . . We were zigzagging' but a torpedo struck the ship and she sank within ten minutes. Lawrey had nine in the cutter of which he took charge. 'We had no sea anchor, so improvised one from two oars lashed together, and this served well. Two men were at the oars to keep the boat's head to sea and I had a steering oar for the same purpose.' When the easterly wind moderated, the sea anchor was taken in and a single lug sail was set. 'We had no compass but I steered North by the North Star.' Despite shipping some water, good progress was made. Before reaching land they were picked up by a Danish three-masted schooner and reunited at Gibraltar with all who had survived the explosion.[9]

The readiness of Merchant Service personnel to defend their ship is indicated by numerous celebrated instances of counter attacks on the submarine predator but it is also revealed in a more modest way by such documents as a certificate showing that apprentice H.N. Taylor had satisfactorily completed a 'Voluntary Gunnery Course for apprentices and cadets'. Perhaps being torpedoed in *Jersey City* at an earlier date led Taylor to volunteer for the course but if this were to be the case, there was a

disappointing sequel. 'In an alarm at night with the gun's crew closed up and the convoy scattered there was an almighty crash, the ship shaking like an earthquake, and those of us aft on the gun were smothered in soot from the funnel.' The Captain, who had lost one ship which went down very swiftly, in reflex action ordered 'abandon ship'! 'The gun sight and breach block were jettisoned' the crew taking to a boat and pulling clear. At dawn, the ship, *Homer City*, was still afloat so back on board they went, the ship being safely brought in to Plymouth, the apprentice deprived of the opportunity of testing his gunnery proficiency.[10]

In April 1918, after the dispersal of a convoy which had been shepherded to within reach of Gibraltar, the steamship *Ramsay* continued south bound for Dakar when at night she encountered a surfaced submarine disguised by hoisted sails. U-boat torpedoes received a prompt response of rapid, accurate gunfire. The submarine was soon in flames and sinking. For *Ramsay*'s wireless operator, the experience, which his wireless duties had not in fact enabled him to witness, was some compensation for being torpedoed in the transport SS *Sturton* in February of that year. Every member of *Ramsay*'s crew received financial reward from the Admiralty and other sources for the achievement which, in terms of gunnery skill at a range of 900 yards, had been superb.[11]

In Chesapeake Bay in October 1917, *Afghan Prince* took fire and Wireless Operator B.C. Bishop was one of those who responded to the order 'All hands to Port boat'. The smoke of the oil fire was blinding and choking. Unfortunately the wireless was all disconnected and sealed up in accordance with American Government rules for ships in their waters but Bishop 'unlocked the drawer and seized phones and connected them to the receiver, unlocked deed box and pulled a crystal out, put it on the receiver and searched for a sensitive point . . . The dynamo had still to be switched on before pulling the starter handle over – she started up thank heaven.' There was more work to do

SS *Afghan Prince* on fire. (B.C. Bishop)

particularly with the aerial before the wireless could be operated. Annapolis wireless station received the distress signal and a tug was ordered out to assist the *Afghan Prince*. The fire at one time had seemed under control but broke out again even more fiercely. 'All of us simply stood and watched the clouds of smoke rising and watching the tug approaching.' Further wireless signals brought out another tug and the two helpers eased *Afghan Prince* to a position off Baltimore where the fire was finally doused. Bishop recorded in his diary that: 'The Engineers and Mates can really be said to have saved the ship. The pilot behaved disgustingly and was in a sheer funk.' Unfortunately, the pilot was ashore first and a different version appeared in local papers.[12]

Q SHIPS AGAIN

Hunting the U-boat was the total preoccupation of the Q Ship. Of the 54 U-boats lost to all causes in 1917, six were destroyed by Q ships, seven by British submarines, nine rammed by surface craft and nineteen lost by detonation of mines. A tramp steamer, SS *Penshurst*, as *Q7*, was well suited to her work of acting as a decoy to destruction. Her three holds were fitted with wood and caulked so that she could float if torpedoed and she had a deep gunwhale which concealed the movements of her crew. She had a complement of fifty-eight. *Penshurst* sank two U-boats and in her own destruction on Christmas Eve 1917 she very nearly secured a third victim as she fought off her killer.

'Not more than three crew members were allowed on deck during daylight hours' recalled A.L. Jones, who had been a boy telegrapher in *Penshurst*. Changes of Watch were carried out

The wolf in sheep's clothing: the crew of Q ship HMS *Hyderabad* in uniform
and in disguise. Built by John I. Thornycroft and Co. Ltd and in service in
1917, *Hyderabad* was commanded by Lieutenant Commander J.K. McLeod
and had a well experienced crew, as denoted by the badges of the ratings.
(Captain J.K. McLeod)

HMS *Hyderabad*'s midship gun was screened from view by a 'deckhouse' of metal sheets which was collapsed to form the gunners' floor for action. Of the popular three-island cargo ship configuration, *Hyderabad* mounted one gun forward on the bow island, one aft on the stern island and one amidships on the bridge deck abaft the funnel. She also had two minethrowers in the forward well deck and two in the after well deck hidden by false deck hatches, and two torpedo tubes to port in the hull side below the bridge. (Captain J.K. McLeod)

HMS *Hyderabad*'s stern gun – like the bow gun – was rotated into a recess in the deck when the vessel was masquerading as a merchantman. She is berthed alongside a larger merchant vessel. (Captain J.K. McLeod)

A Q Ship captain, B.J.D. Guy, in his Merchant skipper disguise. As Guy had won a VC in China in 1900 he had excellent qualifications for his command of the Q Ship *Werribee*. (Per J. Winton)

Ireland, recalled that early in 1917 they had 'not more than 12 I think and it was not yet realised how close to a U boat, depth charges must explode nor what a large number of charges must be exploded to have any chance of success.'[14] On 17 February 1917, *Narwhal* actually took on board two survivors of a U-boat sunk by *Q5*, some of whose crew also took refuge as it seemed that the Q ship would sink too. *Q5* was, in fact, towed and beached at Berehaven, her Commander, Gordon Campbell, being awarded a Victoria Cross for this his third U-boat sinking. De Winton's next appointment to the destroyer *Mosquito* involved him in convoy escort duties. From a Lough Swilly base in Northern Ireland, destroyers met homeward bound convoys needing escort for the Clyde or the Mersey. In six months' convoy work over the turn of 1917–18, de Winton was not to see a U-boat but *Mosquito* was on hand to rescue large numbers of American troops from the British converted trooper, *Tuscania*, torpedoed early in 1918. This rescue may serve as a reminder of the curious fact that overwhelmingly American troops were brought to Europe in British ships.

MINE SWEEPING

Sweeping for the mines laid by the U-boats in sea lanes and close to port entries was done by various vessels but in the main by steam trawlers. The trawlers' task was to cut the wires attaching the mine to a weight keeping it below the surface but at a depth to be struck by a passing vessel. With the mine on the surface, it could be exploded or sunk from a safe distance by rifle fire or less economically by a shell from a small gun mounted on the foredeck. A pair of trawlers together dragged thin cable wire into which was worked at intervals knuckles or stopper knots of wire. When a mine was caught, the trawlers dragged it alternately port and starboard between the knuckles until the mine's weight-attaching wire was sawn through.[15] Three pairs of trawlers working in echelon could cover a wide stretch of water but the ten-

by crawling along the deck and there was a state of tension aboard the ship reflecting the riskiness of the whole work. Double pay, abundant good food and a better leave allocation were some reward and there was potentially prize money, too, but as Jones remembers it, all but two of the crew elected to return to normal duties after their ship's loss rather than continue in Q ship service. To his £50 share of prize money for *Penshurst's* work, Jones added a well deserved Distinguished Service Medal.[13]

Concerning the supply and efficacy of depth charges in the submarine war, Captain F.S.W. de Winton, whose memories are of the destroyer *Narwhal* at Queenstown in south west day period of work was demanding on nerves. For those not bred as fishermen, it took some time to adjust to life on the rolling, pitching deck of a trawler. Of mine sweeping, R.J. Allerton wrote that it could 'mean hours of tension when perhaps no mines were found but when there could be no relaxation. I had seen mines and seen them sunk and twice seen those so close that they had to be warded off with poles.' Allerton, as a telegraphist, served from Lowestoft and then Ardrossan, Kirkwall and Peterhead. He remembered that concern was always expressed by the local naval authorities about the inadequacy of coal and water before going out for a rota of ten days but on one occasion food ran out and: 'We subsisted on odd scraps made into a stew and dry bread flavoured with salt and pepper.'[16] He does not make clear whether this was the occasion when a submarine periscope was pursued only for it to turn out to be a salmon tin with the sun glinting on it!

Much earlier in the war, when a variety of vessels was being used for mine sweeping, some scarcely suitable, a steam yacht, *Sagitta*, was employed. At the wheel of this 'small craft auxiliary', Able Seaman Corry watched an especially valuable deed performed. A German mine, anchored but on the surface, was bravely selected for closer examination. 'The big motor boat was lowered and Stuart Garnett, our Commanding Officer, went off with two others. When near the mine, Garnett jumped into the sea and swam. He found two wires outside the casing, and severed them with pliers, hoping that this would reduce the possibility of an explosion and attached a line to the mine. The derrick was swung out, the mine lifted clear of the water. The detonator could then be pulled out, thereby increasing the safety factor. The anchor wire was cut, but not let go, and the mine landed on board where the primer was removed before lashing the mine on the forward well deck. The wire was led to the windlass and an attempt was made to pull up the anchoring device but the latter was so effective that the wire broke.'[17] A seaman, Alfred Swann, repeated the performance for a second mine and, not

One of the two German mines being hauled gingerly aboard HMS *Sagitta*. (Sir James Corry)

without a certain amount of apprehension among the crew, *Sagitta* brought her twin explosive treasure trove to home port.

In April 1917, Corry, keeping a diary, recorded a mine disaster for a fleet storeship, *Charles Goodanew*, and a particularly narrow escape for *Sagitta* accompanying the drifters with the storeship. Off North East Scotland in a heavy sea, *Charles Goodanew* had struck a mine early on the morning of 17 April. 'I was given order "hard a starboard" and immediately the wheel was round I looked astern but only smoke was visible as she had sunk so quickly, in less than a minute. Soon after another mine detonated, apparently by wreckage of *Charles Goodanew*. We signalled drifters to pick up survivors, there were two, and then steamed through the wreckage on the look out for more. The water was strewn with timber, sweeping kites, barrels, boxes and two Carley floats of considerable size. I was then standing by lifeboat in case we risked lowering it. Suddenly everyone rushed aft. So many were looking over

Able Seaman Donald Bremner apparently loading a 6-pounder gun with a beer bottle, aboard the mine sweeping steam yacht *Sagitta* in 1915. (Sir James Corry)

the side that I went and found a mine within 20 feet of us. Thinking this unhealthy I went to the port side and found another mine floating there about the same distance off . . . Meade King [2nd Officer] took the wheel and steered between them. So close were they that the C.O. was afraid of the Kelvin lead striking the one to starboard while "chippy" had hold of a boat-hook to shove off the port side one.'[18]

While on the subject of mines, it should be mentioned that mine laying commanded even more naval resources than mine sweeping. Unfortunately, in the outstanding instance of this, the 240-mile Northern Barrage between the Orkneys and Norway, the colossal resources committed to it may not have been well directed. The purpose, that of preventing any enemy egress from or ingress to the North Sea was only doubtfully attainable and certainly not with the inferior US mines which predominated in the barrage. In any case, there was Anglo-US discord over the whole concept and its layout in practice.

17
Calamity, Caring and Conveyance

K-BOATS

Of all the innovations of the Royal Navy at sea in World War One, there was nothing to match the technological unlikelihood of the K-boats. K class submarines were essentially submersible destroyers. With a length of 353 feet and a beam of 26 feet 6 inches, they had a threefold propulsion system: diesel, steam turbine and electric. The turbines gave the K boats a surface speed of 24 knots, enabling them to cooperate with the Grand Fleet, but there were inherent disadvantages in the slowness of the change from readiness for surface work to readiness for submersible action. Funnels had to be retracted and capped, turbines stopped and cooled and diesel engines brought into play to accelerate the speed of diving, after which the electric motors could take over. Conceptually, *Fearless*, a four-funnel light cruiser, was to lead her 12th Submarine (K boat) flotilla to within torpedo range of the enemy, the torpedoes would be fired and a hasty retreat would be made. In the absence of armour and with only 4 inch guns for defence, the K boats would have had no chance of surviving a surface fleet action.

The boats had an unhappy record of service, being involved in 'sixteen major accidents and countless smaller mishaps. One sank on her trials. Three were lost after collisions. A fifth disappeared. Another sank in harbour. The loss of life was appalling; the escapes from death were among the most remarkable in the history of submarines . . . in their two years of service

The submarines with funnels! *K16*. (G.T.W. Kimbell)

only one of them engaged the enemy, hitting a U-boat amidships with a torpedo which failed to explode.'[1] An engineer officer who served in K boats recognised in his memoirs their tendency to dive when travelling at speed on the surface into anything of a sea and the unpopularity among old submariners of there being thirteen openings to the hull, each, of course, to be closed before diving, but he nevertheless affirmed that 'considering the tactical role they were designed for, and with officers who did not expect to handle these very big boats in the same way as smaller submarines and appreciated their limitations in this respect, they were a wonderful effort and no more dangerous than any other submarine – if properly handled.'[2]

With regard to life within *K4*, of which he was Engineer Officer, O.W. Phillips has written of the morning headaches produced by the battery gas, the early loss of his teeth which he attributed to an excess of tinned food, the universal constipation from a lack of exercise. Exercise of a quite extraordinary sort was

US battleships of the 6th Battle Squadron and British battleships of the 1st Battle Squadron putting to sea from Rosyth. (Vice Admiral E. Longley-Cook)

actually required of the flotilla's officers by the new Commander in Chief, Sir David Beatty, late in 1917. 'On our being introduced to him he remarked that life was a bit dull on board the *Queen Elizabeth*, that one of his staff officers was getting a bit above himself and if we dressed as pirates, raided the ship's ante room one evening and pulled his trousers off, he personally would have no objection provided he was notified of our arrival on board.' The escapade was duly carried out. 'We spotted our prey, a large and reputedly somewhat pompous officer, reclining in an armchair behind a copy of the *Times*. Without further ado he was seized and firmly held while his nether garment was deftly whipped off. An awed hush fell and his shipmates turned their eyes away from such a dreadful piece of desecration. This was broken by the voice of the Commander in Chief. "Well I think you have been working up for that for some time." Nothing to be said, and our victim, good fellow, joined in the laugh against himself.'[3]

Intimately concerned with the entire short-lived service of one K class submarine was Signalman Kimbell, appointed to *K17*, newly completed in the autumn of 1917. Kimbell's service from training ship in 1910 had been in different types of cruiser, a battleship and a destroyer. With Falkland Isles and Jutland action behind him, he had volunteered for the submarine service, passed searching medical tests and, despite his breadth of experience, felt a really new entry or 'nozzy' at Fort Block-house, Gosport, the navy's submarine head-quarters. He had successfully taken the submarine course examinations and been given a new canvas holdall for his extra quantity of sea clothing, which included a thick white sweater, long thick woollen stockings and a pair of heavy sea boots.

K17 was at Gairloch, her funnelled appearance astounding Kimbell as no such class of submarine had been mentioned in his training course. Apart from his communications work, his diving station and duty operating the Port main ballast valve were explained to him. He was also shown the 6 to 8-feet long bottles of compressed air held in every compartment not only for the operation of machinery but for saving life. Kimbell was to have special responsibilities too related to the preparations for firing torpedoes. After the completion of torpedo trials, *K17* made for Scapa Flow and exercises with the Grand Fleet before being dispatched South to the 13th Submarine Flotilla at Rosyth.

With the arrival of another flotilla of K boats, the 12th, operational orders for the sequence of units leaving the Forth were altered, placing the 13th Flotilla near the van. Kimbell records a general uneasiness being felt in *K17* at their small blue stern light being undetected if any mechanical failure were to affect speed or steering with the looming bulk of battle cruisers and cruisers following them in the darkness of a night movement.[4]

In precisely such circumstances *K17* was struck early in 1918. Kimbell was in poor health and when the shuddering crash came he was returning from yet another of his frequent visits to the 'box', the latrine reached by a long narrow passage with a heavy water-tight door at either end. He could hear water pouring in somewhere. Both doors he found closed and clipped but with a spanner he banged the after door. It was opened for him. In the engine room compartment the Engineer Officer was calmly discussing with the other ten or so men their escape alternatives when the increasing slope made it seem that an involuntary plunge was imminent. With no further ado, all the air from the compressed air cylinders was released and at a given signal the engine room hatch clips were knocked off, the air forcing the hatch open. Each man in turn climbed up the ladder and was shot out like a cork from a bottle. From the engine room all got out but few survived. Kimbell desperately tried to keep afloat but he was weak from his illness. Till his strength gave out he attempted to support a man obviously in a still poorer condition from injuries sustained in the collison. The signalman soon seemed alone. He was covered in black fuel oil but managed to make renewed efforts to save himself when a huge white bow wave indicated the approach of a large vessel bearing down on him. Barely conscious when a rope thrown for him fell across him, he somehow secured himself and was hauled aboard *K7*. Eight men survived from a complement of fifty-six.

In a dreadful sequence of events, two K boats had altered course to avoid two mine sweeping trawlers suddenly detected moving obliquely across the path of the submarines, then the helm of their flotilla leader, *Ithuriel*, temporarily jammed as she correspondingly altered course. *K22* and *K14* then came into collision after which the battle cruiser *Inflexible* crashed into the damaged *K22*. *Ithuriel*, picking up coded distress signals of what was happening astern of her, turned about to give aid, ordering the undamaged boats of the flotilla to follow her on a track judged sufficiently to the south to avoid the outward passage of the rest of the force.

K7 Alongside HMS *Canada*, with HMS *Monarch* in background. September 1918. (Commander J.B. Mitford)

In fact, the inward course brought the vessels directly into a collision path with the capital ships and the escorting destroyers. Frantic evasive action in the darkness secured escape for all concerned until, by further irony, *K17* was hit by the 12th Flotilla leader, *Fearless*, and in a final disaster *K4* was rammed and sunk with further loss of life.

The subsequent court of inquiry apportioned blame for the series of accidents among officers of the K boats concerned. The larger linked issues of the foolproof quality of the movement orders for the force, the suitability of K boats for the role required of them and then the material factor of the design of the boats seem, in retrospect, to have been subjects as deserving of searching enquiry at the time as the officers were of censure.

HOSPITAL SHIPS AND TROOP TRANSPORTS

Hospital ships used during World War One were of several different types from fully converted liners or merchant ships with adaptations for the conveyance of wounded to ambulance carriers which took troops and stores as well and were without the supposed protection of the provisions of the Geneva Convention. There was even a lower denominator in numerical scale in the hospital barges which operated on canals and rivers behind the Western Front.[5]

Hospital ships proper were painted in white with a green band around the hull as well as the huge red crosses on their sides, fore, aft and amidships. The liners *Aquitania* and *Britannic*, distinguished for their work carrying wounded and sick from the Dardanelles, were so marked. *Aquitania* had over 4000 hospital beds and did two years of service between 1915 and 1917. Some of the staff of the hospital ship *Soudan* were from the Royal Naval hospital at Plymouth. Sick berth steward W.G. Olver was with *Soudan* in the ship's support of operations in the Dardanelles from February 1915. On 25 April, the day of the first landings, 'lighters and boats are constantly coming off with wounded, half of whom are dead before they can be got on board. 26 April. There is now 500 wounded in this ship with more or less serious injuries. There is nothing but groaning everywhere and blood is running about everywhere on the decks. The staff is not big enough to cope with so much work in time although everyone is working day and night, we are the only hospital ship here.' On 14 May, working off Anzac beach: the dead had to be left amongst the others for some time owing to the small number of staff to deal with the rush. Burials from the ship's side were of constant occurrence.' After a fortnight's constant work in waters around the Peninsula taking wounded to Lemnos and Imbros, *Soudan* was despatched to Malta and the staff got five days' rest. On their return to the Peninsula there was heavy work off Cape Helles in June and July and then, in August,

Liners on hospital ship and troopship duty: *Aquitania* and *Mauretania* seen at Mudros 1915. (Captain L.A.K. Boswell)

Gallipoli, May 1915: HMS *London*'s Picket Boat ferrying wounded to HM Hospital ship *Gascon*. (Vice Admiral E. Longley-Cook)

Soudan acted as a base hospital for the renewed offensive. Olver allows himself a reflective comment which is incontestable: 'I think it can be honestly said that no one on this ship has ever been called upon to compete with so much work before.' A few days later, the staff was involved in a different form of rescue work, collecting up survivors from the troopship *Royal Edward*.[6]

F.K. Escritt, a senior medical student in 1915, served as a dresser in the hospital ship *Letitia*, run by the Indian Medical Service. *Letitia*, a Donaldson line ship, had been extensively converted. 'All the partitions which formed the walls of the cabins were hacked down and the result was 2 large wards, one aft and one forard of the engine room and one narrow one either side of the latter. The holds were completely empty to conform to the Geneva Convention except a few crates of medical stores which were opened for inspection and located in the centre of the hold. Unfortunately the ballast was near the keel, consequently we swung about like a pendulum.' At Alexandria, *Letitia* was refitted as a British hospital ship and straightway evacuated 500 severely wounded Australian troops from the Gallipoli Peninsula. 'Mortality rate was pretty high. After a couple of days nearly all the cases

Survivors of the loss of the troopship *Royal Edward* about to be picked up by HM Hospital Ship *Soudan*. Note the upturned lifeboat. (Surgeon Lieutenant C.J. Taylor)

Royal Edward troopship survivors aboard HM Hospital Ship *Soudan*. (Surgeon Lieutenant C.J. Taylor)

became septic and the odour of pus was overpowering . . . We worked day and night – very often in rolling seas with trolleys getting loose and discharging bowls, basins and instruments on the deck. The ship's staff in their off-duty hours were marvellous, especially the Chief Engineer who liked to control the trolleys in the operating theatre . . . It was I think the day after leaving Malta that we encountered fog and at 2 a.m. struck an Italian cargo ship amidships. She sank. In the excitement a young apprentice pulled the cord of the siren too hard and for the next two hours the din was terrible and orders could not be heard.' All cases were brought on deck and the boats swung out but *Letitia* reached Gibraltar where she was sufficiently well repaired to continue to the UK.[7]

Britannic was just one of the hospital ships lost after exploding a mine during the war. The first British hospital ship to be torpedoed was *Asturias*, on 21 March 1917, but two were destroyed in this way in a single day in April. *Asturias* was showing all her lights and her Red Crosses were illuminated when she was torpedoed off Start Point, Devonshire. Thereafter, hospital ship markings on vessels in Home Waters were replaced with a naval conformity to the new camouflage of 'dazzle painting'. Even a gun was provided for defence.

The difficult task of evacuating at night the torpedoed naval hospital ship *Rewa* in January 1918 seems to have been managed efficiently but one patient, carefully lowered into a lifeboat, could not understand why his bandaged feet were soon soaking until someone discovered that a small fountain of sea water was jetting up through the hole left for an unplaced bung![8]

Of course, the crowding of troop transports presented very real problems under emergency conditions. The dreadful toll of lives lost in the *Royal Edward* is a grim witness to this but a many-decked liner taking vast numbers of men was usually well escorted. On two occasions, both in 1915 and in the Mediterranean, soldiers and sailors worked together under conditions of action or the result of action to rescue a ship which seemed lost. Reference has already been

made to the *Southland* incident; the other dramatic encounter with a U-boat concluded with the escape of the troop transport *Mercian*. The attack took place on 3 November 1915, east of Gibraltar. Conflicting accounts exist of conduct aboard the ship but there is unanimity of praise for the Commander, Captain Walker, for maintaining under prolonged shell-fire a zig-zag course which evaded some of the shelling. The official history of naval operations records some panic among the Yeomanry troops when they were ordered on deck in the expectation of a torpedo attack,[9] but an almost contemporary account by the Purser denies such a development and describes the troops taking up their positions in an orderly and quiet manner. 'All credit is due to them for their fine behaviour for shells were coming fast now.'[10] It was, in fact, a soldier who responded to Captain Walker's appeal to take over from him at the wheel; soldiers also assisted in the boiler room so that full speed might be maintained and it was soldiers who manned their own Maxims and were eventually given permission to fire on the U-boat. The Yeomanry officer who recorded these recollections also added: 'Unfortunately some of the ship's crew had taken to the boats.'[11] Was there any panic? Where did it originate? It is difficult to establish precisely what did happen, other than that the ship was saved but fifty-three men lost their lives.

A sad episode which reflected some discredit on those principally responsible occurred with the torpedoing of the troop transport *Cameronia* halfway between Sicily and Greece on Sunday, 15 April 1917. According to the evidence of an army padre and an RAMC doctor, there had been no boat drill nor had any boat station directions been given to the officers to read to the men. There was no demonstration to show how the lifebelts were to be put on and when the torpedo struck 'no one among the Merchant Navy crew appeared to know how to launch the lifeboats. Instead of manning them with three or four sailors and lowering them into the water, some sort of order was given for the troops to get into the boats while they were

5   CERTIFICATE OF DISCHARGE   6
Or Certified Extract   from Eng. I. and O.L.

No.	*Name of ship and official number, Port of registry, and tonnage.†	*Date and place of engagement.	*Rating; and R.N.R. No. (if any.)	Date and place of discharge.	Description of voyage.	Signature of Master.
1	BRITANNIC L'POOL. 18749 24592	6/9/16 Soton	ORD.MDR.	1916	Hospital Ship	Chas A Bartlett
2	LONDON	19 DEC 1916 TILBURY	Trimmer	16 MAR 1917 TILBURY.	CAPE MAIL	John W. Hague
3	WALMER CASTLE LONDON	TILBURY	Trimmer	Aug 7 1917 TILBURY	Cape Mail	John W. Hague
4	S.S. "GRANTULLY CASTLE" 129,058. LONDON. T. 4794. H.P. 656.	18.8.17 Southampton	Fireman & Trimmer	12 FEB 1918 SOUTHAMPTON	HOS. TRANSPORT	J George
5	S.S. "GLENGORM CASTLE" 109,290 SOUTHAMPTON. T. 4,299. N.H.P. 497.	2 FEB 1918 PORTSMOUTH.		31 MAR 1918	HOSPITAL SHIP	D H Hosking
6	OLYM. OFFICIAL No. 131 LIVERPOOL TONNAGE 9950	14 APR 1919 SOUTHAMPTON	FIREMAN	2 MAY 1919 SOUTHAMPTON	H. M. TRANSPORT 2810	

*These columns are to be filled in at time of engagement.   † In Engineers' Books Insert Horse Power.

910283

194

Survivors of the troopship *Leasowe Castle* being picked up the day following her loss by U-boat torpedo in April 1918. (A.L. Downes)

still slung in the davits. The result was disastrous, while the life boats were being slung out over the water one of the ropes broke with the enormous weight it had to bear and the whole boatload was pitched into the sea. Or, if the ropes held, one of the boats would start swaying and would be dashed into the side of the ship which was then listing badly. The boat was smashed and again the men were thrown into the water.'[12]

To have obeyed a printed instruction to take to rafts stationed on the deck, rafts which then seemingly would float off as the ship settled,

Opposite top
'Certificate of Discharge' for Merchant Navy Coal Trimmer Henry Hicks, showing his service aboard the 48,000-ton liner *Britannic* being used as a hospital ship but lost after exploding a mine in the Mediterranean. This is a replacement book as the original was lost in the sinking. Hicks was to serve in two other well-known hospital ships, their names clearly marked. (H. Hicks)

Opposite bottom
HM Hospital Ship *Anglia* sinking, having been mined in the Channel on 17 November 1915. (Rear Admiral A. Poland)

would have meant almost certain drowning as *Cameronia*, bow first, dived almost vertically to her doom. Those who waited to see what would happen were to be proved wise as the destroyer *Rifleman* came alongside and took all still aboard to safety. The sea had been calm, the *Cameronia* did not sink for some time, there had been no panic and yet about 200 lives were lost and many were injured when they were pitched out of boats or jumped onto *Rifleman*'s deck.[13] Proper procedures had not been explained and they could scarcely be followed.

A further example of what seems to have been an extraordinary state of affairs concerns the ordering out of Alexandria harbour of the newly arrived troop-carrying liner *Aragon* with 2,700 persons aboard. Presumably the appropriate berth for her was not vacant. Unprotected, she lay off shore easy prey to a U-boat which sank her on 30 December 1917. A mine claimed a bonus prize for the Germans, the destroyer *Attack* which had raced to pick up survivors. Again the price paid was serious loss of life (610 from *Aragon*). That was also the price for the last large-scale naval exploit of the war, the raid on Zeebrugge and Ostend.

18

The Zeebrugge, Ostend and Tondern Raids

Reflective contemplation of the Dardanelles Gallipoli campaign may lead to an unwelcome conclusion that the sum of human endeavour committed to it was unwisely expended. Between Zeebrugge in 1918 and Gallipoli in 1915 there are clear fundamental differences, not least in scale, but there is a parallel beyond the very obvious one of amphibious operations conducted with outstanding personal courage. The parallel can be stated quite simply: not only did the 1918 raids really achieve nothing in material terms but it can be argued that there was no real reason in April and May 1918 for even launching them.

The battered *Vindictive* returning from Zeebrugge on 23 April 1918. (C.A. Mooring-Aldridge)

The Germans had a U-boat base inland of the Belgian coast at Bruges, this city being at the apex of its divergent links to the sea, a canal to Ostend and a wider one to Zeebrugge, a port which had a dockyard and bomb-proof U-boat shelters. Ideas for blocking Zeebrugge had first been advanced in 1914 and more ambitious schemes had been put forward in late 1916. Shelling from monitors was tried in May 1917 and still more adventurous was a large amphibious operation considered but written out of court by the BEF's own plans for an offensive to the coast combined with a landing operation. Had the latter been successfully developed, there would have been no question of the blocking of ports which would, in their liberation, be used by the allies.[1]

The Flanders U-boat bases enabled the Germans to exert a considerable threat to the Channel, despite every effort by the Dover Patrol to counter it. With effect from 1 January 1918, Vice Admiral Sir Roger Keyes was appointed to command of the Dover Patrol, his energy and personality breathing new life into a rather jaded force. Keyes had no great intellectual gifts himself but he selected his staff wisely and the new leadership instituted a far more vigorous policy of massed patrols and brilliant night-time illumination of the minefields. With the surface thus denied to the submarine, her commander was forced to risk the minefield. The policy bore fruit. By 9 February 1918, four U-boats had been destroyed, whereas only two had been dealt with in these waters from August 1914 until a third was sunk on 19 December by which time more intensive patrolling had already started.

The danger of such mass patrol by small vessels was the invitation it offered to a German surface raid and this is precisely what happened in mid-February when German destroyers sank seven drifters and a trawler, damaging other vessels. British destroyers failed to identify the Germans on sighting them in the darkness of the night. Keyes' fury over the German success may have been a reinforcing element in his determination to strike a signal blow, indeed at the Flanders U-boat bases but also a blow for the naval war effort and not least for his command. Convoy patrolling in strength, flares, searchlights and deep laid mines were winning a battle but to win it more swiftly required and 'justified' a bold enterprise.

Towards the end of February, Keyes produced plans superceding those drawn up on the authority of Sir John Jellicoe as First Sea Lord in the previous year.[2] Blockships were to be sunk in the entrance to the Bruges Ship Canal at Zeebrugge and in the entrance to Ostend harbour, while as much damage as possible was to be done to both ports.

The old cruiser *Vindictive*, assisted by two Mersey ferries, *Iris* and *Daffodil*, would land a storming party of sailors and Royal Marines on the strongly fortified mole or pier at Zeebrugge. Success in destroying the mole's defending batteries of guns would enable the three old cruisers *Thetis*, *Intrepid* and *Iphigenia*, as the blocking ships, to approach their designated station for submersion, while two submarines were to fix themselves into the railway viaduct section of the mole, there to be blown up, breaching its link with the shore. A similar blocking operation, but without a landing force, was planned for Ostend. A dark night, high water, a calm sea and some on-shore wind to assist with a planned smokescreen were essential requirements for success. Twice in April the force assembled and was held back because of unfavourable wind or weather conditions. Keyes persuaded his superior authorities to allow him a third opportunity, despite the nigh certainty of the Germans having been forewarned and the likelihood of a moonlit night on the only date when the tide conditions were suitable. The decision to go was taken in the afternoon of 22 April, the force would leave that night.

The sense of a dramatic venture is caught by the diary of Surgeon Probationer Abercrombie, with the destroyer *Warwick*, which flew the Admiral's flag. 'We went out at the head of about 12 destroyers, two of them towing two old "C" submarines loaded with 5 tons of amatol each, and the rest towing C.M.B.'s there were also about 30 motor launches.' Further from Dover they joined up with '*Vindictive*, also five concrete laden block ships and the two boarding steamers.' Abercrombie noted that *Vindictive* had 'protective mattresses everywhere and carried a great number of men each told off for some special job. There were demolition parties, flame throwers and every mortal form of frightfulness: every man had been carefully chosen and was a volunteer and a magnificent looking lot they were. Seamen from the Grand Fleet and Marines only.'[3]

An unkind wind offshore cleared the protection of a smokescreen from *Vindictive* as she approached the mole. Under heavy fire which resulted in serious casualties, she increased

The Mole at Zeebrugge – After the War! (G.J. White)

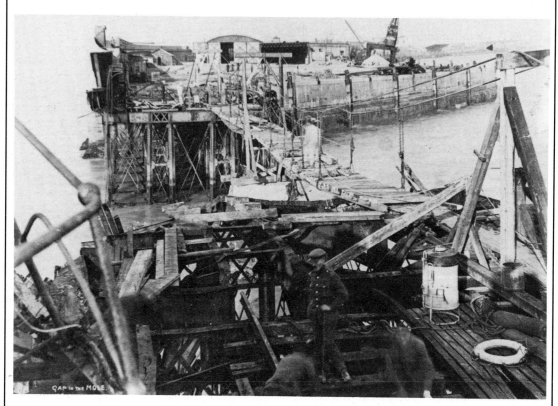

The gap torn in the Zeebrugge Mole by the British submarine explosion was
soon bridged by this temporary structure. (G.J. White)

speed to reach the mole more quickly. In so doing she overshot her assigned point for the disembarkation of her landing party and in this position *Vindictive*'s guns were unable to bear upon the battery defending the mole. 'As a consequence the storming and demolition parties were without support. Pinned down and badly punished by a hail of fire, they were unable to accomplish much.'[4]

Royal Marine Captain A.R. Chater was thrilled by having been selected to take part. He has written that 'towards dusk on the 22nd when the pyrotechnics expert Wing Commander Brock was transferred by whaler to *Vindictive* he had with him a box labelled "Explosives – Handle with great care". This was hoisted on board and handled very gingerly. It was taken down to the Wardroom and found to contain several bottles of excellent vintage port which were consumed with relish.' The spirits of the occasion had also got to one old Marine who may have obtained more than his regulation tot of rum and who shouted at Captain Chater and the Sergeant Major as they made their rounds about the men on the mess decks: 'We are just going over the top. We are all equal now.' Some three hours later Chater caught sight of the same man and remembers thinking: 'What a changed and sober man he looked.'

Chater had been wounded at both Antwerp and on the Gallipoli Peninsula but fortune was to pick him out unscathed from the bursting fragments of a shell which killed the Royal Marine Commanding Officer and the second in command who were standing either side of him. So severe were the casualties that platoon distinction was destroyed. Chater ordered hook ropes to be used for descending to the mole, *Vindictive*'s landing ramps having been destroyed or proving useless. Scaling ladders were taken ashore for the return. Using a rope himself, Chater slid down onto the wall and so to the pier beneath it. To do the demolition work which was their objective, a rush without any cover would have to be made along 200 yards of bare pavement. He and another Royal Marine captain were discussing this daunting prospect for those who had found themselves at one of the sheds on the mole, when a ship's siren blew. It was early for the recall signal and, in any case, the designated morse K signal was not being sounded but Chater returned to the ship and had it confirmed that the recall, after only 45 minutes on the mole, was being ordered. Chater helped to organise the withdrawal: 'units returned steadily to the ship, bringing wounded with them. The enemy were still shelling the sea wall and those who had to cross the mole and climb the ladders had the most hazardous time. Fortunately some of the ladders remained intact until the end. When I could see no more men approaching, I returned on board and reported to that effect. A few moments later the ship left the mole . . . We felt that our part of the operation had been a complete failure. We had lost many good men with what seemed to us no result.'[5]

One of the men lost but not killed was a sergeant of Marines, H. Wright. His account makes clear the strain of waiting to see when *Vindictive*'s approach would be detected. 'Everyone spoke in whispers. There we stood, shoulder to shoulder, rifles in hand ready for the dash forward, not a movement hardly a whisper, and only the noise of the propellers broke the silence.' Sergeant Wright wrote of the 'terrible battery of guns' firing at their ship from less than 100 yards and of a very powerful searchlight from the land illuminating the ship as a target. Of their own guns, 'three crews in succession were wiped out from their post manning the Pom Pom gun in the crow's nest. The *Iris* now came to our assistance and rammed the *Vindictive* into the Mole.' Two gangways were left out of fourteen and 'my officer Lieutenant Stanton having been fatally wounded I had the honour of leading No. 10 platoon onshore.' Of a platoon of forty-five there had been so many casualties that only twelve landed. One gun position was charged but it had been vacated by the Germans. 'Disgusted we now turned our attention to the concrete dugouts and gave them a good bombing. There was a German destroyer lying alongside the Mole on our left, we bombed her also.' Red Very lights were sent up to show that these few men had reached their position and small reinforcements came ashore. 'These brave fellows headed by their officers came through us walking in extended order as cool as if they were on parade and carried their position.' Events now took a grim turn for the Marines with Sergeant Wright: confusion over whether the signal sounded was for recall or not led to their being left behind and motorboats did not come to their assistance. They climbed the wall and there lay feigning death but searching seaward for signs of rescue. None came and they were captured.[6]

Under heavy fire the blockships were duly sunk but none was in its correct position. Of the submarines one was brilliantly handled, its explosion producing a large gap in the viaduct. A letter from the Captain of *Ulleswater*, E.K. Boddam-Whetham, gave an account of the astonishing escape of the crew of the submarine *C3*. Having rammed the viaduct and lit the fuses of the explosive charges the crew got into their motorboat but found its propeller broken. Rowing allowed only worryingly small distance to be made from the submarine but then the Germans opened up 'heavy machine gun fire and Sandford and several of his crew were very badly wounded. Sandford's brother then came along in a picket boat and got them on board and put them into *Phoebe* – a destroyer – just as [German] reinforcements came dashing along the viaduct from the land, the ten tons of T.N.T. [in the submarine] went up and that lot went to where they belong.' Incidentally, it was *Phoebe* which made repeated efforts in the harbour to tow to safety the disabled destroyer *North Star*. She failed but rescued all the crew still alive. '*Thetis* got it absolutely in the neck from the shore batteries and also got entangled in some sort of net boom defence and was sunk before she got right to the canal and I'm afraid all hands were lost.'[7]

Warwick, standing off shore, took aboard from motor launches men evacuated from two of the blockships. Over a third of these men was wounded: 'The first man hauled inboard was dead, two others died almost immediately. For the wounded not very much was possible; their wounds were dressed with septic gauze wrung out in Izal and bandaged: haemorrhage arrested by pressure. Each man was given morphia $\frac{1}{2}$ a grain hypodermically and the worst cases $\frac{3}{4}$ of a grain, blankets to keep them warm. Our iodine was used for small wounds.' While the dressings were being done, 'the Admiral . . . came down and spoke to every soul who had been wounded, cheering them up and assuring them that their work had been the finest thing in history.'[8]

At Ostend, the same untimely wind change exposed the approaching ships and to make matters worse the blockships were not brought in to their correct position. The smoke screen was blown on shore and this, aided by the Germans having moved a key marker buoy, led to the harbour entrance being missed. If gallantry at Zeebrugge were to have achieved little, the thrust at Ostend had achieved nothing. When the Ostend raid was repeated on 10 May, no more fruitful result was obtained. In the attacks on 23 April, 173 men had been killed or died of wounds and thirty-six had been captured. It is quite clear that at Zeebrugge the blockships had not done what was intended; only small and temporary effect had been exerted on the movement of U-boats and even destroyers.

Everyone concerned wanted to believe in a great victory, the Nation, the Press, the Admiralty, Sir Roger Keyes and his command. The depressing events of a renewed German offensive on the Lys that month after the first such blow on the Somme in late March, had left public opinion parched of reason for optimism. Zeebrugge offered this and in this lay its worth. A blow had been struck after all, a blow which damaged the striker's fist rather than injuring his opponent but which uplifted the spirits of a contestant who needed to demonstrate to him-

German opposition at Ostend. (G.J. White)

self above all that he had the will and the capacity to strike back. Jutland, the disappointing victory, had been followed by Zeebrugge, the superb defeat.

OSTEND AND TONDERN, MAY AND JULY 1918

Battle-scarred *Vindictive* was used for blocking in the abortive attempt at Ostend on 10 May and, if this were a completely frustrating failure, there was no lack of sustained endeavour. Amidst all the flashes and lights flickering through the smoke and fog, *Vindictive* was searching for the harbour. 'At one moment under a burst of a star shell, we plainly saw the houses on the sea front, close on our port beam, but we still could not find the harbour entrance.' The ship was being shelled increasingly as *Vindictive* edged along the shore for the harbour entrance. The fire was becoming intense and the officer who wrote of this experience, John Alleyne, was then wounded as was his captain. The ship was abandoned on the order of the unwounded 1st Lieutenant, motor

launches picking up most of the crew but missed Alleyne who, with support from a life jacket, had to struggle back to *Vindictive*. Here he was given unusual shelter by an occupant of the waterlogged end of a ship's boat, the other end hauled upright by rope from its davit. They answered a voice from a searching motorboat, were picked up and so taken clear under heavy fire.[9]

Ostend in May and Tondern in July were unusual exploits and the last British aggressive moves in the North Sea before the Armistice intervened. From the flight deck of the converted battle cruiser *Furious*, seven Sopwith Camels took off on 19 July 1918 for the eighty-mile flight to bomb the German airship sheds at Tondern in Schleswig. The sheds were destroyed as were two Zeppelins within them but only three of the Camels returned to ditch safely near the Fleet for rescue by destroyers. Lieutenant William E. Dickson had been in the team which had practised with 50 lb bombs on a target in the Firth of Forth. He was in the first flight which chose the larger of the two sheds where the two Zeppelins lay. With the bombing

A final resting place for *Vindictive*: Ostend, but not quite in the right spot! (G.J. White)

```
    C in C        to        General        6.12.17.


On the arrival of the U.S.Squadron tomorrow Friday ships's

company are to be massed in the most convenient part of the upper

deck and ships are to cheer independently giving three cheers as

each U.S.Ship passes to take up her berth.   Bands are to be paraded

and play the "Star Spangled Banner". No Guards .  After arrival

the Rear Admiral in Command of U.S.Squadron will call on C in C

who will then return the call.  A further signal will be made as

to Official Call.     The existing procedure for piping the side

for British Officers is to be employed for U.S.Officers as opposed

to the Procedure for Foreign Officers.   On and after Saturday

Dec.8th when colours are Hoisted the following National Anthems are

to be played.

            BRITISH.
            UNITED STATES.(Star Spangled Banner)
            One other Allied Nation.
```

A welcome to the Americans. (Captain L.A.K. Boswell)

Jazz reaches Britain: a US Navy Band aboard the light cruiser HMS *Caroline*. (F.A. Foxon)

them in avoiding internment. Thinking of the Wardroom and then of home, he risked a westerly flight, spotted the white wake of the destroyers, picked the leading one, HMS *Violent*, followed the normal procedure by landing ahead of her and was soon hauled aboard. Dickson and Captain Smart, the earliest of the returning pilots, had the honour of being presented to the King the following day, as he had come north to inspect the fleet at Rosyth. The immediate award of the DSO to Dickson and a bar to his DSO for Smart may have few rivals in the speed with which reward followed the deed. (They were in fact gazetted on 21 September 1918.)[10]

work done, Dickson judged that his petrol gauge reading allowed him a fair chance of return rather than to follow alternate instructions to land in neutral Denmark and make for certain addresses from which help would assist

The drama of these three raids should not obscure the significance of other developments, such as the transfer south of the main Grand Fleet base from Scapa to Rosyth, or the successful cooperation in human and material terms of the American and British navies in the last year of the war from Scapa Flow and Rosyth following upon the good example set by the respective Admirals and their men in the previous year, but the war for those at sea as well as for those on the Home Front and those serving on foreign fields was dragging.

19

The End of a Long Haul

INFLUENZA

For all the personal magnetism which Beatty exerted over the Grand Fleet, retaining to the full those qualities which A.J. Marder regarded as among the determinants of the sea war, 'esprit de corps and strong sense of professional pride',[1] war weariness was there. It was beginning to seem a war without an end rather than a war to end war until the conjunction of the Turkish Armistice and the news of the mutiny in the High Seas Fleet. Indeed there was more than just weariness as the influenza pandemic which was to scourge the world was seriously affecting the fighting efficiency of the navy in the weeks before the Armistice. Plymouth and Devonport, for example, were hit desperately hard; the rows of tombstones of boys from the training establishment there stand today as sad witness that the young and fit were not spared in their vigour. All naval work suffered: if engine room staff were reduced, a destroyer simply could not put to sea, one was so badly affected when at sea that another destroyer had to be sent to bring her back to harbour. Some officers found that the sickness of their fellows meant working a constant four hours on, four hours off rota. On convoy escort duty, the criterion was: 'If you had enough men on their feet, you went to sea even if you could not properly fight the ship – only drop depth charges.'[2]

It is curious that the best accounts of the war at sea make little or no mention of the disturbingly weakened condition of the fleet at this time. In official circles there was a shrewdly-based awareness that the very approach of the end of the war would lead to the High Seas Fleet command bringing its units out for a last desperate throw, something which was in fact only prevented by the mutiny of the German sailors. The influenza-wracked Grand Fleet was not to be tested, instead there was to come within the personal experience of the officers and men of the Royal Navy the evidence of their awe-inspiring victory in a sight which stretched the nerves but strangely numbed the spirit – the processional surrender for internment in British waters of the overwhelming proportion of the seaworthy strength of the High Seas Fleet.

THE ARMISTICE WITH TURKEY

First there was the Mediterranean surrender of the Turks. After complex diplomacy, it fell to the British Commander in Chief in the Mediterranean, Vice Admiral Sir Somerset Gough Calthorpe, to negotiate with the Turks. On 30 October 1918, by the happy accident of fate, the Armistice was signed on board *Agamemnon* of Dardanelles renown and, furthermore, *Agamemnon* lay in Mudros Bay, the great harbour for the Gallipoli enterprise.

As Captain's Coxswain, W.T. Henson had the responsibility of arranging the Captain's quarters for the Armistice meetings and for looking after two Turkish sailors attendant upon their negotiators. It was during dinner that news came through from London for the document to be signed. 'They all got up from the dining table shaking hands. Drinks were served. I cleared the small round table in the after cabin as they wanted to sign on that. The Turks were very emotional. I heard Rauf Pasha say that they should never have gone to war with us as we had always been great allies. He came over to me and gave me a Turkish Treasury note as a souvenir.'[3]

A sailor's view of things ashore: from an autograph album. (F.A. Foxon)

MORALE AT THE END OF THE WAR

Within days of the Turks falling out of their alliance with the Central Powers, the Austro-Hungarian Empire and then Germany were forced to sue for an armistice. It is not unreasonable to see in the severity of the naval armistice conditions which the British insisted in imposing upon Germany a demand for a sort of Roman triumph sufficiently compensatory for the absence of the testing ground of battle.

It has also been suggested that one of the reasons why naval authorities stomached so readily disappointment over the way the war ended, bringing the more obvious credit to the army in France, was the serious decline in lower deck discipline. Pay and other service condition grievances were having some influence upon morale. There is in the letters of sailors as well

as soldiers ample evidence of resentment felt towards the workers at home bettering their conditions by industrial action. A number would also be influenced by events in Russia which heralded a new order, lent enchantment by its distance and worthiness of emulation for a British sailor with a sense of social grievance.

In any case, there are those with a grumble in every walk of life and such an obvious statement can at least be garnished with an appropriate seasoning of 'universality'. If there were not to have been bellyaching about food, pay and authority, envy of those under circumstances perceived to be better, then that would have been quite phenomenal whether in an eighteenth century Man of War, a cruiser in 1917 or a frigate today.

During active service before such grousing descended into real malcontent affecting the performance of duties, there would first be resistance from those whose work increased by having to shoulder the burden of the shirker, then petty officers and then officers would become involved in the exercise of naval discipline. A ship in fact could most ruinously be made unhappy from causes in the Commander's cabin or in the Wardroom. Inefficiency or bad management at the top could cause genuine grievance or aggravate discontent at the bottom; efficiency and good relations established from the top could never eradicate all grumbling. Human nature, especially under close crowding and the performance of monotonous duty, would not be denied its natural expression.

As the end of the war and demobilisation problems presented further causes of discontent it is not easy to generalise soundly on the degree of seriousness of the trouble on the lower deck before Armistice released the taut stringing of active service conditions.

It is also difficult to assess the extent to which the broadsheet *The Fleet*, published to express the views of the lower deck, was itself representative, despite its editors being authorised by the men to submit a 'Petition on their behalf'. Early in September, the editor, Lionel Yexley,[4] produced a pamphlet setting out sixteen causes of discontent and sent copies to all persons of influence from the King and Prime Minister downwards. As Captain Roskill makes clear in his biography of Earl Beatty: 'The outcome was that substantial concessions were made; but it was not until after the war had ended that the whole problem of officers' and men's pay and allowances was tackled systematically.[5]

At Sunderland, I have searched exhaustively in the papers and recollections of ratings and officers for evidence of widespread discontent before November 1918; many men have been questioned and re-questioned and, while the absence of grist to this particular mill can scarcely be taken as a conclusive denial that there was any serious disaffection, I simply cannot put forward a case that there was. That the end of the war came none too quickly for the wartime volunteer sailor is as fundamentally true as it is to note the apprehension of the young career naval officer as he viewed his future in a navy likely to face drastic reduction. Sadly, the rejoicings of the former would soon be stilled by the reality of post war Britain while the apprehensions of the latter would be as cruelly fulfilled in the sharp edge of the Geddes axe and its clinical truncation of officer personnel.[6] Of course, war and peace interact and in our period certainly cannot be examined in isolation but it is worth emphasising that the disillusion of 1914–18 servicemen so commonly referred to was in the main a disillusionment with the conditions under which they attempted to resume a civilian way of life.

NOVEMBER 1918: THE SURRENDER OF THE HIGH SEAS FLEET

As for the ceremonial surrender of the High Seas Fleet, it was anticipated almost disbelievingly. How could such hugely powerful forces, locked in real, however distant combat, finally meet in the open sea with one totally submitting to the other? Could there be such abject surrender or would some incident, if not planned

Hostilities over? 23.40 Hours, 11 November 1918. (Dr A.B. Emden)

design, lead to a shattering resumption of hostilities?

The naval conditions imposed by the Armistice signed on 11 November included the handing over to the allies of all submarines and the disarming for internment of six battle cruisers, ten battleships, eight light cruisers, including two mine layers, and fifty destroyers of the most modern type. The way in which this was to be done was negotiated on 15 November between Sir David Beatty and Hipper's representative, Admiral Meurer, who arrived off the Firth of Forth aboard the light cruiser *Königsberg*. The day of humiliation was fixed for 21 November.

The three stages were remembered by Lieutenant Galbraith of *Queen Elizabeth*, Beatty's flagship. When the Armistice was announced to the full ship's company on 11 November, 'everyone was relieved and thankful that the war had come to an end but the news

Sir David Beatty, Commander in Chief Grand Fleet, prepares to receive Admiral Meurer to arrange for internment of German ships, a signal taken in by HMS *Parker*. (Dr A.B. Emden)

Operation Orders for escorting the High Seas Fleet to internment in November 1918. (Admiral Sir T.H. Binney)

was quietly received, there was no excitement. I think many of us were wondering what our future was to be.' Of 15 November: 'To receive the Germans a cordon of Marines was placed from the gangway close in to the two after turrets X and Y and round them so that the Germans had to pass them on the way to the hatch leading to the flat outside the Commander in Chief's quarters. As the German Admiral stepped onto the Quarter Deck he looked very cast down and nervous, he held out his hand to Commodore Brand who had his hands clasped behind his back and whose only acknowledgement was to say to the German – 'I am instructed to take you to the Commander in Chief' and then turning on his heel, led the way. The German Admiral glanced once or twice at the cordon of Marines, appearing uncertain whether they were a Guard of Honour or something more sinister and gave a half hearted

attempt at a salute – one could not help feeling sorry for him.'

At the actual surrender on the 21st, Galbraith was on the upper or navigating bridge of *Queen Elizabeth*, just above Beatty on the Admiral's bridge. From the compass platform giving him a clear view of those immediately below as well as of the German ships, Galbraith thought Beatty looked shaken by the enemy's near presence in peaceful submission. As in all the British ships, 'action stations' meant that the turrets were cast loose ready to train in any direction, shells were in the loading tray and cartridges in the hoists so that 15 seconds would see the guns ready to fire. Galbraith recorded Beatty speaking to Captain Chatfield: 'If we had met them in October how long do you think they would have lasted?' After a pause Chatfield responded: 'I would give them about 20 minutes Sir.'[7]

In an impressively conducted manoeuvre, the German ships were met, seemingly inspected as they were closely passed on either side by a column of British ships which then turned about to escort the safely penned High Seas Fleet into the Firth of Forth. Lieutenant J.G.D. Ouvry, (*Inconstant*) wrote in his diary that at 8.30 a.m. '"Action" was sounded for the last time. We all closed up seriously to our stations rigged in full war kit – gas masks – anti flash helmets – goggles – shrapnel helmets. Guns were not actually loaded, but all ammunition was up and ready. Guns were trained fore and aft but Directors were kept laid on and ranges etc. passed all ready for opening fire. The excitement was of course intense as it was impossible to tell whether the Hun had something up his sleeve for us or not. It seemed too wonderful for an extremely powerful fleet to give themselves up without a blow.'[8]

There were still individual inspection duties to perform; one such visit did not go with its planned precision. From *New Zealand*, a picket boat took a party of senior officers to one of the German battle cruisers. 'The Germans had manned ship all round their guard rails and the Captain was in tears on the Quarter Deck where also were Commissars or ratings acting as such. The ship was lying across wind and tide and at the last moment approaching the starboard gangway the long swell caught the picket boat, the Cox did not do the right thing and the bows shot under the two ton ladder and left it hanging

Cameras recording the German battle cruiser *Derfflinger* on 21 November 1918. (Captain L.A.K. Boswell)

vertically down the ship's side. The Germans were obviously amused and took 20 minutes to make the gangway useable when our band of Commanders went on board and I took the picket boat to lie off about 200 yards abeam.' Worse was to follow. The officer remained at attention in the picket boat for quite a while before the stoker petty officer reported that if he couldn't be allowed to empty the ashes overboard he and his lads would have to come on deck as there was no space left in the boiler room. Very reluctant permission was given for the lad, a young stoker, to come up, but he was to look as smart as possible. He was of course by this time very dirty and hot. Up he came with the huge bucket. 'He was a large moon-faced chap keen to do his best and threw the ashes but alas his brass-soled boots slipped and the ashes were swiftly followed by the stoker and his bucket into the water.' The stoker and even his bucket were rescued but the intended dignity of the formal inspection could scarcely be salvaged.[9]

Two days earlier, the first U-boats had been escorted into Harwich for inspection and internment at Parkestone, the crews departing homewards in a German transport. The U-boats, flying the British White Ensign, were to remain there but the surface vessels in the Firth of Forth, forbidden to fly their German ensign, were to be escorted to Scapa Flow for a fate, the scuttling of 21 June 1919, which was viewed by some as treachery, by others as fittingly ignominious and by some across the North Sea as a sort of victory in defeat. The peril from U-boats and the threat posed by the High Seas Fleet for twenty years had gone. The Treaty of Versailles attempted vainly to circumscribe its re-emergence.

The crushing nature of a victory which actually secured the surrender of virtually the full capacity of the enemy to wage the war at sea had been earned by a total of just under 600,000 ratings and just over 55,000 officers. They had been supported, of course, by the Merchant Navy and the shipyards and had been a principal element in a total victory by the armed

The enemy still! (Admiral Sir T.H. Binney)

services, the British industrial and social war effort and the efforts of their allies. British naval tradition had been enhanced, its foundation in the outstandingly successful working relationship and interdependence of officers and men had been proved not just in action but in what amounted to a battle lasting four and a half years. There is no need to search for a Trafalgar appearing anachronistically out of her period: the whole war was the decisive battle and it had been won. Sadly, the achievement encapsulated by the grey silhouettes proceeding into the Firth of Forth on 21 November 1918 was to be transient. A generation later, the British sailor was to be tried and tested again. Mercifully, he was not to be found wanting.

End Notes

Preface and Acknowledgements
1. Capt J.W. Farquhar: Letter to author, 2 February 1984.

Introduction
1. A.J. Marder: *From Dreadnought to Scapa Flow*, Vol. V, 298–9.

Chapter 1
1. A.J. Marder: *From Dreadnought to Scapa Flow*, Vol. V, 331.
2. Rear Admiral R.M.Dick: Papers. P.H.L. Archives.
3. Drawn from Vice Admiral Sir Charles Hughes Hallett's 1976 response to A.J. Marder's enquiry to him on the education provided at Dartmouth. A copy is held in P.H. Liddle's archives and in it Hughes Hallet goes on to pay a balancing tribute to the flexibility of mind and the capacity which were also encouraged by naval service in that wide ranging and unconventional responsibilities like landing party leadership and other shore-based duties not infrequently fell to the naval officer. In a final point, he stressed the competitive spirit with which all individual and team games activities were pursued. From coaling ship to gun drill this was of course a dominant feature in every sphere of life in the Senior Service for which the cadet was being trained.
4. Hayward: *HMS Tiger at Bay*, 24.
5. W.H. Campbell, manuscript recall; F.W.H. Miller, typescript and taperecorded recall; F.G. Holvey, manuscript recall, and L.V. Bedford, manuscript recall. P.H.L.
6. In the case of boy artificers, as with all rates, there was the opportunity through the 'Mate Scheme' of rising to commissioned rank and some even attained Flag Rank.
7. Published by Simpkins and Marshall. London, 1940.
8. General Sir H.E. Blumberg in *Britain's Sea Soldiers* provides the information that in battleships and battle cruisers with more than four 12-inch or 9.2-inch guns, the Marine complement was 50 per cent Royal Marine Artillery and 50 per cent Royal Marine Light Infantry. Blumberg makes two further related points of interest: first, the contribution of Marines to wireless and staff work and, secondly, the importance of the varied work undertaken by re-called Marine Pensioners, e.g. as army instructors and NCOs, RND officers, petty officers and ratings, RN commissioned officers, as well as the more obvious clerical staff.
9. Opus cit. Vol. 1, 433.
10. Air Vice Marshal Sir Geoffrey Bromet: Diary for August 1914, P.H.L. Archives.
11. Cdr. A.G.D. Bagot: Midshipman's log. P.H.L. Archives.
12. Rear Admiral K.M. Lawder: 1914 Journal. P.H.L. Archives.
13. Vice Admiral Sir Charles Hughes Hallett: Recollections. P.H.L. Archives.
14. Capt. A.W. Clarke: 1914 Diary. P.H.L. Archives.
15. Pre-Dreadnought battleship.
16. Inspection Parade.
17. A rate of change and deflection instrument, i.e. the amount of 'aim off'.
18. Paint was, of course, a fire hazard.
19. Battle cruisers: *Indomitable, Indefatigable*.
20. In my book, *Men of Gallipoli* (Allen Lane, 1976), pages 25–6, there is the fine account by W.G. Cave, rangetaker in *Dublin*. He graphically recalls the final attempt to launch a surprise destroyer torpedo attack on *Goeben*. *Dublin* and her two attached destroyers were in too much danger once they were spotted to press the attack.

Chapter 2
1. R. Godsell: Letter of 28 August 1914. P.H.L. Archives.
2. Cdr A. G. D. Bagot: Log. P.H.L. Archives.
3. Vice Admiral Sir Lennon Goldsmith: Letter of 6 September 1914. P.H.L. Archives.
4. The author is indebted to Vice Admiral Sir Charles Hughes Hallett for this outline of action stations in a 'K' Class destroyer.
5. An unusual book in some ways, but nevertheless one that is very informative on what had been done to prepare anti-U-boat defences and what was completed by June 1915 to make Scapa Flow safer was written by the naval officer who had a principal responsibility for the work concerned, Captain D.J. Munro: *Scapa Flow, A Naval Retrospect* (Sampson, Marston and Co. London, undated). In a visual sense, *Scapa Flow and a Camera*, by C.W. Burrows (George Newnes, London, 1921) is particularly evocative of the 'Scapa Scene', 1914–19.
6. Lord Strathclyde: Naval Recollections as Lt Galbraith. P.H.L. Archives.
7. Photographs taken from *Olympic* and published in American papers affected the Admiralty's attempt to delay for an appreciable time the release of information of the loss of *Audacious*.

Chapter 3

1. Major General T. Jameson: Recollections. P.H.L. Archives.
2. Major General A.R. Chater: Recollections. P.H.L. Archives.
3. M.A.M. Dillon: Recollections. P.H.L. Archives.
4. Wing Cdr J. Bentham: Recollections. P.H.L. Archives.
5. J.D. Ewings in Lord Sorenson's papers: Letter of 10 February 1915. P.H.L. Archives.
6. A total of 738 lives were lost, twelve men escaping on 26 November 1914, the December Court of Enquiry lending no credence to widespread rumours of sabotage.

Chapter 4

1. A.J. Marder: *From the Dreadnought to Scapa Flow*: Vol. II, 111.
2. L. Hirst: *Coronel and After*, 107–8. Peter Davies. London, 1934.
3. E.W. Bullock: Recollections. P.H.L. Archives.
4. Rear Admiral R.M. Dick: Letter of 10 December 1914. P.H.L. Archives.
5. A.J. Marder: *From the Dreadnought to Scapa Flow*, Vol. II, 123. A sad footnote on the battle is contained in the diary of Able Seaman S. Holvey (HMS *Cornwall*): 'We had our Leading Seaman dipped to Able Seaman lossing [sic] his good conduct medal and three badges for being drunk on the day of action.'
6. Cdr C.F. Laborde (Clerk: HMS *Inflexible*): Letter of 13 December 1914. P.H.L. Archives.

Chapter 5

1. Chief Petty Officer W.G. Cave: Recollections. P.H.L. Archives.
2. Lt Cdr H.K.L. Shaw: Letter of 3 November 1914. P.H.L. Archives.
3. Dr T.G.N. Haldane: Letter of 25 December 1914. P.H.L. Archives.
4. Lt Cdr S.W. Brookes: Diary as a Signaller, 18 December 1914. P.H.L. Archives.

Chapter 6

1. Nor was *Tiger*'s shooting accurate at this stage of the action.
2. The signal for the alteration in course was still being shown from the reduced halyards. *Blucher* was on this course and was clearly the 'rear of the enemy' as indicated by the second signal: 'ATTACK THE REAR OF THE ENEMY'.
3. This report was found later in 1915 in the German Consul's Office, Cameroons, on its capture by the British. P.H.L. Archives.
4. Vice Admiral B.B. Schofield: Letter of 29 January 1915. P.H.L. Archives.
5. *Ref. Cit.*
6. Vice Admiral Sir Lennon Goldsmith: Letter of late January 1915. P.H.L. Archives.

Chapter 7

1. I have written at some length on these themes in *Men of Gallipoli* (Allen Lane, London, 1976). There might have been certain definite military and political advantages accruing from the appearance of a sizeable British force off Constantinople. The Turks might have sued for peace, an hypothesis involving the further question of whether a form of naval bombardment would have been necessary to secure such a request for terms. Turkish surrender would have been of immediate advantage in Egypt and Mesopotamia and would have allayed fears over the security of India. It would in all probability have had beneficial political consequences in the Balkans though one must always bear in mind the conflicting ambitions of those whom it would be ideal to bring in to the allied side in that area. In what I judge to be the really vital area of the war, the Western Front, where the main German military commitment was to be faced, I do not see the increased human and material resources thus available to allied operations making any real difference. It would be difficult to offer a convincing argument that increased resources for the allies in France and Flanders in 1915 would have led to any more swift breaching of the opposing defensive positions. In other words, I believe that success against the Turk would have meant certain significant but limited gains. The very idea of a shortening of the whole war by as much as a year or two years, I regard as something to view with derision, softened or exacerbated, according to one's standpoint, by an awareness of the human cost consequent upon the launching of such an endeavour. How might such gains, the real and the imaginary, have been achieved? It has been argued that success lay within reach of the navy without major military involvement. It is Professor Marder's contention that a failure to resume bombardment and mine clearance at the end of the second week in April, using the 'Beagle' Class destroyers, now fitted with mine sweeping gear, was a sadly wasted opportunity. It is his judgement that, even after the disaster of 18 March 1915 when a close bombardment of forts defending the vital minefield had resulted in the loss of, or serious damage to five allied battleships, the stakes were sufficiently high, the odds sufficiently favourable, to make further determined effort worthwhile. I have a feeling that Marder has lent his considerable academic weight to a myth

which will be as difficult to expunge as some of those which John Terraine has boldly assailed.

2. PRO Cab 22/1 3623. 8 January 1915.

3. Lt Cdr N. Holbrook VC. Recollections. P.H.L. Archives.

4. Petty Officer Stephens: 1915 Diary. P.H.L. Archives.

5. Vice Admiral Sir Peveril William Powlett: Midshipman's Journal. P.H.L. Archives.

6. Air Vice Marshal Sir Geoffrey Bromet: Diary. P.H.L. Archives.

7. Vice Admiral Sir Charles Hughes Hallett. Letter of 2 March 1915. P.H.L. Archives.

8. P.H. Liddle: *Men of Gallipoli*, 42–4. Allen Lane, London, 1976.

9. There had been criticism too of the volunteer crews of fishermen but the task they faced was unenviable.

10. Diary error: *Bouvet* had struck a mine.

11. In fact, by a mine.

12. Cdr H. Banks: Original diaries and typescript of the diaries. P.H.L. Archives.

13. *The Tatler* and *The Sphere*, with dubious artistic impressions of the day, are singled out for scorn.

14. Cdr Fox-Pitt: Letters. P.H.L.Archives.

15. Cdr R.J. Hayward: Recollections. P.H.L. Archives.

16. E. Grayken: Recollections. P.H.L. Archives.

17. E.M. Peacock: Recollections. P.H.L. Archives.

18. 16 April. See *Men of Gallipoli opus* at 90–2.

19. Cdr D.S.E. Thompson: Diary. P.H.L. Archives.

20. Rev. O. Creighton: *With the 29th Division in Gallipoli*, 40. Longman Green, London, 1916.

21. A more senior officer on the left of the line of tows approaching the shore made independent efforts to correct the track of his tow.

22. The weight of equipment was approximately 88 lbs according to the *Official History of Military Operations, Gallipoli*, Vol. I, 172.

23. Cdr C. Drage: Typescript Diary. P.H.L. Archives.

24. The father of another of these First Term Dartmouth cadets who had become Cadet Midshipman, Aubrey Mansergh, had been so annoyed at still having to contribute to his son's Dartmouth fees that he had written to the First Lord of the Admiralty about it. Churchill promised to look into this injustice but was happy to inform the father that his son had been awarded the Distinguished Service Cross for his work at the Dardanelles. (*viz* Admiral Sir Aubrey Mansergh: Recollections. P.H.L. Archives).

25. *Bless our Ship: opus cit.* Chapter IV.

26. Corporal J. Sinclair 10th Bn: Letter of 4 May 1915. Source: South Australia State Library.

27. Vice Admiral E. Longley Cook: Recollections. P.H.L. Archives.

28. Tows from HMS *Implacable* assisted too, though *Implacable*'s fine work was principally at 'X' beach.

29. Capt. H. Wilson: Letter of 4 May 1915. P.H.L. Archives.

30. Captain H. Wilson: log 25 April 1915. P.H.L. Archives.

31. The matter was settled by the mortal wound suffered by the Scot.

32. D.S.E. Thompson: Diary 25–6 April 1915. P.H.L. Archives.

33. Cdr R.V.H. Westall: accounts in Royal Marines Museum, Eastney and P.H.L. Archives.

34. P.H. Liddle: *Men of Gallipoli*, 164.

35. Cdr C.H. Longden Griffiths: 1915 Diary. P.H.L. Archives.

36. J. Falconer: Diary August 1915. P.H.L. Archives.

37–8. Cdr C.H. Longden Griffiths: Diary, 19 December 1915. P.H.L. Archives.

39. G.E. Keeler: Diary. P.H.L. Archives.

40. Air Vice Marshal T Traill: Recollections. P.H.L. Archives.

Chapter 8

1. Cdr C.H. Heath Caldwell: Diary. P.H.L. Archives.

2. Arabistan as well as Baghdad offered possibilities. There were also successful offensive operations on the Euphrates, resulting in the occupation of Nasiriya.

3. C. Cato: *The Navy in Mesopotamia*, 38. Constable, 1917.

4. Capt. P.L. Gunn: Recollections. P.H.L. Archives.

Chapter 9

1. Capt. T. Phillips (MN): Recollections. P.H.L. Archives.

2. Vice Admiral Sir Charles Hughes-Hallett: Recollections. P.H.L. Archives.

3. Cdr R.A.C. Michell: Diary. P.H.L. Archives.

4. Dr J. Shaw: Diary. P.H.L. Archives.

5. M. Nasmith's *E11* had had engine trouble delay and had found the Kattegat too well patrolled to venture it. Max Horton commanded *E9* and Laurence *E1* of which Blacklock was second in command.

6. Capt. R.W. Blacklock: Memoirs. P.H.L. Archives.

7. Rear Admiral A. Poland: Recollections. P.H.L. Archives.

8. J.G. Cox: Recollections. P.H.L. Archives.

9. H.W. Keeler: Recollections. P.H.L. Archives.

10. See later: 1917–18 Q-Ship Operations. A.L. Jones.
11. Air Vice Marshal P.E. Maitland: Log. P.H.L. Archives.
12. H. Hereward: Recollections. P.H.L. Archives.
13. C.C. Crouch: Recollections. P.H.L. Archives.
14. *U-68* by Q ship *Farnborough* off the coast of Kerry.
15. Dr W.W. King Brown: Recollections. P.H.L. Archives. King Brown was in fact repatriated after only two months captivity in Heidelburg. He believes that this decision was a fortunate error caused by his being held as the sole Briton with a large number of French Red Cross personnel released in view of their having been in captivity since the early days of the war.
16. Also known as the high speed anti-submarine sweep.
17. There was poor inter-allied Naval cooperation in the Adriatic and Mediterranean. See A.J. Marder: *From The Dreadnought to Scapa Flow*, Vol. II, 329 *et seq.*
18. It was, of course, not paralleled numerically by the Turkish butchery of their Armenian subjects.
19. Vol. III, 131 *et seq.*
20. Cdr C.G. Steele: Recollections. P.H.L. Archives.
21. *Men of Gallipoli*, 213–15.
22. In 1915, 855,000 tons of British merchant shipping was lost, 748,000 by U-boats, 77,000 by mines and 29,000 by cruisers and other surface craft. A.J. Marder: *From the Dreadnought to Scapa Flow*, Vol. II, 346.
23. W.E.N.H. Westall: Recollections. Royal Marines Museum. Captain M. Farquhar has written to the author pointing out that vessels were ordered out of Malta to search for the 'submarine' and as a result, three more vessels fell victim to the mines.
24. A.G. Newman: Recollections. P.H.L. Archives.

Chapter 10

1. A.J. Marder: *From the Dreadnought to Scapa Flow*, Vol. II, 436.
2. This German raid was not, however, designed to catch Beatty's Rosyth based battle cruisers unsupported by battleships of the Grand Fleet.
3. Capt. J. Crawford: Recollections. P.H.L. Archives.
4. Capt. J.D. Walters: Recollections. P.H.L. Archives.
5. Anonymous: Letter. P.H.L. Archives.
6. Capt. R. Poland: Letter of 9 June 1916. P.H.L. Archives.
7. W.G. Cave: Recollections. P.H.L. Archives.
8. Capt. R. Poland (RM): Letter of 9 June 1916. P.H.L. Archives via Rear Admiral A. Poland.
9. Surgeon Rear Admiral T.N. D'arcy: Recollections. P.H.L. Archives.
10. F. Bowman: Diary. P.H.L. Archives.
11. Capt. E.S. Brand: Recollections. P.H.L. Archives.
12. Rear Admiral R.M. Dick: Account written in June 1916. P.H.L. Archives.
13. Rear Admiral K.M. Lawder: Contemporary Official Report. P.H.L. Archives.
14. Sub-Lt D. Wainwright: Typescript of contemporary account. P.H.L. Archives.
15. Official History, Vol. III, 352.
16. He was to be singled out for the award of a posthumous VC.
17. Vol. III, 334; and also in John Winton's *The Victoria Cross at Sea*, 121 *et seq.*
18. Cdr C.G. Vyner (then named Compton): Recollections. P.H.L. Archives.
19. Capt. R. Poland (RM): Letter to his brother. P.H.L. Archives.
20. J.C. Jones (RML): Contemporary account. P.H.L. Archives.
21. Capt. R. Poland (RM): Letter to his brother. P.H.L. Archives.
22. Dr G.H. Bickmore: Typescript Recollections. P.H.L. Archives.
23. Midshipman (later Captain) A.W. Clarke: Diary, Royal Oak, 'Dreadnought' battleship.
24. Capt. J.W. Farquhar (Midshipman: HMS *Benbow*): Letter of 2 June 1916. P.H.L. Archives.
25. Commodore C.E. le Mesurier: Letter. P.H.L. Archives.
26. Cdr W.J.A. Willis: Recollections. P.H.L. Archives.
27. Vice Admiral Sir Lennon Goldsmith, then Cdr Goldsmith (*Lydiard*): Letter of 3 June 1916. P.H.L. Archives.
28. F. Foxon (Electrical Artificer 1st Class): Diary. P.H.L. Archives.
29. Capt. J.W. Farquhar: Letter of 2 June 1916 to his father, Admiral Sir Arthur Farquhar. P.H.L. Archives.
30. Admiral Sir Harold Burrough: Letter of 7 June 1916. P.H.L. Archives.
31. Commodore C.E. le Mesurier: Letter. P.H.L. Archives.
32. Cdr T.S. Fox Pitt (*Inflexible*): Letters of 2–5 June 1916. P.H.L. Archives.
33. F. Bowman: Diary. P.H.L. Archives.
34. Richard Hough, in his book *The Great War at Sea 1914–18* (OUP, 1983) Chapter 15, 'Jutland: A Retrospection', makes thought-provoking observations on many aspects of the battle. Some of

his judgements may appear partial and subjective (for example, on Grand Fleet Battle Orders and the performance of the High Command) but he is interesting on the contrasting qualities of the British and German ships, on the 'flash' problem, on the effectiveness of British shells, on the potential significance of the absence of the carrier *Campania* from Jellicoe's force and on the generally poor performance of British signalling and communications.

35. While the official History classified *Nottingham* and *Falmouth* as light cruisers, F.J. Dittmar and J.J. College in *British Warships 1914–19* classify them as second-class cruisers.

36. Rear Admiral S.A. Pears: Contemporary Letter. P.H.L. Archives.

37. Dr G.H. Bickmore: Typescript Recollections. P.H.L. Archives.

Chapter 11

1. F.W.H. Miller: Letters. P.H.L. Archives.
2. Dr A.B. Emden: Papers. P.H.L. Archives.
3. C.C. Twiss: Recollections. P.H.L. Archives. 'Housey Housey' was the slang name for the game of House known, of course, as Bingo today.
4. A.W. Thomas: Letters. P.H.L. Archives.
5. A.L. Jones: Recollections. P.H.L. Archives.
6. These rates are for 'continuous' not 'wartime' service for which the rate was slightly lower – in the case of the CPO, the rate was considerably lower, 2/6 per day.
7. If a man were habitually a nuisance to the extent that he was a liability rather than an asset to the Service, he could be discharged on the authority of the Commander in Chief as 'services no longer required'.
8. A.W. Clarke (based at Sheerness): Diary of 11 March 1917. P.H.L. Archives.
9. W.R. Crick: Recollections. P.H.L. Archives.
10. For an extended account of the work of Naval Chaplains in the Great War see Gordon Taylor, *The Sea Chaplains*, Chapter Nine (OUP, 1978).
11. Assistant Clerk Bickmore playing the short, blind seventh hole teed-off before the pair ahead had rung the bell to indicate that the green was clear. The red face of Sir Doveton-Sturdee, victor of the Falklands, appeared over a bank, not to remonstrate with him but to congratulate the young officer for his hole in one. The course was teetotal so Bickmore's success was not costly.
12. W.R. Crick: Recollections. P.H.L. Archives.
13. A porthole which could be opened for ventilation.
14. Capt. H. Dalrymple Smith: Recollections. P.H.L. Archives.
15. In 1917, a sub-lieutenant's pay was 9/- a day.
16. If the class of ship were to warrant a Commander as well as a Captain, he too would have a midshipman attendant upon him.
17. Capt. C.A.G. Nichols: Recollections. P.H.L. Archives.
18. Admiral Sir William Davis: Recollections. P.H.L. Archives.
19. Rear Admiral H.J.B. Moore: Recollections. P.H.L. Archives.
20. See *From Public School to Navy*. Edit. Lt W.S. Galpin. Underhill, Plymouth, no date.

Chapter 12

1. Vice Admiral Sir Lennon Goldsmith: Letters. P.H.L. Archives.
2. Dr.R.H.J.M. Corbet: Recollections. P.H.L. Archives.
3. E. Meyers: Recollections. P.H.L. Archives. As a sad footnote, it might be mentioned that at the time of the tragedy a children's party was taking place aboard the cruiser.
4. Capt. R.F. Nichols: Recollections. P.H.L. Archives.
5. Cdr D.H. Evans: Diary. P.H.L. Archives. Evans was awarded the Albert Medal for his work, a medal exchanged for the George Cross by Royal invitation in 1971 to all its holders.

Chapter 13

1. Dr J. Shaw: Letter. P.H.L. Archives.
2. Brig. G.R. Roupell VC: Typescript recollections. P.H.L. Archives.
3. Capt. A.W. Clarke: Diary for March, April and June 1917. P.H.L. Archives.
4. Capt. H.G. Pertwee: Recollections. P.H.L. Archives.

Chapter 14

1. An idea of the gallantry displayed may be gathered from the fact that a VC, five DSCs, a bar to a DSC, five CGMs, eighteen DSMs and a bar to a DSM were earned by the driftermen. See J. Winton: *The Victoria Cross at Sea*, 145–7.
2. Rear Admiral P.W. Dumas: Diary and Official Papers. P.H.L. Archives.
3. F.E. Hughes (HMS *Hyacinth*): Recollections. P.H.L. Archives.
4. J. Falconer (HMS *Talbot*): Diary for 1916. P.H.L. Archives.
5. H. Beevers: Contemporary account written in hospital. P.H.L. Archives.
6. Commodore David Norris: Letter to A.B. Lee of 5 September 1918. Subsequent letter of 13 September 1918. Capt A.B. Lee: Papers. P.H.L. Archives.
7. Sir James Corry: Diary. P.H.L. Archives.

8. On a later page in the diary, Trotsky's name has been amended to 'Trotsky's brother'.
9. W. Kennedy: Diary. P.H.L. Archives.
10. Rear Admiral R.M. Dick: Papers. P.H.L. Archives.
11. Cdr C. Drage: Diary. P.H.L. Archives.
12. Sir James Corry: Recollections. P.H.L. Archives.
13. Cdr Charles Drage: Diary. P.H.L. Archives.

Chapter 15

1. Patrick Beesley: *Room 40: British Naval Intelligence 1914–18*. Hamish Hamilton, 1982.
2. Professor W.H. Bruford: Recollections. P.H.L. Archives.
3. Miss K. Ussher: Recollections. P.H.L. Archives.
4. Rev. T.C. Gordon: Diary. P.H.L. Archives. Reflecting a different but no more endearing preoccupation, was the wag at the Admiralty who was supposed to have coined a couplet on 'The Naval Officer's Routine':
   Up with the lark
   To bed with the wren.
5. Miss E. Gledstane: Recollections. P.H.L. Archives.
6. Lady Ashton *neé* Gaitskell: Recollections. P.H.L. Archives.

Chapter 16

1. A westbound Scandinavian convoy was caught in October 1917 by German surface units more powerful than the British destroyer and trawler escorts. Both British destroyers and most of the twelve merchantmen (nine of which were from neutral Scandinavian countries) were lost despite a gallant fight by the destroyers *Mary Rose* and *Strongbow*. A similarly serious blow was administered in December when four armed trawlers, a destroyer and six merchant vessels were sunk by German destroyers. The German ships again escape unscathed from attention by British forces attempting to waylay them.
2. Capt. A.W. Clarke: Diary for September and October 1917. P.H.L. Archives. The author deliberately leaves Clarke's destroyer unnamed.
3. Sqn Ldr T.P. York-Moore: Recollections. P.H.L. Archives.
4. Air Vice Marshal P.E. Maitland: Recollections. P.H.L. Archives.
5. Air Vice Marshal Sir Ralph Cochrane: Recollections. P.H.L. Archives.
6. Rev. T.C. Gordon: Diary. P.H.L. Archives.
7. Capt. B.A. Hardinge: Diary. P.H.L. Archives.. The attack took place without warning west of the Scilly Isles.

8. R.D. Hoskins: Diary. P.H.L. Archives.
9. Capt. E.T.N. Lawrey: Recollections. P.H.L. Archives.
10. Capt. H.N. Taylor MN: Documents and Recollections. P.H.L. Archives.
11. G. Mather: Recollections. P.H.L. Archives.
12. B.C. Bishop: Recollections: Contemporary account and Diary. P.H.L. Archives.
13. A.L. Jones: Recollections: P.H.L. Archives.
14. Capt. F.S.W. de Winton: Recollections. P.H.L. Archives.
15. In 1917, the Grand Fleet was equipped with paravanes for cutting through mine fields at high speed.
16. R.J. Allerton: Recollections. P.H.L. Archives.
17–18 Sir James Corry: Diary. P.H.L. Archives.

Chapter 17

1. D. Everitt: *The 'K' Boats*. George Harrap, 1963. Quotation from page 9 of New English Library edition, 1973.
2. Rear Admiral O.W. Phillips: Recollections. P.H.L. Archives.
3. Rear Admiral O.W. Phillips: Recollections. P.H.L. Archives.
4. G.T.W. Kimbell: Recollections. P.H.L. Archives.
5. J.H. Plumridge: *Hospital Ships and Ambulance Trains*. Seeley Service, London, 1975.
6. W.G. Olver: Diary. P.H.L. Archives. For the loss of *Royal Edward* see *Men of Gallipoli*, opus cit, 213–14.
7. Major General F.K. Escritt: Recollections. P.H.L. Archives.
8. E.V.J. Jones (Pte 8th Bn. King's Shropshire Light Infantry): Recollections. P.H.L. Archives.
9. Vol. III, 225.
10. Lincolnshire Yeomanry Papers. P.H.L. Archives.
11. Col. J. Wintringham: Lincolnshire Yeomanry Papers. P.H.L. Archives.
12. Sir Graham Wilson (RAMC): Recollections. P.H.L. Archives.
13. Fr W.O. Fitch (Army Padre): Recollections. P.H.L. Archives.

Chapter 18

1. That there was a relationship between Sir John Jellicoe's fears for the British war effort under the menace of the Bruges-Ostend-Zeebrugge U-boat triangle and the launching and continuance of the Third Ypres offensive is clear, though a subject of continuing debate.
2. In September 1917, Jellicoe directed that plans should be drawn up but his own resignation was called for and given in the last days of the year.

3. Dr G.F. Abercrombie: Diary. P.H.L. Archives.
4. A.J. Marder: *opus cit.* Vol. 5, 55.
5. Major General A.R. Chater: Recollections. P.H.L. Archives.
6. Sgt H. Wright: Account held in Royal Marines Museum. The account goes on to detail that a captain, two sergeants, a corporal and ten privates had been captured.
7. Letter extract of Captain, later Rear Admiral E.K. Boddam-Whetham of 24 January 1918, per Patrick Cordingley.
8. Dr G.F. Abercrombie: Diary and notes. Abercrombie boldly and successfully tackled the men gassed by fumes of some nature by giving them mustard and water which made them vomit and this led to their recovery.
9. Capt. Sir John Alleyne: Recollections. P.H.L. Archives.
10. Marshal of the RAF Sir William E. Dickson: Recollections. P.H.L. Archives.

Chapter 19
1. A.J. Marder: *opus cit.* Vol. v, 331. Sir David Beatty took over from Sir John Jellicoe as Commander in Chief of the Grand Fleet in late November 1916.
2. Vice Admiral Sir Charles Hughes Hallett: Recollections. P.H.L. Archives.
3. W.T. Henson: Recollections. P.H.L. Archives.
4. The editor was James Woods who wrote as 'Lionel Yexley'. A case similarly for special pleading or for being specially well informed might be made for the published research of Cdr H. Pursey on the subject of the mess deck conditions. See National Maritime Museum for documentation of both Yexley and Pursey.
5. Capt. Stephen Roskill: *Earl Beatty*, 268. Collins, 1980.
6. A contributory factor had been the granting of regular commissions to the necessarily large influx of junior officers brought in during the war.
7. Lord Strathclyde, then Lt Galbraith: Recollections. P.H.L. Archives.
8. Cdr J.G.D. Ouvry: Diary. P.H.L. Archives.
9. Capt. C.A.G. Nichols: Recollections. P.H.L. Archives.

Personal Experience Documentation

In assembling the names of all those from whose papers material has been drawn, I have followed a policy of listing any rank held in retirement but not of cataloguing other distinctions or honours. By this means it is hoped to avoid giving cause for offence by error of omission or commission. Listed next, with every endeavour to be accurate, is the date, rank or appointment, rating, ship or station of the person at the time his or her letter or other document was produced. Unless specifically stated otherwise, all material is held in my archives at Sunderland.

Abbreviations

AC	Armoured, or Heavy Cruiser	DB	Dreadnought Battleship
B	Pre Dreadnought Battleship	LC	Light Cruiser
		M	Monitor
BC	Battle Cruiser	ML	Minelayer
C	Cruiser	MS	Minesweeper
D	Destroyer (all classes)	S	Sloop

Abbott, Mrs, 1915: Canteen Worker, YMCA Stornoway, Isle of Lewis.

Abercrombie, Dr G.F., 1918: Surgeon Probationer, HMS *Warwick* (D).

Allen, S.J., 1914: Leading Seaman, HMS *Bacchante* (AC).

Allerton, R.J., 1917: Wireless Telegraphist, HMS *Roman* (MS).

Alleyne, Capt. Sir John, 1918: Lieutenant (Navigating Officer), HMS *Vindictive* (C), being used as a Block Ship (Ostend).

Andrews, Sqn Ldr J.C., 1915: Warrant Officer, RNAS, Gibraltar.

Austin, J.M., 1915: Coal Trimmer, *St Combes Haven* (Drifter).

Ashton, Lady, *née* Gaitskell, 1918: WRNS, WRNS HQ London.

Bacon, C. de L., 1918: Midshipman, HMS *Tiger* (BC).

Bagot, Cdr A.J.D., 1914: Midshipman, HMS *Queen Mary* (BC).

Banks, Cdr H., 1915: Midshipman, HMS *Agamemnon* (B).

Bartlett, Sqn Ldr C.P.O., 1917: Flight Commander, No. 5 Wing RNAS, RNAS Petite Synthe.

Beevers, H., 1918: Able Seaman, Caspian Naval Force.

Bentham, Wing Cdr J.H., 1914: Ordinary Seaman, Benbow Battalion, 1st Royal Naval Brigade, Royal Naval Division (Antwerp); 1917–18, Flight Sub-Lieutenant, RNAS Cattewater.

Bickmore, Dr G.H., 1915: Assistant Clerk, HMS *Warspite* (DB); 1916: Clerk, HMS *Falmouth* (LC).

Binney, Admiral Sir T.H., 1915: Lieutenant-Commander, HMS *Queen Elizabeth* (DB); 1918: Commander, HMS *Queen Elizabeth* (DB).

Bishop, B.C., 1917: Wireless Operator, SS *Afghan Prince*.

Blacklock, Capt. H.W., 1915: Lieutenant, HM Submarine *E1*.

Boddam-Whetham, Rear Admiral E.K., 1918: Lieutenant Commander, HMS *Ulleswater* (D).

Boswell, Capt. L.A.K., 1914: Cadet, RNC Dartmouth; 1915: Midshipman HMS *Irresistible* (B) and HMS *Queen Elizabeth* (DB); 1918 Sub-Lieutenant HMS *Queen Elizabeth* (DB).

Bowman, F. 1916: Naval Instructor, HMS *Colossus* (DB).

Brand, Capt. E.S., 1916: Sub-Lieutenant, HMS *Valiant* (DB).

Braybrooke, Lord (H.S. Neville), 1917: Flight Lieutenant, RNAS.

Bromet, Air Vice Marshal Sir Geoffrey, 1914: Lieutenant, RNAS Westgate-on-Sea; 1915: Lieutenant, HMS *Ark Royal* (Seaplane Carrier).

Brookes, Lt-Cdr S.W., 1915: Signalman, HMS *Doris* (LC).

Bruford, Professor W.H., 1917: Lieutenant RNVR, Admiralty Intelligence, Room 40.

Bullock, E.W., 1914: Chief Stoker, HMS *Inflexible* (BC).

Burrough, Admiral Sir Harold M., 1916: Gunnery Officer, HMS *Southampton* (C).

Burrows, Cdr H., 1916: Midshipman, HMS *Benbow* (DB).

Bush, Capt. E.W., 1914: Cadet, HMS *Bacchante* (C); 1915: Midshipman, HMS *Bacchante* (C).

Buss, Sqn Ldr H.A., 1917: Squadron Commander, RNAS Manston.

Cave, W.G., 1914–16: Able Seaman to Chief Petty Officer, HMS *Dublin* (C).

Chater, Major General A.R., 1914: Acting Adjutant, Royal Marines (Antwerp); 1918, Captain, Royal Marines (Zeebrugge).

Churchill, Capt. C.F.H., 1915: Midshipman, HMS *London* (B).

Clarke, Capt. A.W., 1914: RNC Cadet and Midshipman, HMS *Implacable* (B); 1916: Midshipman, HMS *Royal Oak* (DB); 1917: Sub-Lieutenant, *P14* at Sheerness and in a destroyer based at Lerwick.

Cochrane, Air Chief Marshal Sir R.A., 1917: Lieutenant RNAS (Airship Pilot), Scapa Flow.

Corbet, Dr R.H.J.M., 1917–18: Surgeon Probationer, HMS *Raider* (D).

Corry, Sir James, 1915: Able Seaman, HMS *Sagitta* (Auxiliary Small Craft-Yacht).

Cox, Petty Officer J.G., 1916: Petty Officer, HMS *Abdiel* (ML).

Crawford, Capt. J., 1916: Midshipman, HMS *Valiant* (DB).

Crick, W.R., 1916: Signalman, HMS *Caroline* (LC).

Crouch, C.C., 1914: MN Officer, HM Transport *G.802*.

Dalrymple-Smith, Capt. H., 1917–18: Midshipman, HMS *Ramillies* (DB).

D'Arcy, Surgeon Rear Admiral T.N., 1916: Surgeon Probationer, HMS *Onslow* (D).

Davis, Admiral Sir William, 1917: Midshipman, HMS *Neptune* (DB).

Denham, Capt. H.M., 1915: Midshipman, HMS *Raccoon* (D).

de Winton, Capt. F.S.W., 1917: Sub-Lieutenant, HMS *Narwhal* (D).

Dick, Rear Admiral R.M., 1911: Cadet, RNC Osborne; 1914: Midshipman, HMS *Carnarvon* (AC); 1916: Sub-Lieutenant, HMS *Barham* (DB); 1918: Sub-Lieutenant, HMS *Attentive* (LC).

Dickson, Marshal of the RAF Sir William E., 1918: Captain RAF, HMS *Furious* (as converted Aircraft Carrier).

Dillon, M.A.M., 1914: Acting Adjutant RNVR, Collingwood Battalion (Antwerp).

Downes, A.L., 1918: Trooper, Warwick Yeomanry, HM Troopship *Leasowe Castle*, (torpedoed).

Drage, Cdr C., 1915: Midshipman, HMS *London* (B); 1918: Sub-Lieutenant HMS *Cochrane* (AC).

Dumas, Rear Admiral P.W., 1918: Captain, Senior British Naval Officer, Mudros.

Edwards, Dr H.V., 1916: Surgeon Lieutenant, HMS *Porpoise* (D).

Elmhirst, Air Marshal Sir Thomas, 1915: Midshipman, HMS *Indomitable* (BC).

Emden, Dr A.B., 1916: Able Seaman, HMS *Parker* (D).

Escritt, Major General F.K., 1915: Medical Student, Dresser, HM Hospital Ship *Letitia*.

Evans, Cdr D.H., 1918: Sub-Lieutenant, HMS *Trident* (D).

Evans, Cdr G.F., 1917: Midshipman, HMS *Renown* (BC).

Ewings, J.D., 1914: Able Seaman, Benbow Battalion, 1st Royal Naval Brigade, Royal Naval Division (Antwerp).

Falconer, J., 1915: Able Seaman, HMS *Talbot* (C) (detached for East African land based operations, 1916–17).

Farquhar, Capt. J.W., 1914: Midshipman, HMS *Benbow* (DB).

Farquhar, Capt. M.: Sub-Lieutenant, HMS *Wallflower* (S).

Fitch, Father W.O., 1917: Army Padre, aboard HM Transport *Cameronia*.

Foster Hall, C., 1918: Midshipman, HMS *Collingwood* (DB).

Foxell, Dr H.L.G., 1916: Surgeon, HMS *Kempenfelt* (D).

Foxon, F.A., 1916: Electrical Artificer 1st Class, HMS *Caroline* (LC).

Fox-Pitt, Cdr T.S., 1915: Midshipman, HMS *Lord Nelson* (B); 1916: Acting Sub-Lieutenant, HMS *Inflexible* (BC).

Gledstanes, Miss E., 1918: WRNS Officer (cypher work), shore-based at Immingham.

Godsell, R., 1914: Sub-Lieutenant, Harwich Force.

Goldsmith, Vice Admiral, Sir Lennon, 1914: Commander, HMS *Laertes* (D); 1916: Commander, HMS *Lydiard* (D).

Gordon, Rev. Dr T.C., 1918: Lieutenant (Seaplane Pilot), RNAS RAF Great Yarmouth.

Greig, Miss D.B., 1918: Driver, WRNS Motor Transport Division.

Gunn, Capt. P.L., 1914: Able Seaman, HMS *Clio* (Sloop) and Steam Launch *RN2*.

Haig-Ferguson, Cdr P., 1913: Cadet, RNC Dartmouth;

1914: Midshipman, HMS *Mars* (B); 1915: Midshipman, HMS *Tiger* (BC); 1917–18: Sub-Lieutenant HMS *Teazer* (D) and HMS *Lurcher* (D).

Haldane, Dr T.G.N., 1915: Midshipman, HMS *Doris* (LC).

Hardinge, Capt. B.A., 1916–17, MN Officer, SS *Clan Davidson*.

Harris, Cdr G.C., 1917: Sub-Lieutenant, HMS *Temeraire* (DB).

Hayward, Cdr R.J., 1915: Paymaster Sub-Lieutenant, HMS *Irresistible* (B).

Heath-Caldwell, Cdr C.H., 1915: Lieutenant, HMS *Miner* (Armed Launch).

Henson, W.T., 1918: Petty Officer (Captain's Coxswain), HMS *Agamemnon* (B).

Hereward, Mr H., 1915: passenger survivor of SS *Lusitania*.

Hicks, H., 1916: MN Coal Trimmer, SS *Britannic* (Hospital Ship).

Hoare, Rear Admiral D.J., 1914: Engineer Lieutenant, HMS *Collingwood* (DB); 1916: Engineer Lieutenant, HMS *Birkenhead* (LC).

Holbrook, Lt-Cdr N., 1914: Lieutenant, HM Submarine *B11*.

Holvey, F.G., 1914: Able Seaman, HMS *Cornwall* (AC).

Hoskins, R.D., 1917: MN Officer, SS *Carlisle Castle*.

Hoskyns, Cdr J.W., 1914–15: Sub-Lieutenant, HMS *Yarmouth* (C).

Hughes, F.E., 1916: Able Seaman, HMS *Hyacinth* (LC).

Hughes-Hallett, Vice Admiral Sir Charles, 1914: Cadet, RNC Dartmouth; 1915: Midshipman, HMS *Vengeance* (B); 1918: Sub-Lieutenant, HMS *Hardy* (D).

Hutchinson, Group Capt. T.G.G., 1917: Engineer Lieutenant, HMS *Queen Elizabeth* (DB).

Jameson, Major General T., 1914: 2nd Lieutenant Royal Marines, Antwerp.

Jaques, F., 1915: Engineer Lieutenant, HMS *Swiftsure* (B).

Jones, A.L., 1917: Wireless Telegraphist, SS *Penhurst Q7* (Q Ship); 1918: Wireless Telegraphist, HMS *Hind* (D).

Jones, E.V.J., 1918: Private 8th Battalion KSLI, HM Hospital Ship *Rewa*.

Jones, J.C., 1916: Royal Marine, HMS *Warrior* (AC).

Keeler, G.E., 1915: Able Seaman, HMS *Lord Nelson* (B).

Kennedy, W., 1918: Able Seaman, HMS *Attentive* (LC).

Kimbell, G.T.W., 1917: Signalman, HM Submarine *K17*.

King-Brown, Dr W.W., 1915: Surgeon Probationer, HMS *Maori* (D).

Kingsmith, G., 1915: Sub-Lieutenant, HMS *Manica* (Kite Balloon Ship).

Laborde, Cdr C.F., 1914: Clerk, HMS *Inflexible* (BC).

Lawder, Rear Admiral K.M., 1914: Captain's Secretary, HMS *Defence* (AC); 1916: Assistant Paymaster, HMS *Malaya* (DB).

Lawrey, Capt. E.T.N., 1918: Apprentice, SS *Port Hardy*.

Lee, Capt. A.B., 1918: Lieutenant RNR, Caspian Naval Force.

Le Mesurier, Commodore C.E., 1916: Commodore, HMS *Calliope* (LC).

Little, A.G., pre-1914: Cadet, RNC Dartmouth.

Longden-Griffiths, Cdr C.H., 1915: Assistant Paymaster RNR, HMS *Roberts* (M).

Longley-Cook, Vice Admiral E., 1915: Midshipman, HMS *Prince of Wales* (B); 1918: Sub-Lieutenant HMS *Tiger* (BC).

Lorimer, Dr D., 1916: Surgeon, HMS *Malaya* (DB).

Lugg, R., 1916: Royal Marine, HMS *Defence* (AC).

McLeod, Capt. A.K., 1917: In command of Q Ship, HMS *Hyderabad*.

Maitland, Air Vice Marshal, P.E., 1915: Midshipman, HMS *Dreadnought* (DB); 1918: Flight Lieutenant, 2nd Officer, North Sea Airship No. 3, RNAS East Fortune.

Mansergh, Admiral Sir Aubrey, 1915: Midshipman, HMS *Bacchante* (AC).

Mather, G., 1918: Wireless Operator, SS *Ramsey*.

May, P., 1915: Leading Seaman, HMS *Triumph* (B).

Meyers, E., 1915: Able Seaman/Torpedoman, HMS *Natal* (AC).

Michell, Cdr R.A.C., 1914: Midshipman, HMS *Edgar* (C).

Michelmore, Cdr T.G., 1916: Sub-Lieutenant, HMS *Hecla* (Depot Ship); 1917: Sub-Lieutenant, HMS *Defender* (D).

Miles, Admiral Sir G., 1914: Lieutenant, HMS *Empress of Russia* (Armed Merchant Cruiser).

Miller, F.W.H., 1914–18: Able Seaman to Warrant Officer, HMS *Iron Duke* (DB).

Mitford, Cdr J.B., 1914–16: Midshipman, HMS *Russell* (B); 1916: Midshipman, HMS *Orion* (DB); 1918: Sub-Lieutenant, HM Submarine *K7*.

Moore, Rear Admiral H.J.B., 1917: Midshipman, HMS *Resolution* (DB).

Mooring-Aldridge, G.A., 1918: Lieutenant RNVR, HM Motor Launch *333*.

Newman, A.G., 1914: Pantry Boy, SS *Georgic* (Cattle Boat).

Nichols, Capt. C.A.G., 1917: Midshipman, HMS *New Zealand* (BC); 1918: Sub-Lieutenant, HMS *New Zealand* (BC).

Nichols, Capt. R.F., 1917: Midshipman, HMS *Vanguard* (DB).

Norris, Vice Admiral Sir C., 1918: Midshipman, HMS *Malaya* (DB).

Olver, W.G., 1915: Sick Berth Steward, HM Hospital Ship *Soudan*.

Ouvry, Cdr J.G.D., 1915: Midshipman, HMS *Tiger* (BC); 1918: Lieutenant, HMS *Inconstant* (LC).

Pears, Rear Admiral S.A., 1916: Lieutenant, HMS *Falmouth* (LC).

Pertwee, Capt. H.G., 1916: Ship's Writer, HMS *Arethusa* (LC); 1918: Secretary to the Senior Naval Officer, Caspian Naval Force.

Phillips, Rear Admiral O.W., 1917: Chief Engineer, Submarine *K4*.

Poland, Rear Admiral A., 1916: Lieutenant, HM Submarines.

Poland, Capt. R., 1916: Royal Marine Officer, HMS *Warspite* (DB).

Portal, Admiral Sir R., 1917: Lieutenant, Grand Fleet.

Roberts, W., 1918: Able Seaman, HMS *St Elvies* (MS).

Roupell, VC, Brig. G.R., 1916: Brigade Staff Officer BEF, aboard cross-Channel Steamer *Queen*.

Salter, Vice Admiral J.S.C., 1917: Midshipman, HMS *Ramillies*.

Schofield, Vice Admiral B.B., 1915: Midshipman, HMS *Indomitable* (BC).

Sebastian, Rear Admiral B., 1903: Royal Naval College, Osborne; 1915: Lieutenant, HMS *Inflexible* (BC).

Sellers, J., 1918: Probationary Flight Sub-Lieutenant, RNAS/RAF Great Yarmouth.

Shaw, Dr J., 1915: Surgeon Probationer, HMS *Druid* (D), HMS *Changuinola* (Armed Merchant Cruiser); 1917: Surgeon Lieutenant, HMS *Lydiard* (D).

Shaw, Lt-Cdr H.K.L., 1914: Officer, HMS *Minerva* (LC).

Shearer, G., 1914: Officer, HMAS *Australia* (BC).

Shearer, W., : Surgeon Probationer, Served in the Far East.

Sinclair, J., 1915: Corporal, 10th Battalion AIF Gallipoli, taken aboard HMS *Prince of Wales*, wounded. Source: South Australia State Library.

Steele, VC Cdr G.C., 1915: Sub-Lieutenant RNR, HMS *Baralong* (Q Ship).

Stephens, ?.?., 1915: Petty Officer, HM Submarine *E2*.

Strathclyde, Lord (T.D. Galbraith), 1914: Lieutenant, HMS *Audacious* (DB); 1918: Lieutenant, HMS *Queen Elizabeth* (DB).

Taylor, C.J., 1915: Surgeon Lieutenant, HM Hospital Ship *Soudan*.

Taylor, Capt. H.N., 1918: Apprentice (MN), SS *Homer City*.

Thomas, A.W., 1917: Able Seaman, HMS *Malaya* (DB).

Thompson, Cdr D.S.E., 1915: Midshipman, HMS *Implacable* (B).

Traill, Air Vice Marshal T.C., 1915: Midshipman, HMS *Lord Nelson* (B).

Twiss, C.C., 1916: Writer, HMS *Victorious* (B).

Ussher, Miss K., 1918: WRNS, Naval Base, Gibraltar.

Vetch, Cdr H., 1914: Midshipman, HMS *Prince of Wales* (B).

Vyner, Cdr C.G., 1916: Sub-Lieutenant, HMS *Acasta* (D).

Wainwright, Sub-Lt D., 1916: Sub-Lieutenant, HMS *Nomad* (D).

Walters, Capt. J.D., 1916: Midshipman, HMS *Valiant* (DB).

Ward, H.R.H., 1918: Flight Sub-Lieutenant RNAS, RNAS Capel.

Westall, Cdr R.V.H., 1915: Midshipman, HMS *Goliath* (B).

Westall, W.E.N.H., 1916: Midshipman, HMS *Russell* (B).

White, G.J., 1918: Sergeant Observer, RAF, No. 217 Squadron.

William-Powlett, Vice Admiral Sir Peveril, 1915: Midshipman, HMS *Vengeance* (B).

Willis, Cdr W.J.A., 1916: Petty Officer Gunner, HMS *Calliope* (LC).

Wilson, Sir Graham, 1917: Medical Officer RAMC, aboard HM Transport *Cameronia*.

Wilson, Capt. H., 1915: Midshipman, HMS *Euryalus* (C).

Wintringham, Col. J., 1915: Officer in Lincolnshire Yeomanry aboard HM Transport *Mercian*.

Wright, Sgt H., 1918: Royal Marines, HMS *Vindictive* (C) (Zeebrugge).

Wyndham-Quin, Capt. The Hon. H., 1914: Lieutenant, Commanding Torpedo Boat *037*.

York-Moore, Sqn Ldr T.P., 1918: Captain RAF Airship (Pilot), RNAS/RAF Mullion.

Sources

It is not to be expected that authors, publishers and readers would agree on the precise purpose and usefulness of a bibliography. In every book on an historical theme a lengthy list of published sources will be seen by some as a victory for scholarship over the constraints of economy and by others as a meaningless exercise in academic window dressing. *The Sailor's War* relies above all on the testimony of personal experience from sources which are, with few exceptions hitherto unpublished and I feel it outside the spirit of such a book to lay out a comprehensive bibliography of the Great War at Sea. The number of pages required for Gallipoli and for Jutland would certainly render the exercise ruinously costly as well as being patently false in giving its impression of the real support sources of the book.

Accordingly, I have listed first some general works of which the Official Histories of Naval Operations and Marder's volumes provided matchless guidance and then those books to which specific reference was made in the text or endnotes. Additionally, I have included a small number of books which assisted me towards a clearer understanding of an aspect of personal experience of the war at sea.

General Works

Corbett, Sir Julian S., Newbolt, Sir Henry. *The Official History of the War, Naval Operations*, Vols I–V, Longmans, London, 1920–31.

Marder, A.J. *From the Dreadnought to Scapa Flow*, Vols 1–5, OUP, 1961–70.

Hough, R. *The Great War at Sea 1914–18*, OUP, 1983.

Bennett, Geoffrey, *Naval Battles of the First World War*, Batsford, London, 1968.

General books, monographs, autobiographies and other books of specific relevance

Allison, R.S., *The Surgeon Probationers*, Blackstaff Press, Belfast, 1979.

Aspinall-Oglander, Brig. Gen. C.F., *Official History of the Great War: Military Operations: Gallipoli*, Vols 1 and 2, William Heinemann, London, 1929–32.

Baynham, H., *Men from the Dreadnoughts*, Hutchinson, London, 1976.

Bean, C.E.W., *The Official History of Australia in the War of 1914–18. The Story of Anzac*, Vols 1 and 2, Angus and Robertson, Sydney, 1921–4.

Beesley, P., *Room 40 – British Naval Intelligence*, 1914–18, Hamish Hamilton, London, 1982.

Blumberg, General Sir H.E., *Britain's Sea Soldiers*, Swiss & Co., Devonport, 1927.

Bone, D.W., *Merchantmen at Arms*, Chatto and Windus, London, 1929.

Burrows, C.W., *Scapa and a Camera*, Country Life, London, 1921.

Bush, Capt. E.W. RN, *Bless our ship*, George Allen and Unwin, London, 1958.

Carr, W.G., *By Guess and by God*, Hutchinson, London, no date.

Cato, C., *The Navy in Mesopotamia*, Constable, London, 1917.

Creighton, Rev. O., *With the 29th Division in Gallipoli*, Longman Green, London, 1916.

Cunninghame Graham, Angus, *Random Naval Recollections*, Famedran, Gartochan, Dunbartonshire, 1979.

Dittmar, F.J. and Colledge, J.J., *British Warships 1914–1919*, Ian Allan, London, 1972.

Dixon, T.B., *The Enemy Fought Splendidly*, Blandford Press, Poole, 1983.

Everitt, D., *The K Boats*, George Harrap, London, 1963.

Galpin, Lt W.S., *From Public School to Navy*, Underhill, Plymouth, no date.

Gray, E., *A Damned Un-English Weapon*, Seeley Service and Co. Ltd, London, 1971.

Hayward, Victor, *H.M.S. Tiger at Bay*, William Kimber, London, 1977.

Hirst, L., *Coronel and After*, Peter Davies, London, 1934.

HMSO Official publication, *Navy losses, and Merchant Shipping (losses)*. Reprinted as *British vessels lost at sea*, Patrick Stephens Ltd, Cambridge, 1977.

Keble Chatterton, E., *Q ships and their story*, Sidgwick and Jackson, London, 1922.

Kemp, P., *The British Sailor: A social history of the lower deck*, Dent, London, 1970.

Killen, J., *A History of Marine Aviation*, Frederick Muller, London, 1969.

Knock, S., *Clear Lower Deck*, Philip Allan, London, 1932.

Liddle, Peter, *Men of Gallipoli*, Allen Lane, London, 1976.

McLaughlin, R., *The Escape of the Goeben*, Seeley Service & Co. Ltd, London, 1974.

Moberly, Brig. Gen. F.J., *Official History of the Great War. Military Operations: Mesopotamia*, Vols 1–3, HMSO, London, 1923, 1925.

Morgan, Charles, *The Gunroom*, A. & C. Black, London, 1919.

Munro, Captain D.J., *Scapa Flow, A Naval Retrospect*, Sampson Low, London, no date.

Pitt, B., *Zeebrugge*, Cassell, London, 1958.

Plumridge, J.H., *Hospital ships and Ambulance Trains*, Seeley Service & Co. Ltd, London, 1975.

Raleigh, W. and Jones, H.A., *The Official History of the War. The War in the Air*, Vols 1–6, Oxford, 1922–37.

Shankland, P., *The Phantom Flotilla*, Collins, London, 1968.

Taylor, Gordon, *The Sea Chaplains*, OUP, 1978.

Trystan Edwards, A., *British Blue Jacket: 1915–40*, Simpkins & Marshall, London, 1940.

Winton, J., *The Victoria Cross at Sea*, Michael Joseph, London, 1978.

Index